CROSS AND CRESCENT

in the

BALKANS

CROSS AND CRESCENT

in the

BALKANS

The Ottoman Conquest of South-Eastern
Europe (14th-15th centuries)

DAVID NICOLLE

Pen & Sword
MILITARY

First published in Great Britain in 2010 by
PEN & SWORD MILITARY
an imprint of
Pen & Sword Books Limited
47 Church Street
Barnsley
S. Yorkshire S70 2AS

ISBN 978 1 84415 954 3

A CIP catalogue record for this book
is available from the British Library

Typeset in Times New Roman by S L Menzies-Earl

Printed and bound in England
by CPI

Pen & Sword Books Ltd incorporates the imprints of
Pen & Sword Aviation, Pen & Sword Maritime,
Pen & Sword Military,Wharncliffe Local History, Pen & Sword Select,
Pen & Sword Military Classics, Leo Cooper, Remember When,
Seaforth Publishing and Frontline Publishing

For a complete list of Pen & Sword titles please contact:
PEN & SWORD BOOKS LIMITED
47 Church Street, Barnsley, South Yorkshire, S70 2AS, England.
E-mail: enquiries@pen-and-sword.co.uk
Website: www.pen-and-sword.co.uk

Contents

List of Illustrations

1. The main gate of the Byzantine castle in Trikala, central Greece.
2. Byzantine carved marble relief of a warrior fighting a dragon, 13-14th century.
3. The decision by Greek Orthodox monks to build monasteries on the extraordinary rock pinnacles at Meteora is often thought to reflect fear of the Turks.
4. Alexander the Great leading his army, in the *Iskandername* by Ahmedi.
5. A Kuman horse-archer on a fragment of ceramic tile from Margaret Island, Budapest, 14th century.
6. An early-14th century wall-painting of Saint Theodore Tiro, showing light-infantry equipment mixed with the archaic elements traditionally given to warrior saints in Byzantine and Balkan art.
7. St. Demetrius or St. Merkurios on a wall-painting made between 1338 and 1350.
8. A detail from the first page of the late-15th century Ottoman *Sulaymanname* manuscript.
9. The Martyrdom of St. Demetrius, on a 15th-century Byzantine icon.
10. The Rumanian principalities of Wallachia and Moldavia accepted Ottoman suzerainty but retained a large degree of independence.
11. The recently restored fortifications of the Hisar fortified area, on the eastern side of the Tophane district of Bursa.
12. The Genoese Gattilusi family ruled several Aegean islands and coastal enclaves during the later middle ages, and was closely linked to the Byzantine imperial ruling dynasty.
13. Enez, at the mouth of the river Marica.
14. The fortified inner harbour at Gallipoli.
15. The Ottomans proclaimed their conquests by religious and charitable buildings rather than fortresses.
16. The Kilidülbahir fortress, on the European shore of the Dardanelles.
17. The Baba Vida castle in north-western Bulgaria.
18. Although Anadolu Hisari has been considerably altered, part of the original keep remains.

19. A shield and sword, crudely carved on a 14th- or 15th-century Bogomil tomb from Bosnia.
20. The carvings on the best-preserved and most highly decorated of 15th century Bogomil tombs.
21. The southern circuit walls of Tarnovo.
22. Illustration from an Ottoman *Kulliyat* or 'anthology manuscript' made around 1480.
23. Khusrau hunting, in an Ottoman version by Hatifi, of the traditional Persian tale of *Khusrau and Shirin*, painted around 1498.
24. One of the illustrations in an Ottoman *Kulliyat* or 'anthology manuscript' includes two members of the elite *Kapi Kulu* corps.
25. A fully armoured knight accompanied by two 'figures of death' on a wall-painting made around 1475.
26. After they conquered the Serbian fortress of Smederovo at the end of the 15th century, the Ottomans added three polygonal artillery towers or bastions.
27. The massive land-defences of Constantinople [Istanbul].
28. The armour, weapons and heraldry on a mid-15th century carving on a medieval house in Sibenik.
29. Golubac fortress stands next to a modern reservoir where the Danube flows through the Derdap Gorge.
30. Bodrum Castle was built by the Crusading Order of Hospitallers in the early-15th century, at the end of an easily-defensible peninsula in south-western Turkey.
31. Warrior saints were painted in a very traditional style, though the realism of this late-14th century saint's face suggests some Western artistic influence.
32. Turkish nomads in a manuscript illustration by Siyah Qalam [Black Pen].
33. One of the earliest attempts to illustrate the fall of the Byzantine imperial capital of Constantinople to the Ottoman Turks with any degree of accuracy was a wall-painting on the outside of the church in the Moldavian monastery of Moldovitsa.

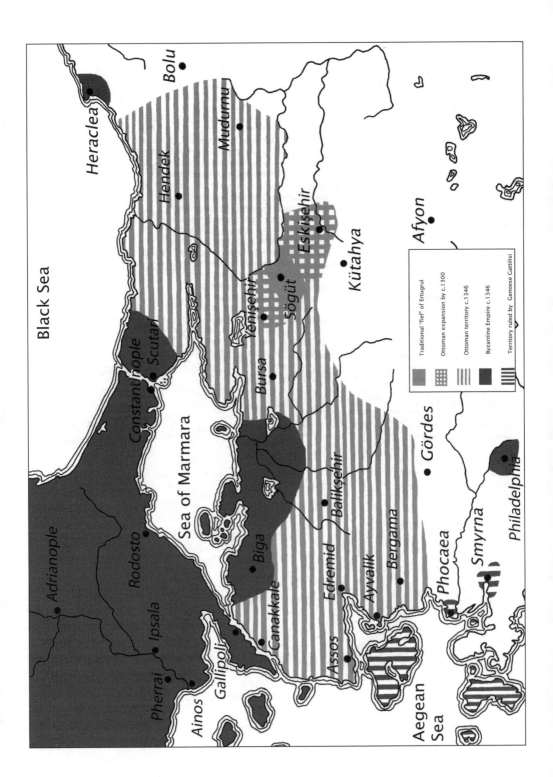

Black Sea

Heraclea

Bolu

Mudurnu

Hendek

Eskişehir

Söğüt

Yenişehir

Kütahya

Afyon

Scutari

Constantinople

Bursa

Sea of Marmara

Adrianople

Rodosto

Ipsala

Pherrai

Ainos

Gallipoli

Çanakkale

Biga

Assos

Edremid

Balıkşehir

Gördes

Ayvalik

Bergama

Phocaea

Smyrna

Philadelphia

Aegean
Sea

Traditional "fief" of Ertugrul

Ottoman expansion by c.1300

Ottoman territory c.1346

Byzantine Empire c.1346

Territory ruled by Genoese Gattilisi

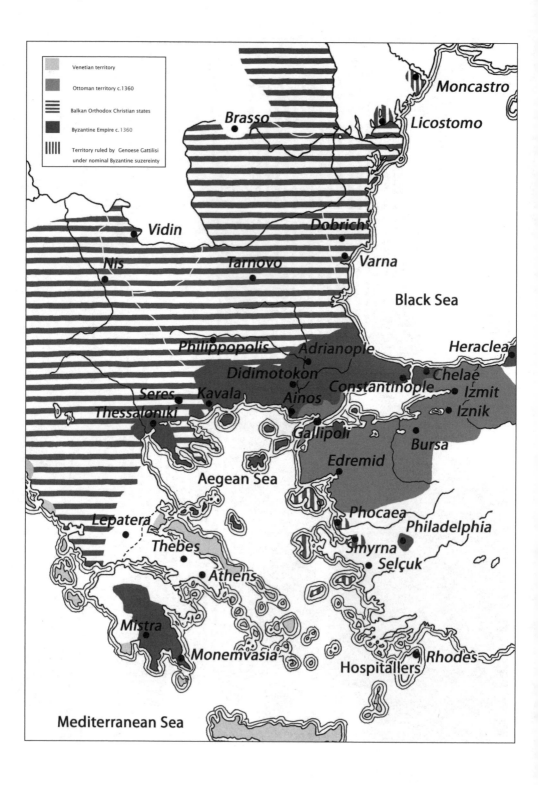

Venetian territory

Ottoman territory c.1360

Balkan Orthodox Christian states

Byzantine Empire c.1360

Territory ruled by Genoese Gattilisi
under nominal Byzantine suzereinty

Moncastro

Licostomo

Brasso

Vidin

Dobrich

Nis

Tarnovo

Varna

Black Sea

Philippopolis

Adrianople

Heraclea

Didimotokon

Chelae

Seres

Kavala

Ainos

Constantinople

Izmit

Thessaloniki

Gallipoli

Iznik

Bursa

Edremid

Aegean Sea

Phocaea

Lepatera

Philadelphia

Thebes

Smyrna

Athens

Selçuk

Mistra

Monemvasia

Rhodes

Hospitallers

Mediterranean Sea

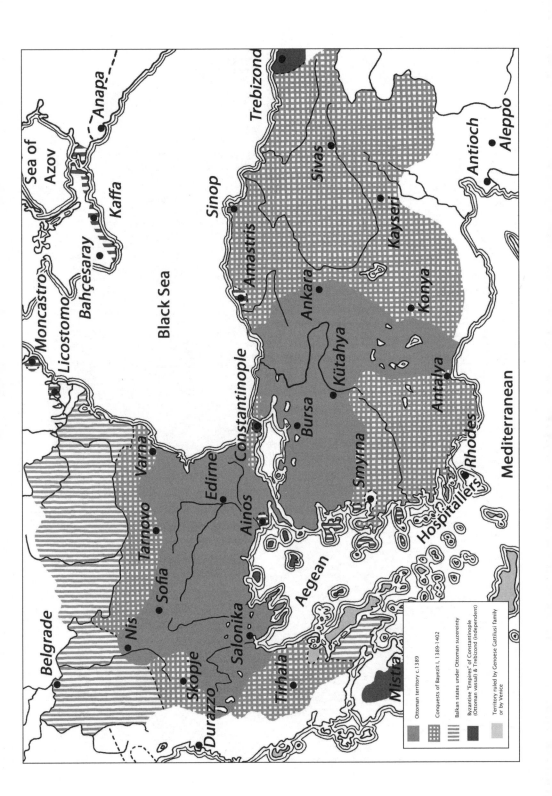

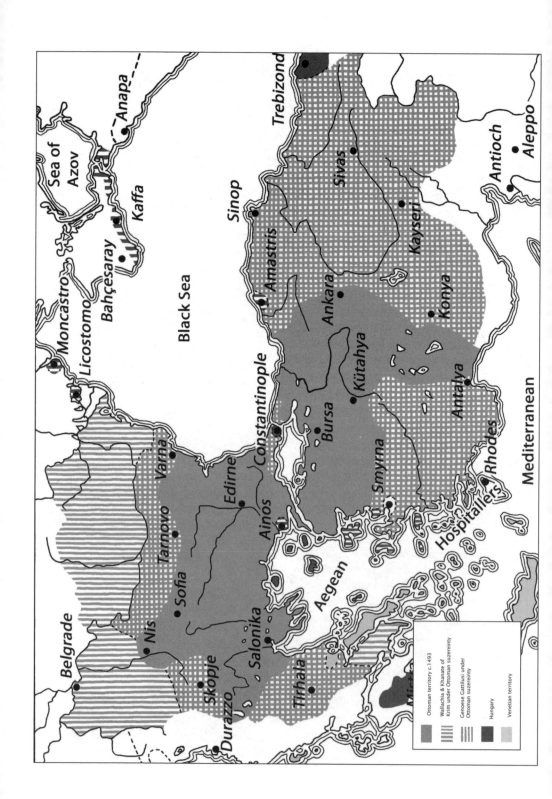

Introduction

*H*istory is full of stories of remarkably rapid conquests, often achieved by small numbers against numerous and varied foes. In the great majority of such cases, however, the conquests thus achieved were almost as rapidly lost once again. The extraordinary expansion of the Ottoman state between the mid-fourteenth and mid-fifteenth centuries is not one of these stories. It was followed by further expansion both in Europe and, with similarly dramatic speed, in the Middle East and North Africa. What is even more significant is the fact that these awe-inspiring military achievements were followed by more than three centuries of consolidation, then by a prolonged rather then precipitous decline.

As a result the Ottoman Empire, as it became, has left a deep impact upon south-eastern Europe, the Middle East, North Africa and beyond; an impact visible in cultural, religious, political and military terms to this day. Within this long and fascinating history, no period is more dramatic and in many ways mysterious than the century between the first Ottoman troops taking control of a small part of the Gallipoli Peninsula and the fall of the final remnants of the age-old Romano-Byzantine Empire. The latter was a more complicated event than is generally realized, there being two 'Byzantine Empires' in existence at that time, plus other fragments or enclaves. Undoubtedly the most important single episode in this collapse was the Fall of Constantinople in 1453, which occurred less than two-hundred and fifty kilometres from Çinbi where those first Ottoman soldiers set up the Ottoman flag around 1352. By 1453, of course, the frontiers of the Ottoman Sultanate, as it then was, had stepped beyond the river Danube, had reached the Adriatic Sea and already encompassed almost half of modern Turkey.

The Ottoman state already had more than half a century of history behind it when it crossed the Dardanelles Strait from Asia to Europe, and this little-recorded early period laid the foundations of what was already in many vital respects a European as well as an Asiatic political, military and cultural system. It could even be said that it was this early combination of east and west which planted the seeds of Ottoman success and durability. This was then followed by a century of remarkable expansion, which began when a tiny force of Ottoman Turkish warriors was invited by a Greek, Byzantine, Christian Emperor to cross the Dardanelles from Asia into Europe to assist him in one of the civil wars which were tearing apart the fast-declining Byzantine Empire. Almost exactly a century later the imperial Byzantine capital of Constantinople fell to what had grown into a hugely powerful and expanding Turkish and Islamic state. Furthermore, the Ottoman rulers of this new state came to see themselves as the natural and legitimate heirs of their Byzantine and indeed Roman predecessors. As a result they became in name and title, as they already were in fact, 'Emperors'.

During the intervening hundred years there had been many other participants in this epic story, winners as well as losers, Christians and Muslims. They included local inhabitants and western European newcomers or settlers, as well as rulers, merchants, long-established local aristocracies and military elites, and resident rural and urban populations who were themselves descended from numerous preceding waves of conquest or migration. Meanwhile the new 'Ottoman' settlers were of similarly mixed cultural or linguistic origins.

Chronology

c.1280	Death of Ertuğrul, Osman I becomes ruler (*bey* and subsequently *emir*) of first Ottoman state.
1301	Ottoman victory over Byzantines at Koyunhisar (Bapheon).
1326	Ottomans capture Bursa; Orhan Gazi becomes Ottoman ruler (*emir*).
1338	Ottomans capture Üskudar (Scutari).
1345	Ottomans occupy Turkish *beylik* (small state) of Karesi; Ottoman force crosses Dardanelles at invitation of Byzantine Emperor.
1353-5	Ottomans occupy Çinbi, Gallipoli and neighbouring towns.
1359	Murat I becomes Ottoman ruler; Ottoman occupation of Ankara.
1361	Turks (not necessarily under the Ottoman ruler's direct control) conquer Edirne.
1364	Ottomans defeats Balkan Christian alliance at River Marica.
1365	Ottomans move capital from Bursa to Edirne.
1371-76	Ottoman conquest of western Thrace and (Greek) Macedonia.
1376	Bulgarian states become Ottoman vassals.
1388	Dobruja becomes Ottoman vassal.
1389	Ottomans defeat Serbians at First Battle of Kosova (Kosovo); Bayezit I becomes Ottoman ruler, asserts independent sovereignty as *Sultan*; Serbia and Bosnia become Ottoman vassals.
1390	Ottomans conquer Turkish *beyliks* of Sarahan, Aydin, Menteşe, Hamit, Germiyan, Teke and part of Karaman in Anatolia.
1391	Wallachia becomes Ottoman vassal.
1392-98	Ottomans conquer Turkish *beyliks* of Konya, Sivas and Kastamonu in Anatolia; Ottomans conquer Thessaly in Balkans.
1396	Ottomans defeat major European Crusade at Nikopol (Nicopolis); note that by this date historians no longer give numbers to such Crusades.

1397   Byzantine Empire (of Constantinople) becomes Ottoman vassal.

1402   Ottoman Sultan Bayezit I defeated by Timur-i Lenk at Battle of Ankara; most Turkish *beyliks* regain independence; fragmentation of Ottoman state.

1402-13   Ottoman civil wars between sons of Bayezit I; finally reunified under Mehmet I.

1413-24   Byzantine Empire (of Constantinople), Serbia, Wallachia and Bosnia again become Ottoman vassals.

1421   Murat II becomes Ottoman ruler.

1423   Unsuccessful Ottoman siege of Byzantine capital, Constantinople.

1426-59   Ottoman reoccupation of Turkish *beyliks* in Anatolia.

1430   Republic of Dubrovnik (Ragusa) becomes Ottoman vassal.

1431-33   Ottoman conquest of Epirus and southern Albania.

1442   Ottomans defeated by Hungarians.

1444   Ottomans defeat Hungarians and Crusaders at Battle of Varna.

1446   Byzantine *Despotate* of Morea becomes Ottoman vassal; Ottomans depose Bulgarian princes and impose direct rule.

1448   Ottomans defeat European Crusade at Second Battle of Kosova (Kosovo).

1450-56   Ottomans conquer islands in northern Aegean.

1451   Mehmet II becomes Ottoman ruler.

1453   Ottoman conquest of Byzantine imperial capital, Constantinople.

1454-55   Ottoman conquest of southern Serbia.

1458-60   Ottoman conquest of Byzantine *Despotate* in southern Greece.

1461   Ottoman conquest of Byzantine 'Empire of Trebizond' (Trabzon).

1464   Bogomil rising against Hungarian rule assists Ottoman conquest of Bosnia and Herzegovina.

1468   Ottoman conquest of northern Albania.

1471-79   Ottoman conquest of most southern Aegean islands.

1472   Ottomans conquer *beylik* of Karaman.

1475   Turco-Mongol Khanate of Crimea becomes Ottoman vassal.

1481   Bayezit II becomes Ottoman ruler.

1484   Ottomans conquer Kiliya and Belgorod-Dnestrovskiy; Moldavia becomes Ottoman vassal.

1499-1501 Ottomans conquer Venetian ports on coast of Albania and southern Greece.

Chapter 1

A Chaotic Background

*T*he Ottoman Empire would one day cover an area remarkably similar to that of the Byzantine Empire at its greatest extent. Many Christians as well as Muslims would also come to see the Ottoman Sultan as the 'new Emperor', and as the legitimate successor of his Greek-speaking Orthodox Christian predecessors. In fact Turks and Byzantines had a very long historical relationship stretching back at least to the so-called 'Fall of the Roman Empire'. This major event in European history is, of course, misnamed since the Roman Empire as a whole did not fall in the fifth century AD, only its western half collapsing in the face of internal decay and external invasion. The Eastern Roman Empire not only survived but eventually flourished as what is now normally known as the Byzantine Empire. Here it should be noted that the citizens of this Later Empire continued to refer to themselves as 'Romans' to the very end, while the first Turks to conquer and settle Byzantine Anatolia were known as the Seljuks of *Rum*, in other words of 'the Rome land'.

The Turks themselves, as a distinct and identifiable people, emerged into history far to the east. During the mid-sixth century AD the *T'u-kiu* or *T'u-chüeh*, as they were known in Chinese sources, lived in the Altai Mountains in and around what is now western Mongolia. Paradoxically most of this original heartland is now inhabited by Mongols who are members of a different linguistic group, while vast lands to the west remain Turkish-speaking to this day.

Of all the peoples who stemmed from Central Asia, none made a greater impact than these Turks whose own origins seem to have been quite mixed. After defeating the Mongol-speaking *Juan-Juan*, who were ancestors of those *Avars* who themselves were masters of central Europe from the late-sixth to the late-eighth centuries, the Turks unified most of the nomadic peoples of eastern Central Asia and established a sprawling realm known as the *Gök* (Blue or Celestial) Turkish *Khaganate*. Around 583 this vast *Gök Turk* empire divided into often hostile Eastern and Western Turkish *Khaganates*.

While the Eastern Turks settled down to agriculture and some degree of urban life, the Western Turks retained their nomadic lifestyle for longer. It was these Western Turks who bore the brunt of the first Arab-Islamic thrusts into Central Asia, as well as being attacked by the T'ang Chinese. As a result their *Khaganate* collapsed around 740, after which the Western Turks were better known as the *Oğuz*, from whom the Seljuks and eventually even the Ottomans would claim descent. While some Oğuz tribes infiltrated the eastern provinces of the Islamic Caliphate and soon became Muslim, others migrated further west to settle in Byzantine Anatolia during the eighth century. They, however, were soon absorbed into Byzantine civilization.

Among those Turco-Hunnish tribes who had remained on the broad steppelands of early medieval south-eastern Europe after the collapse of Attila's ephemeral empire in the fifth century were the *Onogurs* or people of the 'Ten Arrows'. Soon better known as the *Bulgars* (meaning 'mixed people') they established a series of states, the most long-lasting of which was Bulgaria in the southern Balkans, which adopted Christianity, and the Volga Bulgar Khanate in what is now central Russia, which adopted Islam. The history of these peoples and regions is complex, but the Byzantine Empire was often on the receiving end of their raiding, while often also recruiting soldiers from their ranks.

A more permanent state was established by another Turkish tribal people, the *Khazars*, who seized the steppe regions north of the Black Sea in the 670s. Their ruling élite eventually adopted Judaism and a substantial proportion of later Eastern European Jewry was probably descended from these Turkish converts. Weakened by Russian attacks, the Khazars collapsed in the eleventh century and gave way to what is sometimes called the Third Wave of Turkish nomadic migration. This brought the *Pechenegs* to the western steppes and frontiers of the Byzantine Balkans. They had emerged from their ancestral grazing grounds between the River Volga and the southern Ural Mountains back in the ninth century. They were even more mixed than most such tribal groups and although the majority spoke Turkish, they also included Finno-Ugrians and Iranian-speaking nomads.

Despite clashes between Pechenegs and Byzantines, the Byzantine authorities seem to have encouraged some clans to settle along the Danube frontier as *foederati* or resident allies. Elsewhere the Pechenegs gradually merged with other people, including Turkish-speaking fellow nomads such as the *Torks* and latterly the *Kipchaks*. It has even been suggested that the Christian Turks who still inhabit the Dobruja region of eastern Romania are descended from these Pechenegs and Kipchaks rather than from later Ottoman settlers.

A section of the Oğuz Turkish tribal federation known as the *Uzes* were next pushed westward, briefly taking the western steppes from the Pechenegs before being scattered by the Kipchak Turks who followed close on their heels. Short as their history in eastern Europe was, the Oğuz had a very distinctive culture and the Oğuz epic national poem called *The Book of Dede Korkut* would survive in a fourteenth-century form as one of the jewels of early Turkish literature. Oğuz warriors were also serving in Byzantine armies from the ninth century, and in Middle Eastern Islamic armies from the eleventh century, even being recorded as far west as Morocco and Spain.

The Kipchak Turks took over the European steppes during the eleventh and twelfth centuries, roughly the same time that the Seljuk Turks, who were a subdivision of the Oğuz, took control of the eastern provinces of the Islamic world. In Russia the Kipchaks were known as *Polovtsi*, in Byzantium as *Chomanoi* or *Sauromates*, and in central Europe as *Cumans* or *Kun* – names which simply mean 'steppe dwellers'. They now drove the Oğuz from the southern Russian steppes, which they then dominated until the arrival of Genghis Khan's Mongols in the thirteenth century.

Far to the east, however, events had already taken place which would have an ultimately fatal impact upon the Byzantine Empire. The *Karakhanids* were Turks who had emerged from the *Qarluk* tribal confederation during the ninth century, then converted to Islam and established a powerful *Khanate* on both sides of the Tien Shan Mountains. Under their rule the Turkification of the previously Iranian-speaking provinces of Transoxania gathered pace. The Karakhanids thus created the first truly Turco-Islamic state, though their own civilisation also had roots in Buddhism and a dualist faith called Manichaeanism. Powerful echoes of this mixed cultural and religious heritage would survive amongst the subsequent Seljuk Turks, even amongst the Ottomans, and can still be identified in certain aspects of modern Turkish-Islamic as distinct from Arab- or Iranian-Islamic culture.

West of the Karakhanids lay the lands of the Oğuz, who were often also known as Guzz. Some time in the late-tenth century a Muslim convert and leader named Seljuk emerged amongst them. Having quarrelled with his immediate superior, Seljuk led his extended family or clan, and their retainers, to new territory next to the Syr Darya river. For several generations his descendants served various other more powerful leaders more or less loyally. Not until the mid-eleventh century did the Seljuk Turks, as they had now become known, strike out on their own behalf. Yet within a few years they altered the entire political spectrum not only of the Islamic world but also of the Byzantine Empire, defeating the Byzantine army at the battle of Manzikert in 1071.

This battle really was one of the main turning points in European, and perhaps even world, history. The Byzantine Empire lost virtually the whole of Anatolia in a military reversal which came as a huge shock to Christendom as a whole. In fact the Byzantine Empire regained much of this territory before, during and in the aftermath of the First Crusade. At least equally significant, however, was the Seljuk Turkish conquest of most of the eastern and central parts of the Islamic world during the eleventh century. This broke the previous Shi'a political domination of many of these regions and led to a revival of Sunni Islam. It also brought traditional predatory and only superficially Islamic Turkish tribes right up to the re-established eastern frontiers of the Byzantine Empire. Widely known as Turcomans to distinguish them from more settled, civilised and urbanised Turks, these wholly or partially nomadic tribesmen would remain troublesome neighbours.

Meanwhile the Seljuks' tradition of rule and authority was based upon power being shared within the dominant family rather than being concentrated in the hands of one senior member. This system would continue within the Great Seljuk Sultanate which had been established in Iran, Iraq, northern Syria and some neighbouring regions. Though regarded as near barbarians by those Turks already living within the Islamic world, the Seljuks' Central Asian heritage had enabled them to draw upon well established traditions of state-building and rule. Now, as they took over Iran, the Seljuks became increasingly Persian in culture and outlook, though less so in military matters, while adopting a somewhat mystical and often unorthodox form of Islam. This was in many ways significantly different from the 'book-learned' Islam characteristic of the Arab heartlands of Islamic civilisation.

In the immediate aftermath of the catastrophic Byzantine defeat at the battle of Manzikert, what remained of the Byzantine empire was torn by a prolonged series of civil wars and a gradual collapse of imperial authority across Anatolia. Here many isolated Byzantine garrisons clung to fortified strongpoints in the hope of eventual relief while losing control of the surrounding countryside. It was neither a wholesale Turkish conquest nor a complete Byzantine withdrawal. In fact groups of Turkish warriors were often invited to take over a city or region by rival claimants to the Byzantine imperial throne in return for their military support. One such was Sülayman Ibn Qutalmïsh, the founder of the Seljuk Sultanate of Rum, who had been invited to Iznik (Nicaea in Greek) by the Emperor Alexios I. It was this same Byzantine Emperor who a few years later called for military help from Western Europe to eject the Turks, resulting in a campaign better known as the First Crusade.

After Sülayman died, the Great Seljük Sultan Malik Shah took Sülayman's son Qïlïch Arslan as a princely hostage, correctly fearing that the Seljuks of Rum would prove difficult to control. When Qïlïch Arslan was released and returned to Anatolia to reassert Seljük authority, he had great difficulty doing so because other even less amenable Turkish powers had arisen in the area. The most formidable of these were the Danishmandids. Meanwhile, from the 1070s to the arrival of the First Crusade at the close of the eleventh century, several Armenian leaders established their own principalities in south-central Anatolia and northern Syria. Elsewhere elements of the old Armenian military aristocracy, along with descendants of both Greek and Western European soldiers in Byzantine service, accepted Turkish rule. They gradually adopted aspects of Turkish culture, Turkish language and in many cases converted to Islam. Other families remained Christian for several generations while still serving their new Turkish rulers in both civil and military capacities. The Christian Armenians similarly remained a distinct and highly significant group within what would become the Seljuk Sultanate of Rum.

The new Turkish states which had been established in conquered Byzantine territory during the late-eleventh century survived the passage of the First Crusade on its way to Jerusalem. However, the Seljuk Sultanate of Rum was now reduced to little more than the region around the city of Konya (Iconium) which would, from then on, become its capital. From here the Seljuks of Rum gradually regained much of their lost lands to the west and also spread east to take over the territories of their Danishmandid rivals. Thus the Seljuk Sultanate of Rum became one of the most successful states in Islamic history, though certainly not one of the largest, with its success being built upon cultural brilliance and flourishing trade as well as successful military campaigning.

In fact during the early years of the twelfth century the Danishmandids were the leading Islamic military power in Anatolia. Having also lost much less land to Byzantine reconquest, the Danishmandids then swallowed up an entire Christian Crusade which marched on the heels of the successful First Crusade during the summer of 1101. Two lines of Danishmandid emirs emerged by the mid-twelfth century, one based at Sivas, the other at Malatya and Elbistan. Their history remains obscure and they feature more prominently in Turkish folk legends and literature such as the epic *Danishmandname* than they do in strictly historical chronicles.

For their part the Seljuks of Rum soon recovered from their early setbacks, and while generally maintaining good relations with the still powerful Byzantine Empire, they instead concentrated on expanding southwards against the Armenian Kingdom of Cilicia and the Crusader County of Edessa, as well as against the Danishmandid Turks to the east. Nevertheless, in 1176 the Seljuk Sultanate of Rum inflicted a crushing defeat upon an invading Byzantine army led by the over-ambitious Emperor Manuel I Comnenus at the Battle of Myriokephalon. For the revived Byzantine Empire this was almost as great a disaster as the Battle of Manzikert back in 1071 and although the Seljuks of Rum did not immediately follow up their success by invading Byzantine western Anatolia, Byzantine military power never really recovered.

The first half of the thirteenth century marked the highpoint of Seljuk civilization in what is now Turkey, and it was under Seljuk patronage that a distinctive new style of Anatolian Islamic art and architecture emerged. The strongest external influence upon this civilization came, not surprisingly, from neighbouring Islamic Iran and from the Turks' own Central Asian heritage. Nevertheless, influences from both Christian Byzantine and Christian Armenian cultures can be identified. Furthermore, Seljuk Anatolian art, architecture and literature would provide foundations for the Ottoman civilisation which followed.

The century-and-a-half of Seljuk Turkish domination in central Anatolia was a period of striking economic progress, especially in trade. The relatively rapid long-distance communication and trade links by both land and sea not only assisted the spread of new technologies, and cultural and artistic ideas, but also enabled the Seljuks of Rum to take advantage of their prime geographical location at the very heart of several existing and flourishing trade networks. As a result Anatolia became a place to buy, sell or simply to transit goods from virtually the entire known world. By the thirteenth century this 'known' trading world encompassed all of Europe, most of Asia as far as China, Japan, Korea and parts of Indonesia, and a substantial part of Africa. Small wonder that Western European merchants, especially those from Italy, strove to establish friendly trading links with the merchants and rulers of Seljuk cities.

As yet the Mediterranean and Black Seas were both dominated by Christian fleets, largely Italian though the Byzantines were still active in the Black Sea, while Islamic vessels had certainly not disappeared from the eastern Mediterranean. Once the Seljuks and their immediate Turkish successors reached the Mediterranean and Black Sea coasts, they once again took to the sea as both merchants and corsairs, just as their ancestors had briefly done in the late-eleventh century. Sometimes the port facilities they built were remarkably sophisticated, ranging from slipways carved from the rock to entirely covered docks for galleys. Most of these more elaborate structures seem, however, to have been intended for warships rather than merchant vessels.

The conquest of the Byzantine imperial capital of Constantinople (Istanbul) by the Fourth Crusade in 1204, and the Western occupation of that great city until 1261, sapped what remained of Byzantine power and meant that the Seljuks' western neighbour, the Byzantine successor 'Empire of Nicea' was primarily concerned with regaining Constantinople. In turn it enabled the Seljuk Sultanate of Rum to expand once again, reaching both the Mediterranean in the south and the Black Sea in the north. This brought them even greater trading wealth which in turn paid for increased military power and fuelled greater territorial ambitions. Much of this ambition looked eastward towards the ancient heartlands of Islamic civilization, a lure which would eventually pull the Seljuks' Ottoman successors in the same direction.

However, the Seljuk Sultanate of Rum already had several powerful eastern and south-eastern neighbours. The Ayyubids, descendants of Saladin and his family, dominated Syria and northern Iraq. The Abbasid Caliphs of Baghdad had revived as a significant local power in central and southern Iraq and in much of western Iran. Georgia was now a major power in the Caucasus and the current Seljuk Sultan, Kay Khusraw II, had taken Russudana, a daughter of the famed Georgian queen Tamara, as his second wife. His first wife was the daughter of the Ayyubid ruler of Aleppo in northern Syria, but this had been a political match whereas Kay Khusraw's marriage to Princess Russudana is said to have been a love match.

Meanwhile the *Khwarazmshahs* from eastern Iran and Transoxania also had ambitions in these regions. They had been utterly defeated by Genghis Khan and his Mongol hordes in Central Asia, and as a result the current Khwarazmian leader and much of his army had fled westward. Yet they arrived not as refugees but as a still powerful military force which seemed bent on reviving its shattered fortunes in a new part of the Islamic world. In addition to clashing with the Abbasid Caliph and with some of the

Ayyubids, these previously defeated Khwarazmians invaded newly won Seljuk territory in eastern Anatolia.

The Seljuk Sultan of Rum defeated this threat – but a far greater one was already on the horizon. Columns of panic-stricken real refugees were already crossing into Seljuk territory, spreading news of the horrific cruelties committed by the Mongol Genghis Khan's pagan troops as they swept aside all resistance in Transoxania and Iran. This in turn led to waves of religious hysteria against all non-Muslims, including Christians, as well as rebellions against the Seljuk ruler's authority. Perhaps it was also why the Sultan had to rely on Western mercenaries to a much greater extend than he had before.

For several years the Mongols focussed their warlike energies on other targets in Iran, Georgia and southern Russia. In 1221 the Seljuk Sultan of Rum even tried to take advantage of the situation by sending a naval expedition to impose his suzerainty on the Genoese trading outpost of Sudak in the Crimea. In fact the defenders of Sudak, probably with some Seljuk assistance, repulsed a combined Russian and Kipchak Turkish attempt to take control only a few months later. Then, in 1222, the Russians and Kipchaks were themselves utterly defeated by the Mongols at the epic battle of the Kalka River in what is now eastern Ukraine. The following year the Mongol commanders Sübodei, Jebei Noyan and Genghis Khan's own eldest son Jochi were ordered to return to the east and rejoin Genghis Khan. It must have seemed that the Mongol threat to the Seljuk Sultanate of Rum had receded.

Almost twenty years would pass before the Mongols turned their attention to the Seljuks. By now Genghis Khan had died and since 1241 the Mongol Empire had been ruled by Töregene Khatun, the widow of his son Ögedey. The Mongols' career of conquests may have slowed but it had certainly not stopped. Nevertheless some of the Islamic regions they had conquered were already threatening to slip from Mongol control. Soon after Ögedey's death, a Mongol army besieged and took the eastern Anatolian city of Erzerum. Kay Khusraw II realised that he was now a Mongol target, so he assembled a substantial army which he entrusted to the command of the Georgian Prince Shervashidze. The Mongol invaders, under Baydu, also included some Georgian and Armenian troops.

The two sides met at Köse Dag on 26 June 1242 and the battle resulted in a devastating Seljuk defeat. This battle is particularly interesting for military historians because Kay Khusraw's army fought in an almost European manner, and included large numbers of Western European mercenaries, plus others from the Crusader States in Syria. The Mongols, of course, relied upon much the same Central Asia horse-archery and dispersal tactics that the Seljuks' own ancestors had used successfully two hundred years earlier.

What followed was a period of anarchy, with a collapse of Seljuk authority and a rise in the power and independence of various nomadic or semi-nomadic Turcoman tribes. The scene was set for the next phase in Turkish history; that of the *beyliks*. For the last few decades of its existence the weakened and crumbling Seljuk Sultanate of Rum was either a vassal of the huge Mongol *Il-Khanate* or had a Mongol governor imposed upon it. The Il-Khans were themselves only one of several Mongol Khanates which now ruled much of the known world from the Pacific coasts of China to the Polish frontier. After 1307 the fragmentation of Turkish Anatolia became official, with the end of the Seljuk dynasty and the recognized independence of several tiny states called *beyliks*, one of which would soon emerge as a power far great than the Seljuks had ever been. These were the Ottomans.

The first Ottomans were probably one of many nomadic Turcoman groups or warrior bands, rather than true tribes, that moved westward to the Byzantine frontier following the Mongol invasion of Anatolia in the mid-thirteenth century. The most popular myth that the Ottomans themselves told about their origins stated that a young warrior named Osman or Othman fell in love with Malkhatun, daughter of the saintly Shaykh Edebali. Being poor, Othman's only hope of winning her hand lay in earning military fame first. This he did, yet it was only when the young warrior told the Shaykh about a strange dream that the old man allowed Othman to be betrothed to Malkhatun.

In his dream Othman saw the moon, symbolising the fair Malkhatun, rising from Shaykh Edebali's chest and setting in the young man's own. Thereupon a mighty tree sprouted from Othman's heart and soon spread across the entire sky. From its roots four great rivers flowed, these being identified as the Tigris, the Euphrates, the Nile and the Danube. Such a dream clearly drew heavily upon a form of symbolism that had been popular amongst the Turks since their pagan past in Central Asia. However the saintly Shaykh is said to have interpreted the dream as a prophecy of imperial splendour, and so he was happy to allow his daughter to marry the young 'conqueror to be'.

Other more historical, but still perhaps partly legendary, accounts claimed that the Ottomans, or Othmanlis as they called themselves, stemmed from the noble Qayï clan of the Oğuz Turks. Their forebears had supposedly roamed a region of high steppes around the town of Mahan on the frontier of what are now Iran and Turkmenistan in the late-twelfth century. At the time of Genghis Khan's invasion, the leader of this Qayï clan was said to be a man named Sülayman Şah. He and his people now supposedly fled from the advancing Mongols, as huge numbers of nomadic Turcoman tribes certainly did, along with the herds of animals upon which they depended. Sülayman Şah and his followers made their way across Iran into Iraq and into what is now north-eastern Syria. Near the great brick castle of Qala'at Jabar, overlooking the river Euphrates, the band of refugees tried to cross the river but Sülayman was drowned.

Given the historical circumstances of the time, the Turcomans would have been trying to get from the north bank to the south; from what eventually became Il-Khanid territory into that of the Ayyubid Sultans and their Mamluk successors. In fact this part of the Euphrates river would remain a war-ravaged frontier between Mamluks and Mongols for centuries. Sülayman Şah's traditional tomb was, however, on the north bank. According to these traditional tales, Sülayman Şah's sons disagreed about what to do next. Two sons took their followers back into Mongol territory where they supposedly entered Mongol service. The third son, Ertuğrul, took a smaller number of people northward to Erzerum. This might indicate that he had abandoned the idea of crossing the great river into free Islamic territory. Instead they followed the river upstream, westward and then north into Anatolia.

Some time later Ertuğrul and his people are said to have been living near Ankara, perhaps having been given land on the high plains of Anatolian where they could pasture their flocks. It is reasonably certain that Ertuğrul's few hundred warriors were next entrusted with the defence, and perhaps the extension, of a small frontier region further west around the small town of Söğüt. It does seem likely that the earliest historically identifiable Ottomans led a traditional nomadic life on the high plains of central Anatolia during the period when the power of the last Seljuk Sultans of Rum was at best nominal.

During the late-thirteenth century this still small and unimportant people finally emerge into the light of history. For many years European historians generally claimed that the first real Ottoman ruler, Ertuğrul, never existed. However, archaeologists have now found a few coins bearing his name, apparently dating from the 1270s. His tiny state in the mountains around Söğüt soon included the battlefield of Eskişehir (Doryleaum) where the First Crusade had defeated the Seljuk Turks back in 1097. From these humble beginnings the Ottomans would steadily expand their state until they were knocking on the gates of Vienna in the west and sending powerful naval fleets to compete with the Portuguese in the Indian Ocean in the east.

Though Ertuğrul is now known to exist, the early history of the Anatolian Ottomans only start to become clear during the time of Othman Gazi who reigned from 1281 to 1324 AD. By this time the Ottoman *beylik*, named after Othman himself, was just one of several that had emerged from the collapse of the Seljuk Sultanate of Rum. But being one of those located on the frontier with the Byzantine Empire, the little Ottoman state seem to have attracted *gazis* or warriors dedicated to the defence of Islam. Though originally intended to be only defensive, the concept of the *gazi* had by now taken on an expansionist character in many parts of the Islamic world, not least in Turkish Anatolia.

On the other hand it seems that most of the clashes between *beylik* and Byzantine frontier forces were a result of traditional Turcoman raiding and their constant search for better pastures for their flocks. Only occasionally was there official aggression by the rulers of either side. Motivations may have been mixed but the results were clear. The Ottomans, like the other frontier *beyliks*, took control of more and more Byzantine territory. Sometimes they left the fortified towns isolated under Byzantine governors and garrisons who only later submitted to Turkish rule. This they usually did after their nominal ruler, the Byzantine Emperor, had failed or been unable to come to their aid.

In many cases such Christian troops and their officers thereupon entered Islamic-Turkish service. Most were Greek-speaking, but amongst their number were Armenians and Western European mercenaries, eventually including Catalans from far away Spain. Many converted to Islam at once but in some cases these soldiers and their descendants remained Christian for several generations. Such absorption of previous military and aristocratic élites would remain a feature of Ottoman expansion, both in Anatolia and in Europe. It would have a profound impact upon the personnel, organisation, tactics, weaponry and costume of Ottoman armies, as well as on the structure of the Ottoman state itself. Similar fusions of new and old, Islamic and Christian, Turkish and Greek or Balkan Slav, would be seen in Ottoman art, architecture and many other aspects of Ottoman culture.

Although the primary focus of Ottoman expansion was to the north, taking over what remained of Byzantine territory along the Asian shores of the Sea of Marmara and beyond, almost reaching the Bosphoros and Black Sea coasts, the Ottomans were also in competition with neighbouring Turkish *beyliks* to their west and south-west. Several of the latter were engaged in similar expansion against other remaining Byzantine provinces in Anatolia. However, in most cases these other *beyliks* found nowhere else to go once they reached the Aegean coast. So some took to raiding by sea, becoming what European chroniclers inaccurately but perhaps understandably called 'pirate states'.

One of these was the Karasi *beylik* in the north-western corner of Anatolia, which now seemed poised to cross the Dardanelles into Europe. Instead Karasi was conquered by the Ottomans in the mid-fourteenth century, a takeover of a fellow Islamic state which would open up huge strategic possibilities for the Ottomans. Not least the Ottomans inherited Karasi's small but potent fleet, which enabled Ottoman *gazis*, and those who had previously served under the banners of Karasi, to raid Byzantine islands and coasts in the way that other Turkish *beyliks* further south were already doing. The second was to place Ottoman troops on the very shores of the Dardanelles, almost within shouting distance of European soil in the form of the Gallipoli Peninsula only a few hundred metres away.

Chapter 2

Byzantine & Balkan Complexity

*N*ot surprisingly, many of those who wanted adventure and the status of *gazi* warriors offered their services to the Ottomans. At the same time it is likely that the strength and persistence of Byzantine resistance along the Ottoman frontier, which lay so close to the capital and very heart of the Byzantine Empire, may have toughened both the Ottoman armies and the Ottoman administrative system. Perhaps it also gave the Turkish settlers of the Ottoman state time to put down deeper and firmer roots, as well as partially assimilating, and partially being assimilated by, the existing Greek population.

The Byzantine military system which had been defeated by the Seljuks at Manzikert in 1071, and which subsequently failed to contain a renewed Turkish advance into Anatolia, had been much the same as that which had given Byzantium military dominance in the Middle East only a century earlier. What had changed was the quality, training, morale, leadership, composition and numerical strength of the armies involved. A huge emphasis on fortifications had also been characteristic of Byzantine military thinking. Urban militia forces had similarly played a vital role in Byzantine local and provincial defence. They had continued to shoulder a significant burden in the eleventh century but probably reduced in importance during the twelfth, while rising again in the thirteenth and fourteenth centuries.

The high walls and multiple towers of many Byzantine towns may, in fact, reflect the role of relatively untrained militias. Reliance on urban militia forces may have been part of a general decline in Byzantine military power from the mid-eleventh century onwards, this being accompanied by a loss of direct control over many militarily-vital frontier areas to local lords. It seems to have become rare for a Byzantine, rather than a foreign mercenary, to be competent at horse-archery. Most indigenous archery had become an infantry affair, whether in open battle or in siege warfare where the Byzantines' widespread use of numerous small frontier fortresses seems to have been designed to avoid casualties amongst their already insufficient troops. This emphasis on infantry archery also lay behind the widespread adoption of crossbows which would characterize Byzantine forces from the thirteenth to fifteenth centuries. Nevertheless, even after the disastrous battle of Manzikert, Byzantine forces continued to show their traditional discipline and to use well-tried traditional tactics, even though the back of the old military system had been broken.

Armenians had long played an important role in the Byzantine army, and although many deserted Byzantium to re-establish independent Armenian principalities during the twelfth century, others continued to serve the Byzantines in various military capacities. Their importance and numbers declined thereafter, and no new Armenian families entered the military elite after Emperor Alexius' death in the early-twelfth century. Nevertheless, the Armenian term *aspet*, meaning a 'general', was frequently continued to be encountered as a Byzantine family name during the twelfth to fourteenth centuries.

The numerous Western European mercenaries serving in Byzantine armies were far more important than the Armenians, and they too established powerful, long-lasting military families. The most famous Western mercenary force had, of course, been the Varangian Guard, which had originally consisted of men of Scandinavian or Russo-Scandinavian origin. The Varangians were infantry. From the late-eleventh century to the early-twelfth the Varangian Guard became increasingly Anglo-Saxon in composition, and Englishmen, in addition to other Northern Europeans such as Frisians and North Germans, continued to be recruited throughout the twelfth and into the thirteenth century. The offspring of these Varangian guardsmen often retained their distinct identity and followed their fathers into the ranks of this elite unit.

Second in importance only to the Varangians were the Normans, most of whom came from or via southern Italy, though Byzantine sources often refer to them as 'Celts'. As elsewhere, they were among the Empire's most effective troops, generally fighting as heavily-armoured cavalry though they may also be recorded in the role of siege engineers. These Normans were often considered politically unreliable but of course not all of them betrayed their employers and a number of late-Byzantine military families were of Norman origin.

Equally important were mercenaries recruited from the lands east and north of the Byzantine Empire. Perhaps most surprising was the Byzantine employment of large numbers of Seljuk Turks from Anatolia. These contingents were sometimes provided by the Seljuk Sultan of Rum and they proved to be the most reliable of all the Empire's foreign troops. Other Turks arrived as entire tribes or family units, having deserted the Seljuks and Islam to adopt Christianity and serve the Byzantine Emperor.

Following the loss and then partial reconquest of the eastern half of the Empire, a new Byzantine *akritoi* class of minor land-owning warrior families emerged along the Byzantine frontiers, especially in Anatolia. Here they watched over the no-man's-land that lay between Byzantine and Turkish territory until the massive losses of territory which marked the start of the Byzantine Empire's final decline in the later-thirteenth and fourteenth centuries. In the Balkan provinces Thessaly continued to supply effective troops, and was one of the areas least exposed to invasion of the regions remaining under Byzantine control. Since the eleventh century this horse-raising district had been largely inhabited by semi-nomadic and often warlike Vlach clans, who dominated the highlands of central Greece. They spoke a language derived from Latin and are amongst the varied and scattered peoples claimed as ancestors of the Romanian nation. The towns of Thessaly were also important military centres, while the surrounding lowlands were dominated by land-owners whose semi-feudal status as part of a new *pronoia* class was primarily military. The origins of the *pronoia* are still hotly debated, but as a form of land-holding and military obligation it had parallels in both Western European *feudalism* and in the Muslim *iqta* system.

Whether or not the *pronoia* reflected Western or Islamic influence, there is no doubt that from the twelfth century onwards Byzantine military equipment increasingly mirrored that of Western Europe. Even so, after the disastrous battle of Myriokephalon the heaviest styles of fully armoured close-combat cavalry armed with lances never found much favour. They were also hugely expensive to equip and maintain, large numbers of such troops probably being beyond the financial capabilities of later Byzantine and Balkan rulers.

The fact that the Byzantine Empire survived the catastrophic Fourth Crusade and was to re-establish a power-base at Nicea (Iznik), as well as in other regions, says much for the basic strength of Byzantine civil, religious and military institutions. Reduced political and economic power perhaps lay behind a revival of domestic forces, particularly the local troops of Bithynia (approximating to the modern Turkish provinces of Bursa, Bilecik, Izmit, Adapazari, Bolu and Zonguldak). Byzantine Nicea also fielded substantial cavalry armies, some of which were occasionally loaned to the Seljuk Sultan of Rum. During the thirteenth century this Nicean army also seems to have adopted, or perhaps more accurately re-adopted, many Anatolian military styles.

Pagan or recently-converted Turkic peoples from north of the Black Sea were encouraged to settle in Nicean territory in order to enlarge the pool of military manpower, a process which further encouraged what could be seen as a Turcification of the last Byzantine armies. Nevertheless, Western European mercenaries were still employed by the Nicean Empire when political and financial circumstances allowed. There was still some sort of Varangian Guard, though its composition is far from clear, and its main role seems to have been to protect the government treasury at Magnesia (now Manisa). A perhaps token force of 'Axe-bearing Varangians' was even recorded in the mid-fourteenth century, well into the era of the Byzantine Empire's final painful decline.

Balkan areas such as Thessaly increased even further in military importance as the Byzantine Empire lost more territory in Anatolia. Vlach and subsequently also Albanian cavalry of this region played a major role until suppressed by Stefan Dușan following the Serbian conquest of what is now northern Greece in the mid-fourteenth century. Mercenaries were similarly still recruited from neighbouring areas. Alans and Slavs, for example, are recorded in the very early fourteenth century. Turkish prisoners who had been converted to Christianity also fought, rather surprisingly, as infantry archers, perhaps to ensure that they did not desert back to their former comrades. Known as *Mourtatoi*, some may now have used crossbows. However, Western mercenaries were rarely mentioned in the fourteenth century and those that did serve Byzantium proved to be unreliable, probably because of their employer's inability to pay their wages on time.

Byzantine military decline was now acute. Even the local Bithynian militia had been disbanded by Emperor Michael Paleologus in the second half of the thirteenth century, a factor which may have contributed to early Ottoman successes in the north-western Anatolian region of Bithynia. In fact, the Byzantine government largely seems to have lost interest in their remaining Anatolian provinces after recapturing Constantinople from the Crusader or Latin Empire in 1261, and instead paid greater attention to Balkan affairs. The *akritoi* or local frontier leaders were not supported by the central government and many went over to the Turks, as did many of the warlike frontier peasantry.

The Balkans were as fragmented in the medieval period as they are today. Most of the region's inhabitants were Slavs, who included Bulgarians, Macedonians, Serbs, Bosnians, Dalmatians, Croats and Slovenes. Those in the west and north were largely Catholic Christians, except for substantial Bogomil (Manichaean) groups in Bosnia, while those in the south and east were largely Orthodox Christians. Non-Slav linguistic groups included the Albanians, the largely nomadic Vlachs and other ancestors of present-day Romanians, and of course Greek speakers who were largely confined to the Aegean, Ionian and to a lesser extent Black Sea coasts, and the Aegean Islands.

During the early-eleventh century virtually the entire region, except Slovene territory in the far north-west and parts of Dalmatia, was included within the Byzantine Empire. However, the lands of modern Romania largely lay outside Byzantine control, being dominated either by Hungary or by nomadic peoples from the western steppes. By the time the First Crusade marched through their territory, the Serbs had won a large measure of autonomy, and towards the end of the twelfth century the Bulgarians also reasserted their independence. Then, with the Fourth Crusade's capture of Constantinople (Istanbul) in 1204, the whole region fragmented once again. Greece was divided between minor Crusader principalities, the Byzantine *Despotate* of Epirus and within a few decades the revived Byzantine 'Empire of Nicea'. The Serbs meanwhile maintained a relatively small state while the Albanians enjoyed a short-lived independence.

By the mid-fourteenth century, however, Hungary had extended its domination over all of what is now Romania, though much would soon be lost again. Bulgaria had contracted while Serbia had conquered a large if ephemeral empire from the Danube to the Gulf of Corinth. The Crusader principalities held a small part of southern Greece, Venice and Genoa struggled for control of most of the Greek islands, and the Byzantine Empire had shrunk to a few isolated provinces.

Culturally and even politically Byzantium had, of course, been the main influence throughout most of the Balkan peninsula. However, during this period Western and Central Europe made an increasingly important impact, particularly in military matters. This was felt first and foremost in Croatia and Bosnia, but also affected Serbia. In terms of military technology, Western influence came via the expanding Hungarian kingdom and the Republic of Ragusa (Dubrovnik). The latter served as a major channel for the importation of Italian arms and armour, which was then sold on into Bosnia, Serbia, Bulgaria, southern Hungary, Moldavia and Byzantine Greece. The inhabitants of medieval Dalmatia were, in fact, partly Italian in culture and speech though largely now being of Slav origin.

Croatia, having been united with the Hungarian kingdom on terms of near equality in 1091, remained a part of the Hungarian state until modern times. Unsurprisingly, Croatian military equipment therefore echoed that of Hungary, though it generally lacked the horse-archer element of Eurasian steppe origin which distinguished Hungarian military styles from those of other Western countries.

More is known about Dalmatian arms and armour than most other Balkan regions because more documentary sources survive and the art is less influenced by Byzantine archaism. Cavalry seem to have been almost identical to those of the West, and particularly of Italy. Infantry, above all archers with simple and composite bows but later also with crossbows, played a very important role in this urbanized and maritime region. In fact infantry increased in importance from the early-fourteenth century because of greater pressure on the Dalmatian cities by their inland Balkan neighbours. Even as early as 1351 Ragusa (Dubrovnik) was importing firearms from Venice to defend itself from Hungarian attack.

Most unreservedly Westernized of all the Balkan peoples, in terms of military equipment, were the Slovenes. They inhabited the provinces of Carniola, Styria and, until the area was Germanized, parts of Carinthia. All of these had been within the medieval German Empire since they had been recovered from the invading Hungarians back in the tenth century. Only western Istria fell outside the Empire, largely being ruled by Venice.

The Bosnians, being closer to the Adriatic coast and to Italy, were under greater Western influence than the Serbs, whom they otherwise mirrored in military matters. To all intents and purposes Bosnia was independent from the early-twelfth century to 1253, when it fell under Hungarian rule before being incorporated in Stefan Dušan's ephemeral fourteenth-century Serbian Empire. This was, however, a relatively poor, isolated and certainly rugged mountainous area in which archaic forms of warfare survived and distinctive equipment seems to have evolved. An example of the latter might be the large triangular *scutum bosniensem* cavalry shield of the mid-fourteenth century.

Like so many Balkan peoples, the Albanians were dominated by their neighbours throughout most of the Middle Ages. The coastal cities of Albania had survived the urban decline of the early Middle Ages, remaining large as well as commercially and militarily important until the end of the eleventh century. The lowlands were in some respects feudally organized under Byzantine rule, with local warriors already serving as *stradioti* under various categories of Byzantine leadership. The Albanian military role seems to have been quite significant, but a sense of national identity was hindered by the fact that some Albanians were Catholic while others were Orthodox. Nevertheless, independence was won around 1190 during a general period of Byzantine decline, only to be lost again to the *Despotate* of Epirus in 1216. The next phase came with an invasion by the Angevins of southern Italy who, in 1272, established another Albanian kingdom under Angevin patronage. This was followed by a considerable wave of southern Italian and French military influence which was at first eagerly accepted by the local military elites. Angevin control, however, never extended far beyond the coastal plains and cities, while the highlands continued to be dominated by local, sometimes almost nomadic peoples. In the fourteenth century Albanian nomads had spread as far south as Thessaly and they had long dominated the wild highlands of Epirus. When both Angevin and *Despotate* Albania fell under Serbian control in the early 1330s the area was said to support no less than 15,000 cavalry, almost all being lightly-armed tribesmen fighting with spear and sword. Such troops would later make a dramatic impact, usually under the Venetian flag, in fifteenth century Italy, where they were again known as *Stradioti*.

The medieval Hungarian state was very large, and included many provinces inhabited by non-Magyar (non-Hungarian speaking) peoples, though some of these latter areas also had substantial Magyar Hungarian minorities. Many cities also included German minorities and could almost be described as Germanic islands set in a Hungarian sea. In fact the Hungarian state had many of the characteristics of an empire. The most important non-Magyar regions were Transylvania (which had a mixed Hungarian, Romanian and German population), and Zips (Slovakia-Ruthenia), Croatia, Bosnia, Temeşvar (northern Serbia), and northern Dalmatia, all of which were essentially Slav. To the east, Wallachia and Moldavia were for some time under Hungarian suzerainty, but this was relatively short-lived.

The original Hungarians, or Magyars, were a nomadic people of basically Finno-Ugrian origin, though incorporating a large Turkic or Khazar element. After an era of intense warfare, in which the Magyars raided across much of Central Europe and the Germans tried to destroy the nascent Magyar state, the Magyars had suffered a major military defeat at the Battle of Lechfeld in 955. Part of their military aristocracy was slaughtered by the victors and from then on the Magyars were gradually integrated into Christian European civilization.

Hungary officially became Christian in 1001 with the accession of its first king, Stefan. Previously it had been a duchy or principality. Western European feudal institutions were introduced and most of the elite came to adopt Western military systems and styles. While remaining on the defensive along its western frontier, the new Christian Kingdom of Hungary started to press against its northern, southern and eastern neighbours. Following the Magyars' first occupation of the central Danubian Plain, their boundaries had rested upon the crests of the Carpathians to the north, east and south-east, though there is some doubt about the effectiveness of Magyar control over eastern Transylvania which was probably inhabited by semi-nomadic Vlach tribes.

To the south the River Danube and the River Save normally formed the frontier between Hungarian and Croatian, Serbian, Bulgarian and Byzantine territories. From the mid-tenth century the western frontier incorporated Slovakia but not Moravia. It then ran slightly west of the present Hungarian-Austrian frontier. By the mid-thirteenth century Croatia and Dalmatia had been drawn into the Hungarian kingdom by marriage alliance, while Bosnia would be conquered from the Serbs and western Wallachia fell under Hungarian suzerainty. Hungary next felt the full effect of the Mongol assault in 1241, but the country was never incorporated into the Mongol World Empire. In fact Hungary recovered quickly, and during the fourteenth century developed into a powerful centralized state structured almost entirely along Western European lines. Bosnia was retaken, temporarily, in 1328, both Wallachia and Moldavia remaining under Hungarian suzerainty until the 1360s.

Traditional Magyar military styles had relied on a small tribal elite of cavalry, mostly lightly equipped horse-archers though a minority might have used heavier armour. Tactics were basically in the Eurasian steppe tradition, though in the version characteristic of the western rather than eastern steppes. In addition early-medieval Hungary had many characteristics in common with Iran rather than with the Central Asian Turks. Bows were also closer to the Sassanian, Caucasian, Byzantine or early Islamic style than to the Turkish form, as were several aspects of Magyar-Hungarian arms and armour. There is also evidence to suggest that Magyar horse-archery tactics were closer to those of the Middle East than to those of Central Asia. Cultural as well as trade contacts with the Islamic world had, in fact, been very important in tenth-eleventh century Hungary and would remain so throughout the rest of the medieval period.

The first phase of the 'Westernization' of Hungary up to the twelfth century had probably only affected the royal household, mercenary troops, and some leading barons. Many sections of Magyar society, particularly in the Great Plain, remained tribal and at least semi-nomadic well into the twelfth century, if not longer. However, the majority of the population, especially in the Slav areas, had always been agricultural. Many Magyars also now settled down, which in turn led to increasing feudalization of the country and of the army. Light cavalry did not disappear but they declined in importance, while arms and armour became largely, though not entirely, central and western European.

In fact this process of military 'Westernization' was most characteristic of the Slav provinces of the Hungarian kingdom. Here arms, armour and military traditions had never ceased to be within the wider European tradition. By the twelfth century Hungary was making use of Balkan troops drawn from areas which had been under Western European influence since Carolingian times. Despite a considerable Magyar impact, the military traditions of the northern Carpathian mountains also remained essentially Western.

The same process continued through the thirteenth to fifteenth centuries. By then the traditional or steppe elements had been revived or reinforced by the arrival of large numbers of Cuman (Kipchak) refugees at the time of the Mongol invasions. Nevertheless, the dominant feudal nobility of Hungary were almost indistinguishable from their German or Italian counterparts, as of course were the German settlers and German Teutonic Knights in such areas as Transylvania.

Hungary's long experience of warfare against nomads from the steppes just across the Carpathian mountains probably accounted for a continued employment of numbers of relatively lightly-armed horse-archers of various origins. The thirteenth century Hungarian army had, in fact, many characteristics in common with Byzantine forces. Infantry crossbowmen played some part, though most such troops came from Slav areas like Slovakia. The crossbow then rapidly became popular throughout the kingdom, though even in the fifteenth century it had not completely ousted the composite hand-bow. The Hungarians also used other tactics associated with peoples of the western steppes such as wagons drawn up to form field fortifications, although this particular idea may never have been abandoned since early Magyar times. Many so-called oriental features seen in late-Medieval Hungarian armies are sometimes thought to reflect Ottoman influence, although the Hungarians hardly ever met the Ottomans face-to-face until the late-fourteenth century. Meanwhile various features of late-fourteenth and early-fifteenth-century Ottoman military practice, such as the use of wagons as field fortifications and the adoption of firearms, could correspondingly be seen as examples of Hungarian influence.

Whereas the military elites on the western side of the Balkan peninsula became progressively more Westernized, those of the eastern Balkans were less affected by this process. The latter were closer to the centre of Byzantine civilization, as well as being under considerable military influence, not to say pressure, from the nomadic Turkic peoples of the western steppes. For example, the basic military styles of the Second Bulgarian Empire from the late-twelfth to the fourteenth century seem to have evolved when the area still formed part of the twelfth-century Byzantine Empire, at which time Bulgarian warriors naturally served in Byzantine armies. There were also similarities with medieval Russian arms, though these are likely to have reflected mutual contact with Byzantium and the shared threat of the steppe nomads. Nevertheless, horse-archery did play a minor role in later medieval Bulgaria, probably in the hands of allied or subordinate nomadic tribesmen. The military situation appears to have been similar in Macedonia which, after a brief spell of independence early in the eleventh century, had once again fallen under Byzantine, Bulgarian and finally Serbian domination.

The Serbs themselves initially emerged as two distinct principalities in the eleventh century but evolved into a unified state after ousting Byzantine authority in 1172. Serbia later rose to regional dominance after defeating the Bulgarians in 1330. However, its weapons and tactics seem to have been strongly influenced by Italy and central Europe, if not being fully within the Western tradition. The most important weapons were spears, maces and straight swords for horsemen; Serbian infantry using spears, staff weapons, bows and later crossbows.

The later medieval Serbian army consisted of feudal forces under local lords, strengthened by mercenary units made up of both locals and foreigners. Most of the latter were Germans, though Catalans and other Spaniards played a significant role during the mid-fourteenth century. The Serbian army was also theoretically divided into units of 25 or 50, 100 and 1,000 men, its main strength lying in cavalry and infantry archers. An armed levy of peasants existed but was rarely summoned. The fourteenth century would see a number of new developments in Serbian military equipment and perhaps even organization. However, this was probably a result of indirect Turkish nomad influence; the Ottomans themselves not yet having invaded the Balkans. Or it could have come from Hungary, which was similarly under the influence of Eurasian steppe peoples. The resulting changes included the adoption of curved sabres and composite bows.

The nomadic Vlachs had much in common with the Albanians, in addition to being a similarly ancient people predating the Slav conquest and colonization of the Balkans. They too were tribally rather than feudally organized and were often semi-nomadic pastoralists, though some lived as settled village communities. Vlachs also inhabited areas far beyond present-day Romania, including parts of Greece and Bosnia. Many are said to have preserved some Classical, almost Romano-Greek, military traditions, including military displays or 'funeral' games by jousting horsemen. Vlachs had long served in Byzantine armies and continued to do so during the twelfth to fourteenth centuries, and by the late-fourteenth century they were in the forefront of the struggle against the Ottoman Turks.

The emergence of Vlach principalities in what was later to become Romania began in the thirteenth century when the old tribal structure was already breaking down and feudal systems were evolving under local *hospodars* or magnates. Of the three regions of modern Romania, Transylvania west of the Carpathian mountains had long been ruled by Hungary, while Wallachia to the south-east and Moldavia to the north-east had meanwhile been under the domination of various Turkic peoples from the western steppes, such as Pechenegs, Kipchaks and more recently the Mongols. In an effort to escape increasingly effective Catholic Hungarian feudal control, many Orthodox Vlachs from Transylvania migrated across the Carpathians in the late-thirteenth century to establish the Wallachian principality on the southern slopes of the mountains. Here they may have been joined by Vlach groups from other parts of the Balkans. Wallachia nevertheless remained under Hungarian overlordship until 1330 and Hungarian military influence was naturally very strong. So was that of the Kipchak Turks. A second Vlach state emerged slightly later, under much the same circumstances, on the north-eastern slopes of the Carpathian mountains. This principality of Moldavia won its independence from Hungary in 1359. However, Moldavian military and political systems were also under strong Slavic influence from Russia. Furthermore Moldavia soon had to devote most of its energies to resisting Polish domination.

Given the huge significance for European history of the Ottoman Turks' first permanent toe-hold on the Gallipoli Peninsula it might seem surprising that this event did not cause more of a stir at the time. Yet for many decades the enfeebled Byzantine Empire and its rulers, like some of their rivals in the Balkans and Greece, had been inviting Turkish troops – Muslim or otherwise – to support them in their mutually destructive struggles and their self-defeating civil wars.

The fort of Çinbe (Tzympe) on the Gallipoli Peninsula, which was the first Ottoman outpost in Europe, did not even have to be conquered; its occupation being the result of a long association between the Byzantine

Emperor John VI Cantacuzenos and the Ottoman *emir*. On the death of Emperor Andronicus III in 1341, John Cantacuzenos had enlisted Serbian and Turkish mercenaries in an effort to oust his co-Emperor John V Paleologus. Most of these Turkish troops came from Aydin rather than the Ottoman state, but they were allowed to raid across much of Macedonia before returning to Anatolia with rich booty. The *beylik* of Aydin went into steep decline after the death of its famous ruler, Umur Bey, so the next time Cantacuzenos needed help he turned to the Byzantine Empire's immediate neighbours, the Ottomans. Orhan was supposedly encouraged to take 5,500 troops over the Dardanelles into Thrace. With this small but effective army he cleared Cantacuzenos' enemies from the Black Sea coast north-west of Constantinople and enabled his paymaster-ally to regain the Byzantine imperial throne. As part of his reward, Orhan was allowed to marry the new Emperor's daughter Theodora. Meanwhile Ottoman troops under Orhan's son Sülayman were allowed to ravage those parts of Thrace and Gallipoli which did not acknowledge John VI Cantacuzenos as their ruler. It seems that they raided other places as well, including some that recognised Cantacuzenos who was, however, in little position to complain.

John VI Cantacuzenos continued to request Ottoman aid, having inadequate military resources of his own, and in 1349 Sülayman's men were ferried to Thessaloniki by the Byzantine fleet in order to regain that city from the Serbs. Three years later Orhan himself helped Cantacuzenos to defeat his rival, Emperor John V and his Serb and Bulgarian allies outside Didimotokon. It was as a reward for this assistance, and as a means of ensuring that his Ottoman allies would always be ready at hand on the European side of the Straits, that Cantacuzenos allowed Orhan to garrison the little fort at Çinbe (Tzympe) on the Gallipoli Peninsula around 1352 or 1353.

Orhan naturally recognised that this outpost, though small and vulnerable, was a very valuable strategic asset. In fact his followers, and perhaps other enthusiasts not entirely under the Ottoman ruler's control, promptly began raiding the surrounding territory. In 1353 Orhan's son Sülayman reportedly rode north as far as Tekirdağ (Rodosto), apparently in alliance with Genoese ships; the latter presumably hoping that this new alliance would undermine the position of their Venetian rivals in Byzantine trade. Of course Cantacuzenos complained, and stated that Çinbe was only supposed to be a temporary base for his troublesome Ottoman allies. Orhan agreed that the over-enthusiastic Sülayman should come home, but also claimed that it was against Islamic law for him to abandon 'infidel territory' that had been conquered by Islamic arms. He was particularly insistent that the more important town of Gallipoli and its strategic harbour must remain in Ottoman hands. Then on 2 March 1354 the Gallipoli Peninsula was shaken by a severe earthquake that brought down many local fortifications, including those of Çimpe. This in turn prompted Sülayman to reply to the Byzantine Emperor's demands, saying that the earthquake was a sign from God that the Turks must remain – which they did.

With few exceptions, medieval Byzantine military architecture was not on the same scale as that of many of its neighbours. Most exceptions, such as the massive land walls of Constantinople, dated from earlier centuries. In fact, medieval Byzantine architects inherited so much from their Roman and early Byzantine predecessors that most of their own work consisted of upgrading existing structures. As a result the craftsmanship of Byzantine fortification tended not to be very impressive, nor indeed very innovative. Some of the most obvious exceptions were in the design of fortified private dwellings rather than feudal military architecture. The emergence of such fortified dwellings, sometimes in the form of tower-houses, was of course a reflection of declining security in most parts of the later medieval Byzantine world.

Nevertheless, although a great deal of Byzantine religious and military architecture still exists, far fewer domestic buildings survive. The great majority of houses were not fortified and those of ordinary people were probably similar to those of the previous Roman period. At one extreme the poor either lived in small houses with rushes strewn on the floors or in tenements up to nine storeys high. Most homes were of brick, with only the wealthy using stone, though in forested regions such as the coast of the Black Sea, almost all were of wood. Houses of the rich had sloping tiled roofs, while ordinary homes were flat-roofed, at least in the drier regions. The villas of the Byzantine elite were given strong gates for fear of riots and banditry, while the fortified houses resulting from a widespread collapse of law and order during the fourteenth and fifteenth centuries often had strong similarities with Italian urban architecture.

Most of the downstairs windows looked inwards towards a central courtyard, though the higher rooms also had external windows, often glazed with small panes of glass. Stables faced the courtyard where there would be a cistern or well. The homes of the particularly well-off generally had toilets which, in some cases, were linked to a system which drained into the sea. There was often a small bathhouse designed as a separate structure, while the wealthy had small shrines or chapels in their gardens. The layout of the house itself was of ancient origin and consisted of a central hall with other rooms leading off. Some of these formed smaller halls where the men of the household received guests, while the private family rooms were upstairs and had galleried windows overlooking the courtyard. Many had a special room which could be heated for use in winter, either by charcoal braziers or, in wealthier houses, by an underground hypocaust. Byzantine palaces seem to have looked less magnificent than might have been expected, at least on their plain exteriors, but inside they were light and airy with a great deal of colourful decoration ranging from marble panelling to brilliant mosaics. Balkan domestic architecture was very similar to that of the Byzantines and these traditions would then be inherited by the Ottoman Turks in the fifteenth century.

Chapter 3

Aegean Crusaders &
Naval Crusades

or hundreds of years western European knights had been taught to despise their Muslim foes as cowards who fought from a distance, supposedly because they had so little blood in their veins that they feared being wounded. Such propaganda had decreased during the thirteenth century as the Church, and the more educated sections of the ruling aristocracy, came to see Muslims as heretics rather than pagans. Close contact with Islamic civilization had also led to doubts about making war upon Muslims simply because of their different religion. One religious scholar who expressed reservations was named Ricoldus who, around the year 1294, wrote: 'We have been amazed that amongst the followers of so perfidious a law, deeds of so great perfection are to be found.' During this same period, however, anti-Byzantine prejudice had generally increased, with Orthodox Greeks in particular being portrayed as devious, cowardly and effete.

Nowhere were these confused and conflicting ideas more apparent than in the so-called 'Crusader' or Latin States of the Aegean region. These had been established in the wake of the Fourth Crusade of 1204. Thereafter they survived in a state of almost permanent warfare against their Orthodox Christian Byzantine or Bulgarian neighbours, and latterly against the invading Ottoman Turks. Meanwhile a partially Catholic, partly Orthodox Kingdom of Albania was created by the French-Angevin rulers of southern Italy from 1272 to 1286 when it collapsed, and again from 1304 until this ephemeral state was conquered by the Serbs in the 1340s.

The knightly elite of Crusader Greece, like that of the Holy Land, was not only few in number but mostly held small fiefs with relatively few peasants. Even most of the elite themselves were of modest origins, mostly stemming from France, with a smaller number from 'The Empire' in what is now Germany, Austria, Bohemia and the Benelux countries and the easternmost regions of France. Others stemmed from Italy, the Crusader States of the Middle East, Crusader Cyprus and Cilician Armenia.

At first the knightly families of the Aegean Crusader states seem to have been more willing to assimilate existing Slav military elites, and indeed to welcome Turkish settlers if they converted to Christianity, than they were to accept the more numerous resident Greek military elite known as *archontes*. However, as the decades passed and the Crusader elites' shortage of manpower became ever more acute, some *archontes* were knighted and given hereditary fiefs despite remaining members of the Orthodox rather than the Latin or Catholic Christian Church. A rather different situation developed further north in Epirus and Albania. Here a spread of Latin Christianity led to the emergence of two rival communities, the Catholic *Albanenses* and the Orthodox *Graeci*. During the fourteenth century the Albanian military elite also became feudalized along almost Italian lines, with its military forces including large numbers of light cavalry apparently led by local lords who enjoyed the effective if not necessarily the official status of knights.

The mercantile outposts which the Italian maritime republic of Venice and Genoa established along the eastern seaboard of the Adriatic, around the Aegean and the Black Seas, like those established within the Crusader States of the Middle East, were largely defended by troops of Italian origin, in some cases assisted by locals. The main difference was that here in the Near East, such mercantile outposts and colonies were effectively independent of the neighbouring powers – the Venetian 'colonial empire' being under strict control from Venice itself.

Another more shadowy Aegean force could simply be described as pirates. They had been operating with virtual impunity even before the Fourth Crusade and the creation of 'Crusader States' in Greece. They continued to do so, sometimes as independent agents, sometimes as naval mercenaries. One such was Roland of Pisa, who became known as 'The Knight of Thessaloniki'. Even more famous and effective was Licario, a poor knight from Vicenza in Italy, who fled the Venetian island of Evvoia following a blighted love affair and entered Byzantine service in 1271. Licario then reconquered various Aegean islands for the Byzantine Emperor, while other 'pirate knights' served Venice or Genoa. Amongst the most successful were the Zaccaria brothers, who controlled several ports along with the hugely profitable alum mines of the Anatolian coast. They built a formidable fleet and in 1304 seized the prosperous island of Chios in the name of Genoa.

The jewel in Genoa's colonial crown was nevertheless the southern coast of the Crimean peninsula in the Black Sea. Most of the smaller Genoese colonial outposts were governed by associations of wealthy shipowners known as *mahonesi*. Some of these men were of knightly rank while others came from the urban merchant class, and in most cases they were remarkably successful in winning the support of existing local military elites by allowing them a share in the huge profits from long distance trade. Amongst these *mahonesi* were men of extraordinary geographical knowledge. For example, Tedisio d'Orio of Kaffa in the Crimea was said to be interested in opening a trade route to China by travelling westwards, having learned what so many Arab geographers already knew – namely that the world was spherical – a full two centuries years before Christopher Columbus. Whether Tedisio truly hoped to reach China by sailing across the Atlantic nevertheless seems unlikely, and his dream of sailing west from Genoa probably envisaged the circumnavigation of Africa, which Muslim sailors already knew to be a theoretical possibility.

The great majority of the knights of the Latin or Crusader States in the Aegean were more down to earth in their motivation, many having simply abandoned the Latin Emperor in Constantinople when he could no longer afford to pay them. Several generations later the Catalan Grand Company which invaded the Aegean region similarly found no moral difficulty in making long-term alliances with the Muslim Turks of what is now western Turkey. Indeed by the 1330s the Italian rulers of some Aegean states, outposts or islands had accepted the status of *illik kafirleri* or 'non-Muslim frontier lords' under Turkish Muslim suzerainty.

Military pay varied considerably across the Crusader Aegean but in general a mercenary knight received twice or three times as much as a crossbowman, this reflecting the knight's superior status and the cost of his arms, armour and horses. In the Latin Principality of Achaia, which covered most of southern Greece, the 'Ordnance of Nicolas de Joinville' was drawn up around 1323-5 and tried to fix pay for cavalry at 800 *hyperperes* for a year's service by a knight recruited overseas, 600 *hyperperes* for a local knight, and from 300 to 400 *hyperperes* for squires.

Although the Latin states of the Aegean lacked troops rather than horses, they still had to import great numbers of animals as well as items like horseshoes, the majority of both probably coming from southern Italy. Where horse-feed was concerned, these Crusader states had to use whatever was available and as a consequence feed-grain was often said to contain so much grit and rubbish that it had to be sieved before use. On the other hand, grass and straw from the fields may have been more nutritious than it is today because primitive medieval harvesting techniques left a great deal of grain on the ground, which then sprouted.

It is also interesting to note that polo was adopted as a form of cavalry training in several Crusader States. Known as *tzykanion* in Byzantine Greek, it eventually entered medieval French as *chicane*. At the same time the typical western knightly form of cavalry training and entertainment known as *jousting* by pairs of horsemen was even more popular; a particularly famous and splendid tournament being held on the Isthmus of Corinth in 1302. This festival lasted for twenty days.

Meanwhile the Latin elites' enormous sense of their own superiority over indigenous peoples gave them military confidence long after their real dominance had been lost. Though there had been an increase in class consciousness amongst the aristocracy of the Latin east since the later-twelfth century, the declining wealth of many knights made it difficult for them to marry outside the Crusader States. This was just as apparent in Greece at it had been in the Holy Land and consequently the Pope was sometimes asked for special dispensation so that blood relatives could wed. In contrast intermarriage with Orthodox Christians was resisted and in some cases banned outright. Punishments similarly reflected this rigid class structure; rebel knights in Venetian Crete losing their fiefs and non-noble Latins their assets, while rebel Greeks lost a hand or a foot.

At first most of the military elite of the Crusader Principality of Achaea lived in isolated mountaintop castles or strongly fortified manor-houses, at least until much of the rural interior was reconquered by the Byzantines. Here it is worth noting that the finer examples of architectural decoration from Latin Greece show Islamic rather than Byzantine influence, suggesting that architects and masons as well as knights had fled to Crusader Greece from the declining Crusader states of Syria and Palestine during the later-thirteenth century.

In Greece the Latin elite also took pains to differentiate itself from the Greek majority, enforcing laws which supported them in this effort by limiting the right to wear various symbols of knighthood such as spurs, sword, sword-belt and even cloth-of-gold fabric. Nevertheless, religion remained the main divide between the Latin military elites and those they ruled, even though many Latin settler families were eventually absorbed into later-fourteenth and fifteenth century Orthodox Christian Byzantine society. Before that, however, the Crusader elites tried to follow the ideas and fashions of Paris as closely as they could.

Literature, wall-paintings and social events like tournaments all helped this small and somewhat isolated 'western' aristocracy keep in touch with their peers in the western heartlands of medieval European civilization. The art and architecture of these Crusader states was, however, primitive compared to that of its more sophisticated neighbours. Quite a lot of wall paintings survive while others, now lost, had been described in literary sources. The Siege of Troy was, for example, a favoured theme in Crusader Greece, while the 'Castle of St. Omer' in Thebes was decorated with pictures of the Crusader conquest of Syria. Its artists may actually have come from Antioch with the Duke's wife.

Though there were plenty of troubadour poets moving around the Latin East, the question of original literary production is more difficult. Stories about Ancient Greek heroes were also popular, particularly those involving battles against female Amazons or relating to the Trojan War. Surviving texts show that the literature in Latin Greece was most similar to that of French-dominated southern Italy, often involving tales of King Arthur and his Knights of the Round Table. During the fourteenth century, however, Italian began to challenge French as the language of the aristocratic elite in Latin Greece.

At first the feudal hierarchy had been simpler in Crusader Greece than in Western Europe, but things changed when the Duchy of Athens fell under Catalan rule in the early-fourteenth century. Thereafter the main officers were a political *vicar general* and a military *marshal* who was always selected from the knights of the Catalan Grand Company, an initially mercenary but latterly independent army which had conquered the area. After the Catalans themselves accepted the overlordship of the Aragonese Kingdom of Sicily the system was again modified, with each district having its own political *vaguer* (vicar) and military *castellano* or captain.

According to the feudal legal code of Crusader Greece, a knight's obligatory military service involved four months in a castle garrison, four months guarding the frontier, and four months at home as an emergency reserve. Meanwhile military obligations in the Italian mercantile outposts mirrored those in their mother cities back in Italy. Garrison service must have been tedious and the food could clearly be poor. On the other hand the real effectiveness of medieval fortification largely depended upon the quantity and quality of its provisions of wheat, wine, iron, steel and leather – at least as much as the strength of its walls and towers. During the day the gates were normally guarded by knights or non-noble men-at-arms and were probably shut at *Compline* which was the last religious service of the day. Knights formed just over a third of the cavalry in most such castles, horsemen being about a third of the total fighting force which was in turn around a quarter of the total inhabitants. In contrast some Italian trading outposts were defended by remarkably small garrisons, though the most important Genoese settlements did have their own military *baylia* in charge of defence.

During the thirteenth and fourteenth centuries naval warfare became more important for the scattered Latin or Crusader outposts than were campaigns on land. Yet naval raiding was usually on a small scale with the local military aristocracy engaged in little more than piracy. Most of the marines aboard Angevin galleys were, for example, mailed knights recruited in Provençe, but they proved less agile than their non-noble lightly armoured Catalan rivals known as *almogavers*. The crews of ships manned by Latin settlers in the fourteenth-century Crusader States of Greece, especially those based in the Venetian colonies, were summoned by a public crier a week before sailing, then again on the day of departure. Thereafter they were fined if they did not turn out properly armed. Such maritime expeditions involved considerable hardship even for the knights, the basic food being hard biscuit, though figs and wine could be purchased along the way. In winter the fragile war-galleys were almost always taken out of the water, to be placed under cover and guarded by the local garrison. It is also worth noting that galley-slaves had not been used since the fall of the Roman Empire. Until almost the very end of the medieval period Byzantine and Muslim navies remained volunteers except for the personal servants of senior officers. In fact it was the Crusading Order of Hospitallers based at Rhodes which reintroduced galley-slaves to the Mediterranean, and even they should more accurately be described as galley-serfs since service as oarsmen was one of the obligations imposed upon the Hospitallers' Greek Orthodox subjects. Muslims were rarely used as galley slaves for the simple reason that the Hospitallers very rarely took any prisoners when at war with their Muslim Turkish neighbours – captives were simply slaughtered.

Naval tactics were quite simple, with crossbowmen forming the main defence while marines, including knights, attempted to board enemy vessels. Knights were more important in the naval landings which often involved *taridas*, a specialised horse-transporting galley of Arab origin in which the animals stood in stalls down the centre of the vessel. By using its oars a *tarida* could back on to a beach and disgorge its troops directly into battle like a modern landing craft. Meanwhile, larger ships stood offshore, unloading their cargoes of men, horses and supplies into small boats.

Most historians highlight Italian naval dominance as being a key strategic consideration in the history of the Aegean region during this period. However, the Christians' naval superiority is too often overstated, just as it is in relation to the history of the Crusader States in the eastern Mediterranean. The idea that Christian fleets dominated the Aegean and Black Seas well into the fifteenth century is also simplistic and exaggerated. While it is true that Turkish Islamic fleets could rarely challenge Italian or Crusader fleets face to face until the rise of Ottoman naval power in the later-fifteenth century, they rarely attempted to do so. Instead pre-Ottoman Turkish and early Ottoman naval expeditions took advantage of their numerous and almost invariably smaller ships to raid Christian-held islands and coasts while the more powerful but less numerous Italian, Crusader or indeed Byzantine, warships were elsewhere. This had a profound impact upon the location, supplying, defence and garrisoning of Christian fortifications as small forces put ashore by so-called Muslim 'pirates' sometimes penetrated deep inland.

On land tactics also remained quite traditional. The part-Byzantine Greek, part-Latin prince Theodore Palaiologos wrote a military treatise in 1326 in which he advised that if a force was caught unawares its fighting men should not try to form separate units. Instead they should quickly gather into a single body while the squires and pack animals drew up a short distance to the rear where they could collect and guard any prisoners and secure any riderless horses. Individual skills remained paramount, but clearly it was not always the fully armoured knight who dominated. On one occasion early in the fourteenth century a captured Catalan *almogaver* infantryman was pitted against a fully armoured Angevin knight in a particularly ruthless form of 'tournament' or military test in Latin Greece. On that occasion the unarmoured *almogaver*, armed with a spear, light javelin and light sword, awaited the horseman's charge then at the last moment threw his javelin into the horse's chest and dodged the rider's lance. As the knight tumbled from his wounded horse the Catalan cut the knight's helmet thongs and held his sword at the man's throat. As a reward for this success the captive *almogaver* was given fine clothes and set free.

Since there was virtually no arms industry in the Crusader east, neither in the Holy Land nor in the Aegean region and Greece, almost all military equipment had to be imported from Western Europe. The only other source was captured enemy material, much of which was unsuitable for western-style troops. On the other hand the perishable wooden, leather or fabric parts of arms and armour were made locally, certainly in Latin Greece. For example, the Angevin ruler of Naples had established a local armoury in the Greek castle of Clarence in 1281, while a local armourer in Crete was subsequently recorded manufacturing *curacijs* cuirasses or body-armours in 1336.

The bulk of arms and armour nevertheless came from Italy, which had been a major centre of production since at least the twelfth century, Genoa being the main export centre while Milan and some neighbouring cities were the main places of manufacture. During the fourteenth century Albania and Epirus similarly imported large amounts of arms from Italy.

The lighter arms popular in the Aegean region were highlighted in the military treatise written by Theodore Palaiologos, who wrote;

> Indeed in the matter of mounted soldiers... each with his armour and equipment, he should have two small horses like those of the Greeks and the Turks, that is to say geldings, or at least two mares, and that he be armed to match the strength of his horses. That is to say with doublet, haubergeon and gorgeret, cuirass and gambeson, chapel de fer, sword of one type or another at his side, greaves and cuisses and his lance and shield. And if he wishes to have great horses, that is to say destriers in Latin style, let him be armed with heavy armour suitable for that purpose.... And in this connection let their surcoats be provided with a badge like that on their banners, ensigns and the pennons of their lances to make a good show of their people, and this I would also apply to mounted lesser people of the said districts. Vassals and knights should have three horses, a destrier, a good palfrey and a good packhorse to carry their necessary equipment. Barons and those of higher rank should each have at least five horses with their harness, and each should have a good squire to keep him company by his side, and none of them should spare expense for in bearing himself well it turns to his honour and profit, and his renown is increased.

During the mid-fourteenth century this European heraldic system spread beyond the Crusader States to some of the indigenous leaders of the Balkans. One such was Charles Thopia, ruler of the Albanian principality of Dürres, who incorporated the French fleurs-de-lys into his coat-of-arms, partly because his mother was Helen of Anjou and partly as a mark of allegiance to the Angevin rulers of southern Italy. Thereafter the fleurs-de-lys spread further and recently formed the basis of the new Bosnian national flag.

Chapter 4

Religion and the Sword

*R*eligion played an absolutely central role in Byzantine civilization. The schism between the Orthodox and Catholic, Greek and Latin, Churches dated from 1054, but feelings of difference if not separation had been increasing for centuries and continued to do so. The Fourth Crusade of 1204, when a Western European army conquered Constantinople, made Orthodox Christians even more antagonistic towards Catholics. Nevertheless, many efforts at reconciliation were attempted in the following years but all failed, the last one dating from 1453 – the year the Byzantine capital of Constantinople finally fell to the Ottoman Turks.

Orthodox Christians had a deep belief in the power of faith and ordinary people considered that miracles, great or small, were an almost everyday occurrence. They also had a very literal view of the Bible but what most distinguished them was a faith in the power of *icons* or religious images. During the *iconoclastic* or 'icon breaking' controversy of the early medieval period, the Byzantine Empire had been the stronghold of the *iconoclasts* who felt that faith in religious images was misplaced. Paradoxically the stronghold of the *iconophiles*, or those who approved of holy images, was in what would become the Catholic West. By the eleventh century, however, *iconoclasm* was a thing of the past and icons now played a major role in the religious life of people from the Byzantine Emperor to the humblest Balkan peasant. As a result Orthodox Christians were regarded as little more than idol-worshippers by many of their Muslim neighbours.

Monasteries also played a fundamental role in Byzantine life, though Orthodox monasticism remained closer to the ascetic ideals of the first Christian monks than did Catholic monasticism, Byzantine monks being almost entirely concerned with prayer, religious study and the making of icons. It was also quite normal for members of the ruling elites to enter monasteries when they retired from public service. Even the warrior Emperor John Cantacuzenos became a monk after his abdication in 1354, adopting the name of Ioasaph.

The Byzantine Church was a strictly hierarchical organization headed by the Patriarch of Constantinople, who had a close religious and political relationship with the Emperor. This enabled the Byzantine Empire to use the Orthodox Church to influence other Orthodox states and, as a result, the position of the Patriarch of Constantinople became a highly political one. In contrast, Orthodox monasteries were spiritual retreats, often in extremely inaccessible places such as Mount Athos on the easternmost finger of the Khalkidiki peninsula in northern Greece. The other-worldly character of many Orthodox monasteries did not, however, stop them growing rich from donations of money and land. Nor were their leaders reluctant to interfere in the outside world when they felt that political morals were slipping.

As the Byzantine Empire crumbled, some groups of monasteries became virtually autonomous, the most famous being Mount Athos. This area was handed over from the Emperor to the Patriarch in 1312 and would preserve its separate status even after the Balkans were conquered by the Ottoman Turks. Because they owned huge estates, many Orthodox monasteries had large staffs of servants and agricultural labourers. Many monasteries also employed their own garrison troops, and it was common for the monks themselves to take up arms in a crisis. In fact some parts of eastern Europe were dominated by the monastic economy.

Despite the frequently appalling oppression which the Byzantine peasantry endured at the hands of its own aristocracy, there were few revolts because of the people's unswerving loyalty to the Church, particularly in the face of Muslim encroachment. When loyalty did collapse, it was usually seen amongst non-Greeks, often resulting in complete changes in religion or adherence to extreme heresies. For example, the Paulician heresy, which had flourished amongst the Armenians of early medieval eastern Anatolia, spread to the Balkans where it led to the emergence of the Bogomil movement. This flourished particularly amongst Bosnian Slavs and Albanians, which would be precisely those communities where Islam later won its greatest number of converts following the Ottoman Turkish conquest in the 1460s.

In some respects Islam could be seen as a polar opposite of Orthodox Christianity, yet these differences were often superficial rather than fundamental. Muslims believe in One God, whom they call by the Arabic name *Allah*, but whom they regarded as the same God worshipped by Jews and Christians. In fact many Muslims would say that all religions, even the most primitive, worship Allah though in ways which have become corrupted across thousands of years of human interference. For this reason Muslim toleration, though sometimes more theoretical than real, could extend to any group which acknowledged the existence of a Supreme Creator.

Muslims also regard Muhammad as the Seal of the Prophets, in other words the last in a line of prophets going back to Adam himself and including Old Testament Jewish prophets, Jesus Christ, several pre-Islamic Arabian prophets not recognized by Jews or Christians, and, in the eyes of some Muslim thinkers, the founders of all the world's earlier religions. The other basic aspects of the Muslim faith are prayer, fasting, giving alms to the poor and, where possible, making the *Haj*, or pilgrimage, to Mecca.

However, within less than a century of the Prophet Muhammad's death in 632, the Islamic community split into two factions; the Sunni, sometimes called 'Orthodox' Muslims, and the minority Sh'ia, but apart from small differences in doctrine and ritual, disagreement between the two primarily concerned religious authority on earth.

For ordinary medieval Muslims, however, religion continued to dominate everyday life, as it did that of their Orthodox Christian neighbours, with obligatory daily prayers, congregational prayers each Friday, fasting during the month of Ramadan and saving up for the pilgrimage to Mecca. The mosque, meanwhile, was not considered sacred like a Christian church or a Hindu temple, merely being a place of communal prayer which needed to be respected and kept clean. Some mosques did, nevertheless, take on the character of shrines for other reasons, usually because they included the tombs of important religious figures. Other mosques served as religious colleges, or as centres where *sufi* mystic brotherhoods would gather to celebrate in their own somewhat unorthodox manner – celebrations which could include religious music and dance. The latter would become a major community within Ottoman Islam.

Many parts of the medieval Muslim world also held unorthodox beliefs, which could include beliefs in *jinnis* and demons, even amongst the ruling classes. *Jinnis* were thought to be creatures created from fire, just as mankind was created from clay and, like humans, they included male and female, good and bad, Muslims and non-believers. There was a similarly widespread belief in magic, talismans, and prediction of the future.

On the other hand Islam was not structured in the same way as Christianity. Even the Abbasid Sunni *Caliphs* of Baghdad (750-1258) had lost most of their temporal power by the eleventh century, but survived as little more than puppets in Cairo until shortly after the Ottoman conquest of Egypt. Basically the Islamic religious establishment consisted of the *Sharia* legal system and junior *imams* who led prayers in local mosques. These men were not, however, priests, as no such people existed in Islam, but were individuals with sufficient religious education to be accepted by their local communities as religious leaders. Beyond that, the *imam* had virtually no official spiritual authority within Sunni and thus Ottoman Islam.

Another characteristic of later medieval Turkish Anatolia was the large degree of Christian influence upon Islam at the village or tribal level, resulting in some highly unorthodox practices. On the other hand, these made conversion from Orthodox Christianity to Islam much easier. A spread of religious mysticism was, in fact, one of the most notable features of later medieval Islamic society in many countries. It not only flourished in the towns, but also involved wandering dervishes, extreme ascetics, disaffected tribal groups and downtrodden peasants. Shi'a doctrines had by now been largely driven underground and, in their more extreme versions, served as a sort of revolutionary undercurrent.

The powerful Ottoman Sultans only really joined the orthodox Sunni Muslim community in the fifteenth century and, even then, the Ottoman Empire remained home to a large number of varied dervish sects. One of the most unusual was that of the *Bektaşis* whose doctrines and practices included some Buddhist concepts dating back to the time before the Turks converted to Islam. Not only did the *Bektaşi* movement welcome Christians and Jews into the lower ranks of its brotherhood, but they also developed a close relationship with the Janissaries, the Ottoman Sultan's elite infantry troops.

Ever since the days of the Seljuk Sultanate of Rum, Anatolia had been home to several mystical Islamic movements or *dervish* sects. Also referred to as *Sufis*, 'woollies' or 'wearers of rough woollen clothing', some of these groups again reflected the Turks' own pre-Islamic beliefs, including shamanist and Buddhist influences. Others owed more to early Persian-Islamic mysticism and several clearly incorporated elements of the somewhat unorthodox 'folk' Christianity seen in Byzantine Anatolia before the Seljuk conquest.

Shi'a Islam had similarly been strong in early Turkish Anatolia, especially amongst *gazi* or religiously motivated frontier communities and within nomadic Turcoman tribes. It was for these reasons that early Ottoman rulers, though proclaiming their Sunni Muslim orthodoxy, only really became 'mainstream' Muslims in the late-fifteenth century. Such orthodoxy strengthened after the Ottomans defeated the Mamluk Sultans and took over the ancient Middle Eastern heartlands of Islamic civilisation.

Three *dervish* or *sufi* movements would play a notable role in the conversion of many Anatolian and subsequently Balkan Christian communities to Islam. They were the *Mevlavis*, the *Baktaşis* and the *Melamia*. The *Mevlavis* are today the most famous of such *sufi* sects, being popularly known as the 'Whirling Dervishes'. This sect was founded by the renowned Persian poet and mystic, Jalal al-Din Rumi, at Konya in Turkey in the thirteenth century. During the Ottoman period the *Mevlavis* were more prominent in Turkish Anatolia and some parts of the Arab world, while the other two sects were widespread in both Anatolia and the Balkan provinces known to the Turks as Rumelia.

It is difficult to separate truth from legend where the origins of the *Baktaşi* dervishes are concerned. They clearly had a close association with the elite Janissary corps from its very earliest days and were even credited with responsibility for the Janissaries' distinctive tall, white felt caps. Headgear had been a form of religious identification for many years and the tall red hats worn by most early Ottoman troops, including the older and even more prestigious regiment of *Silahtars*, had also been worn by revolutionary Shi'a sects in previous decades. This may, in fact, be evidence of Shi'a influence during the earliest years of the Ottoman state.

First recorded with certainty in thirteenth century Anatolia, the *Baktaşis* were widely regarded by orthodox Sunni Muslims as suspect and even sometimes heretical – an attitude which survives to this day in several parts of the Islamic world. On the other hand, they were very popular amongst the recently converted, ex-Christian and often only superficially-Islamic populations within the expanding Ottoman Sultanate. Christian influence can almost certainly be seen in a ceremonial distribution of bread, cheese and even sometimes wine when a new member was accepted into the *Baktaşi* order. The movement was also characterized by what modern Europeans would describe as a liberal attitude towards the role and status of women.

The original centre of the *Melami* movement was, like that of the *Bektaşis*, in central Anatolia. They had *tekkes* or meeting places in Üskudar on the eastern side of the Bosphoros facing Istanbul, as well as in several other major cities. A refusal to be bound by the external forms of religion was a notable feature of *Melami* belief, and this often got them into trouble with the Ottoman authorities. Perhaps for such reasons most other *Melami* centres were near the European frontiers of the Ottoman state, in Albania, Bosnia and in Budapest during the relatively brief period of Ottoman rule over Hungary.

The Latin or Catholic Christians who dominated relatively small amounts of territory within the Near East and Balkans included communities who were seen as entirely normal in the Middle Ages, but whose beliefs and actions seem shocking to modern European Christians. Above all there was the Crusading Order of Hospitallers which, originally founded as a pious charity to help sick or injured pilgrims in the Holy Land, had become a thoroughly warlike, frequently ruthless and generally oppressive presence in the fourteenth- and fifteenth-century Aegean region.

When Foulques de Villaret was elected Master of the Hospitallers in 1305 the Order entered a more active phase of naval warfare, almost entirely targetted against the Mamluk Sultanate of Egypt and Syria. Both Foulques de Villaret and the Master of the Templars favoured an attack on Egypt using Cyprus, the Hospitallers' new but temporary headquarters, as a base. For his part Pope Clement V clearly had a high opinion of the Masters' Crusading expertize, though their opinions differed. Whereas the Templar memorandum was rather overconfident and even cocky in tone, that by Foulques de Villaret was very different – longer, more carefully argued, less direct and more subtle, reading like a bureaucrat's report rather than one written by a military leader. It emphasized prudence and careful preparation, hinting that a series of small-scale operations over a prolonged period by professional, and where necessary mercenary forces, would be more effective in wearing down enemy power than the sort of all-out Crusading invasion which had so often come to grief.

How far De Villaret's ideas reflected the attitudes of the Hospitallers as a whole is unclear. Yet they suggested that the Hospitallers, under his Mastership, were now an organization which was willing to lower its idealistic sights to accommodate current realities. Such pragmatism would stand the Hospitallers in good stead for centuries, while their Templar rivals would soon be disgraced and disbanded.

It was probably pragmatism which prompted the Hospitallers to conquer the Byzantine island of Rhodes, which was actually further from their Mamluk foes than was Cyprus. It would, on the other hand, provide the Order with its own effectively independent base; something which the Teutonic Knights were currently establishing in the Baltic and which the doomed Templars never achieved. Rhodes was a large and fertile, almost self-sufficient island, set in seas which were still controlled by Christians. Furthermore, it was ideally placed next to the vital trade-route from the Black Sea to Egypt, a shipping lane which not only supplied the Mamluk Sultanate with wood and iron but with the largely Turkish slaves who, once trained and freed, became the backbone of the Mamluk army and state.

Rhodes had long been a fief of Genoese admirals in Byzantine service, and the piracy which had been endemic through the Aegean for a century had grown worse since the Byzantines regained many of the smaller islands. Meanwhile Western merchants and pirates were also active around Rhodes which Venice, as ruler of nearby Crete, similarly coveted.

More recently, Turkish forces had seized part of Rhodes so the Hospitallers were entering an already chaotic region. Various small Turkish *beylik* states had reached the Aegean coast only a few years earlier and they may have been trying to make the pirate-infested off-shore islands into a sort of depopulated no-man's-land along their new and vulnerable coastal frontiers. This was a long-established strategy and the Turks would certainly have regarded the emergence of a warlike new Hospitaller state within this zone as a dangerous threat. Thus the Hospitaller invaders found themselves up against two enemies; the Muslim Turks and the Orthodox Christian Byzantine Greeks whom the Hospitallers, as Latin Catholic Christians, regarded as Schismatics. As a result the Hospitallers probably did not fully control Rhodes until around 1309.

Once established on Rhodes, however, the Order of the Hospitallers not only acquired a new Convent or headquarters, but also a new role – something which their rivals, the Templars, again never achieved. Unfortunately Foulques de Villaret now started to behave like a despotic sovereign rather than the elected leader of a Crusading Military Order. This provoked a rebellion by many Hospitaller brethren in 1317 and the crisis was only solved after the Pope himself intervened. De Villaret resigned, a new Master, Helion de Villeneuve, took over and the Order was finally able to focus on its new role.

As early as 1313 the Hospitallers had offered land, yet to be conquered, to would-be colonizers in return for military service. This differed according to the status of the settler, be they nobleman, freeman, labourer or those who would maintain a fighting galley and its crew. Efforts to carve out a presence on the Anatolian mainland failed, but other islands were seized, stretching from Lerro (now called Léros) in the north to Castelrosso (now called Kastellórizon) in the south-east. Scarpanto (now called Kárpathos) in the west was, however, handed over to the Venetian authorities in Crete.

The conquest of Rhodes had been an impressive combined sea-land operation, and in 1319 Hospitaller ships defeated a Turkish flotilla which was apparently attempting to retake the island. Nevertheless it took the Order many decades to become truly 'naval minded', relying instead on Sicilian, Provençal, Venetian and Genoese ships.

In fact once the Hospitallers were established in Rhodes and the neighbouring islands, their military activity remained limited for many years. Nevertheless Rhodes could already dominate several hundred kilometres of the Anatolian or Turkish coast, and during the 1320s the nearby Turkish *emirate* or *beylik* of Menteşe was virtually denied access to the sea. The main centre of Turkish naval operations now shifted northwards to the *beylik* of Aydin which, as yet, lay beyond the Hospitallers immediate zone of operations. As a consequence flotillas of relatively small raiding ships from Aydin dominated various parts of the Aegean for years. Eventually, in 1344 the Hospitallers joined other recently arrived Crusaders in seizing Aydin's main port of Smyrna (Izmir), so the focus of Turkish naval operations shifted northwards yet again to what had been the *beylik* of Karasi. Ten years later it was from here that the rapidly expanding Ottoman *emirate* crossed the Dardanelles and occupied its first toe-hold on European soil.

Until this point the Hospitallers still apparently regarded their traditional enemy, the powerful Mamluk Sultanate in Egypt and Syria, as the greatest threat. In 1365 the Order took part in a devastating but largely pointless attack upon the great Egyptian port of Alexandria. Hospitaller Rhodes had itself now become a centre of piracy or privateering but, as Latin Crusader territory shrank elsewhere in Greece and the Aegean, so the importance of Rhodes rose. Hospitaller relations with the Mamluks also improved and would eventually develop into something approaching an alliance during the fifteenth century. Meanwhile the Order's relations with the Anatolian Turkish *beyliks*, including the increasingly powerful Ottomans, remained fundamentally hostile.

Relations between the Hospitallers and the local people of Rhodes were dominated by two factors. The first was the cultural and religious gulf which separated the dominant Catholic Hospitallers and the Orthodox Greeks. The second was the mutual concern for defence in a dangerous environment which brought them together. This dichotomy was visible in the city of Rhodes itself where the local Orthodox population had been expelled from the Old City, which was now reserved for the Hospitallers, and instead inhabited a neighbouring suburb, which was nevertheless given a strong defensive wall by the mid-fourteenth century.

Throughout eastern Europe antagonism between Catholics and Orthodox had been increasing since the thirteenth century, reaching such a pitch that some Westerners hated 'Greeks' even more than they did Muslims. In Rhodes the Hospitallers insisted that the local Orthodox Church recognize the supremacy of the Pope in Rome. Eventually the urban

Greeks did so, and in 1437 there was a Uniate Metropolitan (leader of the local Orthodox Church) alongside the Catholic Archbishop. The rural Greek villagers never, apparently, recognized this state of affairs but even so they and their religious leaders became part of the feudal and defence structure which the Hospitallers imposed upon their islands. Yet the different status of Greeks and Latins was still shown in the size and value of the estates they were granted; those of Greeks being tiny while those of Latin Italian settlers sometimes being very large.

Despite these tensions, Rhodes prospered under Hospitaller rule. It became a major transit point in the slave trade from the Black Sea, some of the slaves even being non-Catholic Christians. Many European families settled in the islands, including mercenary soldiers, privateers with their ships and crews, lawyers, bankers, gunners, swordsmiths, armourers, all sorts of other craftsmen and medical staff for the famous Infirmary. There was a particularly large contingent of Florentine, Catalan and southern-French merchants in the early-fifteenth century, while Jews were listed amongst the physicians, surgeons, and apothecaries, as well as craftsmen making clocks, locks, astrolabes and maps. In addition there were Armenians, Cypriots and Syrians who were probably Maronite Christians.

Despite earlier competition between the Military Orders of the Hospitallers and the Templars, the Hospitallers continued to have a high opinion of their now-disbanded rivals. Having inherited so much ex-Templar property, the new Hospitaller owners also felt themselves honoured to follow in the footsteps of what they described as 'so noble a body'. Meanwhile in Rhodes the fighting rather than administrative arm of the Order – who were, of course, often the same men – created a remarkable and rather romantic haven of chivalry. This happened at a time when the ideals of chivalry were under threat elsewhere in Europe, and ultimately became the subject of mockery.

By the fifteenth and sixteenth century there was little more than a veneer of chivalry in Western European warfare, but the Hospitallers of Rhodes continued to see themselves and portray themselves to others as *propugnacula fidee* or 'bulwarks of the faith'. Rhodes itself became a sort of idealized Arthurian citadel where true knights could follow the true code of chivalry. Master Dieudonné de Gozon, for example, came to Rhodes as a young man and was said to have slain a 'wicked worm' or serpent which had been eating young maidens and had already killed several knights. The reality behind this legend appears to have been the young De Gozon's training of some hunting dogs to find and kill a troublesome snake. He and other fourteenth-century Hospitaller leaders tried to fill the Master's court with the noblest blood in Christendom, while also spreading the fame of Rhodes, its fertility and beauty as a sort of 'garden' in which the Knights of Christ could rest after fighting God's foes.

Yet it would be wrong to see the Hospitallers as abandoning their deep if rather naive faith. The Order tirelessly tried to keep the ideal of the Crusade alive, much to the annoyance of more secular minded rulers like those of Venice. The knights on Rhodes also cultivated a mystique of martyrdom, well illustrated in a speech by the Papal Legate before the Hospitallers and other Crusaders sacked Alexandria in 1365. 'Chosen Knights of Christ', he proclaimed, 'be comforted in the Lord and his Holy Cross. Fight manfully in God's war, fearing not your enemy and hoping for victory from God, for today the gates of Paradise are open.'

Normally the fanaticism, if not the supposed chivalry, of the Hospitallers meant that they killed almost all male Muslim prisoners except for children, who were enslaved. There seems to have been a slight change in attitude during the fifteenth century, with captured Muslims, male and female, been sent to slave markets in Italy. From the mid-fifteenth century, with the abolition of the failing *servitudo marina* levy of Rhodian Greek oarsmen, Turkish captives were used as galley slaves. From then on the oarsmen in most Hospitaller galleys consisted of two-thirds slaves and one third *buonavoglia* volunteers who had usually enlisted to pay off their debts. Meanwhile the crews of Turkish war-galleys still consisted entirely of volunteers.

Relations between Hospitaller Rhodes and the fast expanding Ottoman Empire were complicated by the Order's insistence that their only earthly sovereign was the Pope. While other Latin rulers in the Aegean area recognized reality and hurried to congratulate Sultan Mehmet II on his conquest of Constantinople in 1453, the Hospitallers alone refused to do so. Instead they tried to dabble in Ottoman politics, giving refuge to one of Mehmet II's sons, Prince Cem, during the civil war which followed Mehmet's death in 1481. Cem remained in the Order's hands as a pensioned exile while his brother, Sultan Bayezit II, ruled as Sultan. Eventually Cem was taken to France, where he lived in a Hospitaller house.

For their part the Turks did not normally kill Christian prisoners. There are also records of Western European knights having experience of fighting in, rather than against, Ottoman armies, but these obviously would not have included Hospitaller brethren. Whereas there seems to be no direct evidence of Hospitallers being taken alive by the Ottomans, the Venetian Emmanuel Piloti who visited Egypt in 1420 reported that some two hundred French and Italian captives had converted to Islam and had risen to prominence within the Mamluk military system. They currently formed part of the Cairo Citadel garrison, but are unlikely to have included ex-Hospitallers.

Despite the chivalric reputation which grew up around Rhodes, and the important political or diplomatic role of Hospitaller leaders, the Order's military activities were very limited during in the fourteenth century. Much fighting in the Aegean was actually done by mercenaries in Hospitaller service rather than by the brethren themselves. Although much of this lack of action during the fourteenth century could be attributed to slow and distant communication as well as corrupt and inefficient administration, there was inevitably widespread criticism.

Some critics struck at the very purpose of the Military Orders, arguing that their belligerence was immoral, illegal and actually hindered efforts to convert Muslims to Christianity. A few critics of noble birth also resented the way in which men of relatively humble origin could rise to such prominence in the Order that they could 'abuse' knights of nobler birth. Even the Pope contrasted the 'sloth' of the Hospitallers with the vigour of the Teutonic Knights. In 1352 the poet Petrarch wrote, 'Rhodes, Shield of the Faith, lies unwounded, inglorious'. Criticism from the Italian merchant republics was more worldly, with the Venetian Marino Sanudo accusing the Order of harbouring pirates at Rhodes because they had so few ships of their own. Accusations of protecting pirates became even fiercer in the fifteenth and early sixteenth century and as a result Venice, which ruled the large neighbouring islands of Crete and Cyprus, stood passively by during the final Ottoman siege of Rhodes in 1522, even closing its ports and stopping Venetian volunteers from going to Rhodes' assistance.

Despite the cult of chivalry encouraged in Hospitaller Rhodes, almost all the actual fighting seen by the brethren was either at sea, or attacking coastal positions, or in defence of their own fortifications. Paradoxically, perhaps, some of the best accounts of Hospitallers at war are found in Turkish. For example the *Destan of Umur Pasha*, written in the mid-fifteenth century, describes the Hospitallers and other Crusaders attacking a Turkish position outside Izmir a century earlier;

> In the morning the enemy put on their cuirasses and arms. Their horse-armour, their cuirasses were amazing. Their gauntlets, their arm-defences, their leg defences, their helmets, all shone and twinkled in the light. Those who carried small crossbows came in front, those who carried large crossbows and arrows followed. There were an infinite number carrying javelins and shields, and as numerous were those with swords and daggers. The drums, the

cymbals and the trumpets sounded. They surged up from the sea and
made their assault. In the wink of an eye they reached the ditch. They
carried fire to burn the mangonels. They wielded very long axes and
broke all the palisades in the ditch.

Naval tactics were based upon raiding enemy coasts and ambushing his
merchant ships. The relatively small *galiote*, with twelve to twenty-two
rowing benches, was best for raiding. Larger galleys may often have been
used to ambush sailing ships, particularly as the latter tended to increase in
bulk and height during the fourteenth and fifteenth centuries as a way of
protecting themselves against pirate attack. Strong local knowledge was a
major reason for the success and high reputation of Hospitaller galleys.
This was obviously necessary when, as was normally the case, two galleys
worked together. One would lie in wait behind a headland or small island
while the second harried the victim into the jaws of this ambush. Here it
should be pointed out that almost all shipping lanes still lay along the
coasts, with deep water voyaging being relatively rare. When Hospitallers
did meet the enemy at sea they would have used the same boarding tactics,
usually relying upon the raised *calcar* 'beak' rather than a ship-breaking
ram which now formed the prow of a Mediterranean galley.

Coastal raids could involve substantially larger forces, and if an enemy
fortification was to be attacked crossbowmen would again play a primary
role. Ships had to turn and backwater to enable a raiding party to disembark
from the stern, not from the prow as in a modern landing craft. The *Destan
of Umur Pasha*, written in Turkish around the same time, again described
just such a descent upon Izmir harbour by Crusaders, Hospitallers and
others; 'Thirty galleys were sent to Izmir, all filled with men in full
armour.... These innumerable Franks were dressed in iron from head to
foot.' During a subsequent attack upon Izmir town; 'Many coats of mail,
shields, cuirasses and helmets were made in the lands of these enemies.
They took also swords, javelins and daggers. They wanted to form an army,
they took also the great crossbows and small crossbows, bows, arrows and
hand-guns. They built many galleys.' In a later verse the Turkish poet
described the sound of these hand-guns or *tüfeks* in battle – '*shat! shat!*'.

When beached stern first a flotilla of such galleys was also in a very
strong defensive position if threatened from the sea. Battles between fleets
at sea were, however, rare in this period. References to ships being linked
by cables only seem to occur inside a harbour or in very enclosed waters,
and even then they were not tied closely to one another as Viking ships had
been. Normally such galleys formed a loose line, with larger transport

galleys and sailing ships in reserve, while small vessels carried messages from ship to ship. Even so these tactics were rarely necessary for the Hospitallers because the Turks tended to use large numbers of smaller ships in rapid raiding operations. These were not really capable of taking on larger Christian galleys or even larger merchant ships. Furthermore the rulers of rival Turkish *beyliks* rarely cooperated and larger Turkish fleets only appeared when the Ottomans took control of the entire Anatolian coast. Even then, the early Ottoman navy remained designed for raiding or for transporting the land forces which steadily conquered the Aegean islands one by one.

The demands imposed on the Rhodian Greeks ranged from felling and transporting timber to repair ships and building work on castles, to the *servicium generale*, which was a general obligation to help defend Rhodes imposed on both the Greek and Latin or Western European residents of the islands. Many Greek families were also bound by a hereditary *servitudo marina* which obliged them to man the Order's galleys, probably as oarsmen. This was only abolished in 1462, when its demands became so great that men fled the island in such numbers that women could not find husbands to marry. During the fourteenth and fifteenth centuries many Greeks also served in Turkish fleets, not only because they lived in areas now ruled by Turks, but because hostility to the Latins such as the Hospitallers ran so deep. In the late-fifteenth century Greeks from Rhodes itself were amongst those who urged the Ottoman Sultan Mehmet II, conqueror of the Byzantine imperial capital of Constantinople, to invade Rhodes. In 1522 most of the local Greeks of Rhodes reportedly wanted to surrender to Mehmet's successor, Sultan Sülayman, and so fought unwillingly in the island's defence. They had their way and the Hospitallers were forced to evacuate their Aegean islands. Nevertheless part of the Orthodox Greek elite in the city of Rhodes was by then so westernized that it chose to leave Rhodes with the Hospitallers in January 1523, some even following the Order to its new home on Malta.

Chapter 5

Turks, Nomads & Peasants

*M*any of the small Turkish states or *beyliks* which had been established in Anatolia during the second half of the thirteenth century continued to flourish throughout the fourteenth century, while others disappeared after only a brief existence. Meanwhile on the north-eastern coast of Anatolia the Byzantine 'Empire of Trebizond' (after the Ottoman conquest known as Trabzon), rival of the main Byzantine Empire of Constantinople and long-standing ally of the Christian Kingdom of Georgia, prospered in relative peace. Georgia itself was, during this period, a huge state which dominated most of the Caucasus mountains and a substantial part of the interior of what is now north-eastern Turkey. South and east of Georgia lay the even larger realm of the Jalayrid dynasty, which was one of the successor-states of the fragmented and now lost Mongol Il-Khanate. These Jalayrids were themselves of Mongol origin but had emerged as a deeply Islamic ruling elite with the ancient Caliphal capital of Baghdad as their main city.

Meanwhile the two large Turkish *beyliks* of Eretna and Karaman ruled the central regions of Anatolia during the early-fourteenth century. Two other substantial *beyliks*, Dulkadir and Ramazan, had emerged further to the south-east, while the western half of Anatolia was far more fragmented. Each region and *beylik* also had a slightly different military or political heritage and in some cases also a slightly different culture.

Karaman, which was the name generally given to the realm of the Karaman Oğullari or Karamanids (c.1265-1475), occupied the old centre of what had been the Seljuk *Sultanate of Rum* and was in many respects its most direct successor. The Karamanids would, in fact, prove to be the most powerful and long-lasting of the *beylik* dynasties which emerged from the Sultanate of Rum; their Ottoman rivals actually emerging in what had been Byzantine rather than Seljuq frontier territory. The father of Karaman Ibn

Nur al-Din, their first ruler, was a renowned *Sufi* or Islamic mystical teacher, and dervishes continued to flourish under Karamanid rule. For many decades this state was a serious rival to the Ottomans, making military and commercial alliances with powerful states to the east and west, before eventually being absorbed by the Ottoman Sultanate.

The Eretna Oğullari (1336-1380) occupied much of the territory which had once been the centre of the Danishmandid state, which itself had been a serious rival of the Seljuqs of Rum in the late-eleventh and twelfth centuries. Some have maintained that the name of their founder, Eretna Ibn Ja'far, stemmed from the Sanskrit Indian word *ratna* meaning 'jewel', and that he was a military leader of Uighur or Eastern Turkish origin from Central Asia. It has even been suggested that he himself was of Buddhist parentage and had originally served either the Mongol Il-Khanids or their local vassals the Çobanids who ruled northern Anatolia before the rise of the Eretna Oğullari themselves.

The state set up by the Dulkadir Oğullari (1337-1521) lasted even longer than that of the Karamanids. Their founder was an Oğuz Turkish chieftain whose name, Qaraj Ibn Dukadir was later Arabized as Dhu'l-Qadr, meaning 'Possessor of Power', though its original Turkish meaning remains unclear. These Dulkadir Oğullari endured so long partly because they held the same inaccessible mountainous territory which had earlier served as a final bastion for the Armenians of Cilicia. They were also fortunate in being strategically placed to form alliances with more powerful neighbours, most notably the Mamluk Sultans of Syria and Egypt to their south-east and the Ottoman Turks to their north-west. Meanwhile their most persistent foes were the Karamanids of central Turkey and the Aq Qoyunlu, 'White Sheep', Turcomans of western Iran.

The Ramazan Oğullari (c.1378-1608) were relative latecomers to this complex political and military scene, though Ramazan Bey, the father of their founder, had been mentioned in written sources from the 1350s. He is again said to have stemmed from the Oğuz Turks of the Central Asian steppes and thus claimed high status in the family- or clan-rankings of the Turkish peoples. The Ramazan Oğullari built their state in what had been the prosperous economic heartland, rather than the mountainous retreat of the previous Cilician Armenian Kingdom. At first they were enemies of the Mamluks, but the Ramazan Oğullari later adopted a generally pro-Mamluk policy and eventually formed a buffer-state between Mamluks and Ottomans. They seem fortunate to have survived the Ottoman conquest and the overthrow of the Mamluks in the early-sixteenth century, after which the Ramazan Oğullari played the role of submissive vassals of the

Ottomans for nearly a century before their lands were annexed as a directly ruled *eyelet* or province of the Ottoman Sultanate.

The situation was far more fluid and complex in western Anatolia where the Ottomans first emerged. There were simply too many short-lived *beyliks* to describe them in detail, but amongst the most significant were the Candar Oğullari (1292-1462). Like several other tribal leaders, the founder of this dynasty seized power and then won recognition by becoming a vassal of the Mongol Il-Khans. The centre of Candar power was Kastamonu and the neighbouring Black Sea coast. After throwing off Il-Khan suzerainty, this dynasty established themselves as rivals of the rising Ottomans and extended their own territory along the coast eastwards to take the vital port of Sinop (Sinope). After briefly being dispossessed by the Ottoman conqueror Bayezit I in 1393, they were restored by Timur-i Lenk and somewhat confusingly adopted the new name of Isfandiyar Oğullari. Even after their final annexation by the Ottoman Sultan Mehmet II in 1462, the Candar or Isfandiyar family continued to wield considerable local power and influence for many years.

The Germiyan Oğullari (1299-1428) were the closest neighbours, suzerains and eventually rivals of the Ottomans. They had first appeared in the chronicles as a Turkish tribe in the service of the Seljuq Sultans of Rum at Malatya, at the eastern edge of the Seljuq state, but during the late-thirteenth century they migrated westward and eventually established their own *beylik* around the powerful fortress-city of Kütahya. Initially content to be vassals of the Seljuqs and then of the Il-Khans, the Germiyan Oğullari took advantage of the decline of the former and the distance of the latter to carve out what became for a while the most extensive Turkish state in western Anatolia. Here they gained great wealth from their geographical position astride several important trade routes to and from the Aegean coast. The ruler of Germiyan was even able to impose his suzerainty on some of his smaller neighbours, and for a while no less a person than the Emperor of Byzantium was his tributary. However, the rise of small but rich and powerful *beyliks* on the coast as well as of the Ottomans on their northern frontier, led to the decline and fragmentation of the Germiyan Oğullari. Their last ruler, Ya'qub II lost his throne to Bayezit in 1390, was restored by Timur-i Lenk, but then bequeathed the Germiyan state to the Ottoman sultan once more, Murat II actually taking over on the death of Ya'qub II in 1428.

The Hamid Oğullari (c.1301-1391) and the Teke Oğullari (c.1301-1423) were related, their states being ruled by the sons and descendants of a Seljuq frontier commander named Ilyas Ibn Hamid. He himself had carved out a short-lived *beylik* in south-western Anatolia in the late-thirteenth century. The two resulting *beyliks* remained small in territorial terms, but sometimes wealthy because of their strategic location on the trade routes from the Aegean and Mediterranean coasts. Their history was generally more peaceful than that of their larger neighbours but both were conquered by the Ottoman Sultan Bayezit I, after which Hamid disappeared permanently. Teke was, like so many other *beyliks*, restored by Timur-i Lenk, only to be finally reconquered by the Ottomans a generation later. On this occasion the last independent ruler was not absorbed into the Ottoman system, but was killed.

The Menteşe Oğullari (c.1280 to 1424) ruled, at least nominally, the exceptionally rugged and indented coastal region immediately west of Hamid and Teke. The father of Menteşe Bey, the founder of this dynasty, may himself have been the *Amir-i Sawahil* or 'Governor of the Coasts' for the later Seljuk Sultans of Rum, though this may just as well have been a family legend designed to justify Menteşe Oğullari rule. Given their geographical position it is hardly surprising that they soon took to the sea, raiding Venetian maritime trade-routes and the island possessions of the Crusader Hospitallers of Rhodes. Their troops were also involved in a struggle for control of the vital Aegean port of Izmir (Smyrna). Perhaps it was this naval orientation which enabled Menteşe to survive for some years even after the Ottomans conquered their neighbours further inland. However, they were still amongst the Anatolian *beyliks* seized by Bayezit, restored by Timur and then reconquered by the Ottomans within a single generation.

The Aydın Oğullari (1308-1426) had an even more epic naval history than Menteşe. Aydın Oğlu Muhammad Bey had been an army commander in Germiyan service before creating his own small state on the Aegean coast. His son, the famous Umur I Bey, captured Izmir and built a small but remarkably effective fleet with which he seems to have challenged all the Christian navies of the Aegean, and some from further afield. As a result he became the hero of an epic, the *Destan of Umur Paşa*, which remains one of the finest examples of medieval Turkish literature. Eventually Umur and his fleet were defeated and Izmir was retaken for a while by a Crusader and Hospitaller army. Aydın subsequently suffered identically the same fate as most of its Turkish neighbours, before being finally annexed by Murat II in 1426, after its last ruler backed the wrong side during an Ottoman civil war.

The history of the Saruhan Oğullari (1313-1410), whose *beylik* lay immediately north of Aydın, was similar to that of the Aydın Oğullari. As a minor naval power in the Aegean the Saruhan sometimes fought against and sometimes traded peacefully with the Genoese and the Byzantines. The Gattilusi-Genoese coastal enclave of Foça (Phocaea) was, in fact, surrounded by Saruhan territory.

Squeezed between Germiyan and Aydın was another remarkable outpost of Christian rule. The city of Philadelphia (Turkish Alaşehir) and its immediate surroundings remained an isolated pocket of Byzantine territory until 1390 or 1391, long after the rest of western Anatolia had been lost to the Turks. This survival was largely achieved by diplomatic means, playing one neighbouring *beylik* off against another. However the Byzantines, or rather the Catalan Grand Company of mercenaries in their pay, marched all the way from the Sea of Marmara to Philadelphia in the spring of 1304, decisively defeating a Turkish army which was besieging the city. Thereupon the Catalans pillaged the entire region, preying on Turks and Byzantines alike, until the Emperor finally persuaded them to withdraw to Europe. These Catalans again raided parts of Anatolia in the following year but their leader, Roger de Flor, was murdered in the palace of the Byzantine Emperor Michael IX, after which the infuriated Catalans turned against their former paymasters. Soon reinforced by Turkish raiders eager for a share of the spoils, the Catalans went on to ravage large parts of what was left of the Byzantine Empire before taking over one of the Crusader states in Greece. Meanwhile Philadelphia was left in relative peace until Sultan Bayezit I decided to mop up all non-Ottoman territory in western Anatolia in the late-fourteenth century.

Despite the fact that the Turks had first entered Anatolia in the late-eleventh century and taken control of many of the eastern provinces of the Byzantine Empire as nomadic tribes, they were even then socially, military and of course religiously different from their ancestors who had roamed the steppes of Central Asia. Even then the Turks were not simply nomads. They already had urban elements, a strong interest in trade and a highly regarded tradition in various crafts, especially metalworking. Furthermore, the Turks almost certainly learned something of more advanced agriculture as they migrated across the Islamic Middle East and then settled in Anatolia which, though it already had its own transhumant or semi-nomadic traditions, was also a land of settled peasants and farmers. Hence it is no surprise that, despite several periods when agriculture slumped and nomadism increased, the Turkish states which existed in fourteenth-century Anatolia were no longer dominated by nomadic or even strictly tribal ways of life. Circumstances differed from one *beylik* to another, but in all of them there was a mixture of urban and rural, settled, semi-nomadic transhumant and, quite rarely, true nomadism.

An agricultural revolution had, in fact, started in the Middle East during the seventh and eighth centuries. It then spread rapidly across the entire Islamic world, having a profound impact on life in many distant and sometimes surprising regions from what are now Spain and Portugal in the west, to Afghanistan and Central Asia in the east. This agricultural revolution led to a massive increase in population size in almost all areas as a result of a general improvement in diet and in standards of health. On a more personal level, this Islamic agricultural revolution changed methods of cooking as well as the food crops available, while new crops permitted the development of new industries.

The phenomenal expansion of irrigation in what was an essentially dry part of the world meant that more abundant and newer systems of raising or moving water were needed. This in turn contributed to the gradual evolution of a complex and sophisticated legal system to ensure a fair distribution of water for irrigation and consumption. These laws grew out of practices which already existed in parts of the Middle East in the pre-Islamic times and were based upon the principle that the closer a farmer was to the source of the water, the greater were his rights. Any seeming unfairness in this concept was balanced by the fact that larger and wealthier landlords tended to be found in the more fertile lower valleys rather than in the poor, backward and often still tribal upland regions.

In Anatolia, following Turkish conquest after the battle of Manzikert in 1071, the new Seljuk rulers soon tried to reverse an agricultural decline which had characterized the previous Byzantine centuries. They encouraged a revival of irrigated agriculture as a source of taxation revenue, but their success was cut short by the Mongol invasions of the mid-thirteenth century. These had already devastated much of the eastern Islamic lands as part of a deliberate Mongol policy of returning large areas to pastoralism so as to maintain their own nomadic way of life and the huge armies which could be raised from it. Although in some parts of the Middle East the Mongols did not destroy agriculture in such a determined manner, the wars which came in their wake dispersed the peasantry who maintained the existing irrigation canals. Once these delicate systems declined beyond a certain point it became virtually impossible for the peasantry to return since they could no longer grow enough food to maintain themselves. Thus a cycle of decline started in the thirteenth century which in some areas continued well into the twentieth century.

Of course agriculture did survive, and continued to be organized along lines which had largely been established during the pre-Mongol centuries. In almost all regions share-cropping was the most common form of agriculture. Here a landlord's tenants generally had a contract to grow grain on unirrigated land for only one season. Four-fifths of the crop then went to the landlord. Share-cropping contracts meanwhile tended to be for longer periods where fruit-growing land was concerned, whereas irrigated fields were, of course, the most fertile and valuable of all. The distribution of land was even more complex, though in some tribal areas it consisted of freehold farms belonging to individual members of an extended family or the tribe as a whole.

Most land ownership was agreed on the basis of established custom and written documentation was only kept by government for high-value estates in the immediate vicinity of towns or cities. Perhaps as a result these fertile groves tended to be the subject of endless litigation, and intricate deeds of sale, gift and inheritance.

In some more barren, outlying or war-ravaged frontier regions the condition of the local peasantry could be desperately poor. Consequently these were precisely those areas which responded most eagerly to unorthodox religious teachings. Here wandering dervishes and various Shi'a sects found a ready audience and although most governments tried to crush heretical movements they generally failed.

In more favoured regions the new food crops and agricultural techniques often permitted double cropping, where only one had been possible earlier. The extensions of existing irrigation systems also enabled land to be cultivated which had lain idle for decades if not centuries. Meanwhile, oranges and lemons spread westward from India to Spain, along with sugarcane, cotton, rice and the growing of mulberry trees for the new silk industry. Existing cash-crops like almonds, figs and cork from the cork-oak also became increasingly important. There were similarly new vegetables such as aubergines and asparagus. As in Byzantine territory the basic Mediterranean plough changed little, since it remained suitable for most shallow and light Middle Eastern soils. New technical and theoretical books were, however, written on farming and botany, drawing upon knowledge from India and even further east. These discussed different kinds of soil, their manuring, watering and the most suitable crops, as well as more advanced methods of grafting trees and moving live plants over long distances.

There were fewer changes in animal husbandry but the importance of meat, above all mutton, to the Islamic diet, way of life and religious practice meant that the economies of even the remotest peoples could become market orientated. Perhaps partly as a result, the wool and skins from these animals prompted further developments in the textile and leather industries.

The firmly established patterns of long-distance trade which had characterized medieval Islamic civilization since its first century similarly contributed to the market-orientated nature of agriculture. Large quantities of basic foodstuffs, as well as smaller volumes of high-value herbs and spices were transported over huge distance by land and sea. Within the Middle East, for example, dried fruits, honey and nuts were carried from country to country, while snow to cool the drinks of the elite was packed in lead containers and carried on camel back before being stored in efficient 'ice-houses' throughout the year, even in the hottest regions.

Chapter 6

Byzantine Life & Balkans Rivalries

The cultural differences between Catholic or Latin societies in Western Europe and Orthodox societies in the Near and Middle East had grown considerably wider since the great religious Schism of 1054. In the east, as in the west, individuals identified themselves primarily by their religious faith, then by membership of an extended family network. Indeed for ordinary people life revolved around religious celebrations and festivities, including those associated with family life, and of course the agricultural seasons of the year. Within the Byzantine Empire, these patterns were still largely rooted in the Roman past.

On the other hand, costume had changed considerably since Roman times, largely as a result of Persian and Turkish influence. Perhaps the most obvious example amongst men was the wearing of beards. Meanwhile women's costume had changed less and continued to retain a strong and traditional Romano-Greek element. Paradoxically, the wearing of veils by women was a Byzantine fashion, perhaps of Persian origin, which had subsequently been adopted within the Islamic world. Both sexes wore jewellery, if they could afford it, while wealthier women also used facial makeup, which was still virtually unknown across most of western Europe. This included rouged lips and poisonous belladonna (deadly nightshade) to dilate the pupils of the eyes.

Fashions continued to change of course, and towards the end of the medieval period Christian costume in the Balkans and what remained of the Byzantine Empire became virtually identical to that of the Ottoman Turks, even to the extent of adopting turbans and various forms of Turkish headgear. Here, of course, it should be noted that Ottoman costume differed from that of other parts of the Islamic world in several respects, some of which clearly reflected Byzantine and eventually eastern European influence. Cultural exchange across the religious divide was, in fact, not merely a military matter but continued to have its impact on almost all aspects of life.

As in western Europe, and indeed the Islamic world, the Byzantine household was really run by the women. Richer houses normally had more than one guest or public room where the men could relax and receive guests while the women and children generally remained in the private sections of the house. Meanwhile servants tended to live at the top of the building. Many Byzantine houses had flat roofs which were used as terraces in the heat of summer, while their internal walls were often decorated with religious texts or motifs. Secular paintings only seem to have become popular in the later Middle Ages, perhaps as a result of western-European aristocratic cultural influence.

Byzantines, again like the Muslims, took personal cleanliness far more seriously than did westerners. Public baths were abundant, particularly in the main cities. Here some public baths were large and impressive structures which included private cubicles, clean lavatories, and hot and cold pools big enough to swim in. These were used by men during the day, and by women in the evenings. The similarity with the *hamams* of traditional Islamic cities like Damascus even today is quite striking.

Education was another vitally important matter to Byzantine social, economic and political elites. In a wealthy household, a young child would start to learn to read, write and speak clearly in the women's quarters, before he or she was old enough to socialise with older men. Three forms of the Greek language were used; these being the vernacular or *Romaic* of uneducated people, classical *Attic* which was used when writing, and a more elaborate version used for formal speech. Basic education was built around the Greek classics, particularly Homer, which even the Byzantine middle classes quoted widely, while Latin was used only by lawyers and was hardly regarded as a truly 'cultural' language.

Byzantine emperors had themselves attempted to continue the long-established tradition of founding schools for orphans, while bishops and many monasteries also ran their own schools. Primary education was more widely available, even for middle-class children, than it was in western Europe. Those who stayed at school beyond the age of twelve attended a different institution to study Greek, while a minority continued their education from the ages of sixteen to twenty, attending a university, to study rhetoric, law and philosophy.

Here at university, Byzantine education was again based upon disciplines inherited from the Roman past, though it remained essentially religious. Philosophy formed part of the curriculum in all universities, though the study of Plato was only added to that of Aristotle in later centuries. Furthermore, ancient secular scholarship and scientific works were not confined to libraries, as they almost invariably were in western Europe. Instead they were widely read with genuine interest. At the same time Byzantine scholars learned from neighbouring Muslim civilization and, following the Mongol conquests of the thirteenth century, even had access to some Chinese thought. Emperors, senior churchmen, the political, social and merchant elites of Byzantium all patronized scholars, collecting men of learning as ornaments to their households.

Since pagan Roman times, Christianity had improved the status of women within what was in reality the surviving eastern part of the Roman Empire. Nevertheless, most marriages were still arranged by parents or guardians, girls from the age of twelve upwards, boys from fourteen. On her wedding day, a bride was veiled and richly dressed, this being a chance for the bride's family to display their status. The marriage procession then walked to church accompanied by friends and musicians. Rings were exchanged and since the eleventh century an official marriage contract was also signed. Back at the bride's family's house there would be a banquet where men and women sat at separate tables. Next morning the guests woke up the newlyweds with loud and joyful singing. Where more practical matters were concerned, the bride's dowry was kept separate from her husband's wealth as a form of insurance, divorce being legal and in fact increasingly easy from the eleventh century onwards.

Byzantine tastes in food were remarkably similar to those of modern Europe. Anyone who could afford to do so ate three meals a day, with a widespread liking for roasted meat, pork, and ham imported from the Crimea. Here a semi-independent Byzantine outpost survived in the coastal mountains until 1475, a full twenty-two years after the fall of the Byzantine imperial capital of Constantinople. The Byzantines were also said to have had a very sweet tooth. In some areas like Trabzon on the Black Sea coast of what is now Turkey, fish was abundant, with a species of anchovy appearing in such huge and unpredictable shoals that they were sometimes even used to manure the fields. All medieval Orthodox Christian peoples, except the Russians whose agricultural situation was very different, ate a great deal of vegetables, cheese, fresh or stewed fruits, and nuts, while methods of cooking were essentially the same as those still used in Greece and Turkey. The diners, meanwhile, mostly ate with their hands in what would today be regarded as a Middle Eastern manner. Wine was produced in a great many regions, though the Greek island of Chios was a particularly famous centre of wine-making, producing something similar to today's sweet red Mavrodaphne.

Various forms of public entertainment had continued uninterrupted since Roman times, including chariot races which were held in Constantinople's famous Hippodrome, but the last of these to be recorded was in 1204, shortly before the arrival of the disastrous Fourth Crusade. Between each race, bawdy comedies were put on instead of the serious drama supposedly typical of ancient Greece and, unlike the chariot races, this liking for earthy comedy continued long after the restoration of Byzantine authority in Constantinople (Istanbul). *Tzykanion*, or polo, was introduced from the Turco-Muslim world and was played by the military elite. A few western-style military tournaments were similarly recorded in the twelfth to fourteenth centuries, but never really caught on, either with the military elite or with the Byzantine public. Instead Byzantine soldiers preferred cavalry games copied from their Muslim neighbours, these still being played in public only a few decades before the final fall of Byzantine Constantinople to the Ottoman Turks.

In both town and country, meanwhile, religious, semi-religious or semi-official gatherings or celebrations provided an excuse for ordinary people to take a day off work. These ranged from a parade of icons of a local church to almost pagan festivals where masked men lit bonfires in the streets and young people jumped through the flames. There were also the fairs and markets linked to agricultural events such as harvesting the fields or picking grapes.

Not much is known about the secular music of the Byzantine Empire. Organs and flutes were certainly played, while some performances seem to have had features in common with opera. Most, however, were more like cabaret shows and the Byzantines had a reputation, at least amongst some of their neighbours, for enjoying disgracefully erotic dancing. The Church of course tried to ban all such dubious performances, but failed miserably – except on Saturdays and Sundays. On a more innocent note, children's toys are known to have included model carts and animals made of clay, knucklebones, bouncing balls, hoops and tops, as well as musical instruments and dolls made of wax, clay or plaster.

By the later decades of the fourteenth century the Byzantine Empire of Constantinople consisted of little more than the city of Constantinople itself plus the adjoining coasts, southern Greece and a few Aegean islands. Other rival Byzantine or quasi-Byzantine states meanwhile existed, including the 'Empire of Trebizond' on the north-eastern coast of Anatolia and the *Despotate* of Epirus in what is now north-western Greece and southern Albania. Similarly little was by now left of the Crusader States in Greece, while Bulgaria had fragmented into small competing statelets which would rapidly fall under Ottoman domination. The extensive but fragile Serbian Empire had similarly fallen apart even before the Ottomans thrust deep into the heart of the Balkans.

In fact it proved almost impossible for the Orthodox Christian Balkans states to join forces with their Catholic Christian neighbours from central and western Europe against the Ottoman threat. Whereas many of their ruling elites looked northwards for help, most of the ordinary people often preferred Ottoman-Islamic rule to that of the Catholic Hungarians who seemed to be the only viable alternative. Within the fragmented relics of the once mighty Byzantine Empire, confusion and petty squabbling reached epidemic proportions. Most of the Emperors were, at one time or another, vassals of the Ottoman Sultan. Some, in fact, spent their entire reigns as such vassals. Everywhere in what remained of Byzantine territory there seemed to be hostility between the military and the civilians, between the ruling classes and the common people. Furthermore, the crushing of various peasant uprisings and urban revolts had left large parts of Thrace and Macedonia practically uninhabited except for a few fortified towns and their immediate surroundings.

The Serbs had carved out a short-lived but extensive regional empire during the fourteenth century while the Bulgarians, though never repeating the glories of their 'First Empire' of the seventh to tenth centuries, established an effective and highly cultured state in the thirteenth and early-fourteenth centuries. Other players on this confusing Balkan scene included the Albanians, Croatians, Bosnians, Macedonians, Wallachians, Moldavians and Transylvanians. The latter three peoples or regions today form the extensive state of Romania. In addition there were various nomadic or semi-nomadic peoples from the steppes, most of whom were of Turkish origin though some spoke Iranian languages. Then, of course, there were the Crusaders and various other western Europeans from Italy, Spain and elsewhere, all of whom faced the Ottoman Turks at one time or another. All were ultimately defeated, at least temporarily.

Here the role of Hungary was quite significant. Unlike the major Balkan states which were largely Orthodox Christian, Hungary was Latin Catholic. It also became an enthusiastic participant in the Later Crusades. Not that Hungary's sights were set solely on its southern frontier. Part of the Russian Principality of Galich was temporarily conquered by a Hungarian feudal élite which was itself under increasing French cultural and military influence. With the death of King Andrew III in 1301 the Arpad dynasty, which had ruled Hungary since the creation of the state in the late-ninth century, came to an end. Now, after a brief struggle, a member of the Italo-French Angevin family which already ruled southern Italy and parts of Greece, became king of Hungary as Charles Robert I. For Hungary this marked the start of brilliant age. The power of the barons was curbed while French and Italian Gothic culture spread across the country, along with more up-to-date military ideas.

Louis the Great, who succeeded Charles Robert in 1342, also recruited German and Italian mercenaries. These were used against Venice in Dalmatia, pagan Lithuanians and Catholic Poles in the north, and Orthodox Serbs in the south. Louis presented himself as a champion of the Church, but his dreams of leading a great Crusade against the Ottoman Turks were frustrated by chronic divisions within the Christian camp. Instead, Louis' successors had to face the full might of the Ottomans in a struggle which brutally highlighted the failings of the Hungarian army. This was particularly clear when King Sigismund of Hungary, who ruled from 1387 to 1437, called for a Crusade. In the event the resulting ill-disciplined multi-national force met total disaster at the battle of Nikopol in 1396 (see Chapter 10).

South-west of Hungary lay Catholic Croatia which, though a Slav-speaking state, remained almost entirely within Western European cultural and military traditions throughout the Middle Ages. Following a brief period of independence in the eleventh century, the Croatian Kingdom had been formally united with the Kingdom of Hungary in 1091. Nevertheless, Croatia retained a considerable degree of autonomy, though its *bán* or viceroy often had considerable difficulty controlling a turbulent feudal nobility who tended to pursue their own ambitions within Dalmatia and neighbouring Bosnia. By the fourteenth century a local form of light cavalry had evolved and this would stand the Croats in good stead against the Ottoman Turks during the following century.

Bosnia was culturally, religiously and militarily more mixed. Emerging from tribal confusion in the late-twelfth century, it was dominated by local chieftains or *zupans* who accepted – when it suited them – the leadership of the regional *bán* or viceroy. 'Lower' or northern Bosnia was organized as two duchies under the Hungarian crown, these having been established as outposts against Serbian expansion. Meanwhile more mountainous and rugged 'Upper' or southern Bosnia generally retained its own anarchic independence.

Militarily and culturally the bulk of Bosnians had more in common with the neighbouring Serbs than with the Croats or Hungarians. Another peculiar feature of this region was the *Bogomil* heresy, which had features in common with the early medieval *Paulicians* of Anatolia and the more recent *Cathars* of southern France. Bogomilism survived Christian persecution and Crusader assaults but would disappear with the arrival of the Ottoman Turks when most Bogomils apparently converted to Islam. Though fundamentally different in terms of theology, Islam and Bogomilism shared a deeply egalitarian outlook. Thereafter Bosnian cavalry continued to serve with terrifying effectiveness under the Ottoman banner.

Despite it rugged terrain and cultural isolated, somewhat backward Bosnia nevertheless had its own brief golden age in the fourteenth century, though it only achieved real independence under Stephan Tvrtko (1353-91). During his reign the Bosnians conquered part of Hungarian-ruled Croatia and won an outlet onto the Adriatic Sea. Then, when the sprawling Serbian Empire fragmented, the Bosnian *bán* or autonomous governor adopted Byzantine court ceremonial and titles, defeated an Ottoman army at the Battle of Plocnit in 1386 and briefly became the most powerful state amongst the western Balkan Slavs. In reality, however, this glory merely reflected the weakness of the other Balkan states. Serbia would fall to the Ottomans in 1459 and four years later Bosnia itself would be conquered.

The Albanians claimed descent from the ancient Illyrians and were, throughout the Middle Ages, divided into numerous mountain tribes. The development of a sense of national identity was also hindered by the fact that some Albanians were Catholic Christians known as *Arbanites* while others were Orthodox Christians generally known as *Epirots*. After a short period of independence under local *archontes*, which itself followed a collapse of Byzantine authority, Albania and some neighbouring areas were briefly united under a *magnus archonte* before being reabsorbed into the Byzantine Despotate of Epirus in 1216. A degree of autonomy followed an Angevin invasion from southern Italy which established a smaller Angevin-Albanian kingdom on the Adriatic coast. But this rarely controlled more than a few towns and gradually faded away in the face of local revolts. The Angevins of southern Italy nevertheless returned in strength in 1304, and this time they allowed greater freedom to the local Albanian leaders. Meanwhile most of the mountain peoples of the interior remained semi-nomadic, which enabled them to migrate to Greece in large numbers when a series of famines struck their country during the fourteenth century.

Most of Albania was then incorporated, at least nominally, into the huge but fragile Serbian Empire of Stefan Dușan, but when this fell apart in the mid-fourteenth century Albania again broke up into virtual anarchy. The Albanians, perhaps with Ottoman Turkish support, were even able to defeat an army of invading Hospitaller Crusaders in 1378. On the other hand, relations with the Turks were not usually so friendly and it was the Albanian leader Skanderbeg's defiance of the Ottomans in the mid-fifteenth century which most caught the imagination of Christian Europe.

Although Bulgaria country had enjoyed peace and a considerable economic revival as part of the Mongol 'World Empire' during the mid- and second-half of the thirteenth century, its political decline continued, just as the power of neighbouring Serbia grew. Eventually Bulgaria broke into three principalities: Dobruja in the north-east, Vidin in the north-west and Tarnovo in the south. A few places flourished through international trade, but heresies persisted and much of the Bulgarian lowlands were depopulated as a result of wars, nomad raiding and a sequence of plagues. As a result, fragmented Bulgaria was not really in a condition to resist the Ottoman invasion. Plovdiv fell in 1364 and the rest of the country soon accepted Ottoman suzerainty. Perhaps paradoxically, the surviving peasant communities of the eastern lowlands and of the Black Sea coast now entered an era of prosperity under their new Ottoman Turkish lords. Meanwhile a few of the old Bulgarian aristocracy fled to the western mountains where they maintained a precarious autonomy for a few decades, but eventually their persistent revolts led to the imposition of direct Ottoman rule on the last of the autonomous Bulgarian principalities in 1396.

Chapter 7

The Ottomans' First European
Conquests – A New Way of Life

*O*nce they had secured control of Çinbe and Gallipoli between 1353
and 1355, Ottoman troops went on to raid further afield, deeper into
Thrace. They soon seized Çorlu, Tekirdağ, Lüleburgaz and Malkara,
each of which became a forward base for further raids. While Ottoman
Turkish rule was gradually imposed upon the surrounding villages, a more
solid bridgehead was established in and around the Gallipoli Peninsula.
This would thereafter be the launch-pad for the Ottoman state's eventual
conquest of the entire Balkan peninsula. Even after this had been achieved,
Gallipoli, its harbour and hinterland remained vital to secure the Ottomans'
still vulnerable communications link across the Dardanelles Strait
separating Asia and Europe.

At the very start of this process, however, the Byzantine Emperor John
Cantacuzenos recognized the mortal threat posed by an Ottoman base on
European soil. Although these Ottoman Turks were still nominally his
allies, he now turned to his old enemies, the Serbs and Bulgarians, looking
for help.

John VI Cantacuzenus, who ruled as Byzantine Emperor from 1347
until 1354, is often cast as the villain of the piece, but, as is so often the
case, such a view is grossly oversimplified. He first emerged as a
significant historical figure when, as a wealthy magnate and successful
soldier, he purchased the governorship of the important province of Thrace.
John Cantacuzenus then took part in the tortuous Byzantine civil wars of
the early-fourteenth century, rising to become *Grand Domestic* or
Commander in Chief of the Byzantine army under Emperor Andronikos III.
He soon then became the effective, if not yet the official, ruler of what
remained of the Byzantine Empire of Constantinople.

John Cantacuzenus was also a typical product of his age, being the most astute political operator in a time of tangled intrigues. In addition he continued to prove himself an effective military leader but, being a military as well as political realist, he urged the Byzantine Emperor to accept a treaty in 1333 which obliged Byzantium to pay tribute to the Ottoman Sultan. John Cantacuzenus then made an alliance with the Muslim Ottomans to save what was left of Byzantium from a looming Serbian takeover. Furthermore, he relied upon Ottoman support when he had himself crowned Emperor following yet another Byzantine civil war. He appears to have been selfless in his attempts to save the Byzantine Empire, putting his own considerable fortune behind efforts to pay the enormous arrears of salary which were already owed to the remaining soldiers. John Cantacuzenus also employed many foreign, particularly Spanish and Turkish, mercenaries. As if these efforts, if not achievements, were not enough, John Cantacuzenus was a noted historian, though his writings tended to justify his own actions rather than being truly objective.

Within the Byzantine ruling class, both civil, military and religious, the Emperor was widely blamed for inviting the Ottomans into Byzantine territory in the first place. He was consequently forced from the Imperial throne and replaced by an old rival, John V Palaeologus who, as his 'name and number' suggest, had already been Emperor before. However, the situation was now out of control and John V fared no better in his attempts to eject the Ottoman Turks. Eventually he had to recognize the legitimacy of their new acquisitions before the Ottoman ruler, Orhan, would allow food to be brought into the city of Constantinople from what remained of Byzantine territory in Thrace.

The seriousness of the Ottomans' intentions at last began to be appreciated within Europe and some rulers as well as senior churchmen started talking about another Crusade to drive them out. Nothing happened for several years, and in the meantime Orhan's eldest son and designated heir, Sülayman, was killed in an accident, followed only two years later by the *Emir* Orhan himself. This might have proved a vulnerable moment for the young Ottoman state and its still fragile hold on parts of eastern Thrace. In the event Orhan's successor, his second son Murat, proved to be an even more effective and more ambitious leader than his father had been.

Murat had already taken over command of the European *Uc* or 'front' but on becoming ruler he first focussed on consolidating the Ottoman position in central Anatolia, in what is now central Turkey. One of the most significant developments in this region came when the virtually independent *ahi*, or religiously based militia and urban authorities, of

Ankara decided to recognize the Ottoman *Emir* rather than Germiyan *Bey* as their ruler. Other extensions of Ottoman rule also strengthened what would eventually become the Ottomans' 'base area' for their forthcoming conquest of both east and west.

This done, the *Emir* Murat dedicated himself to extending Ottoman authority ever deeper into Thrace, Macedonia, Bulgaria and Serbia, eventually becoming one of the most remarkable conquerors in medieval European history. At the start of this process, Gallipoli was still the Ottomans' main base in Europe, its harbour remaining essential to transport troops and horses across the strait. Nevertheless, the tiny Ottoman fleet could not have retained control of the narrow Dardanelles' waterway if the far more powerful Christian fleets had been determined to break this vital link between the Turks' old and new territories. The Ottomans' strategic weakness was fully understood in Europe and in the Byzantine capital, but the competing Christian powers were never able to combine for long enough to actually control the Dardanelles or to permanently retake Gallipoli. Instead the Ottoman ruler forged valuable though temporary alliances with one or other Christian naval power, taking advantage of their rivalries to strengthen his own still vulnerable maritime link between *Anatolia* and *Rumelia*, Asia and Europe.

In the wake of Murat's conquering armies, the by now almost empty plains of Thrace and the valleys of eastern Macedonia would be recolonised by people from the Anatolian provinces of the Ottoman state. They included Turkish nomadic groups who merged with existing nomadic or semi-nomadic peoples to become the *yürük* warrior-herdsmen who would dominate several Balkan upland regions for centuries. Others included Muslim and Christian peasants from Anatolia, some of whom arrived voluntarily, while others were forced to colonize the new Ottoman territories. The role of those *Bektaşi* dervishes who accompanied many Ottoman armies was also more important than is generally realized, not only as Muslim missionaries but also because they encouraged the settlement and recultivation of abandoned agricultural lands. Much of the latter had, of course, been devastated by wars and plague long before the Ottomans appeared on the scene.

Through this prolonged process a new and Islamic way of life developed in lands which had been Orthodox Christian for centuries. In the Muslim world shared lineage, the extended family, and real or fictitious tribal affiliations, were the foundations of society and were second in importance only to an individual's religious identity. Family, clan and to a now declining degree 'tribe' provided support in business and in resisting government interference. Within the family, relationships were based upon custom, which differed from place to place, and upon Şeriat (Arabic *Sharia*) or Islamic Law, which was essentially the same throughout the Muslim world. Women exerted enormous influence from behind the scenes, this 'power of the *harim*' being the normal way of conducting family or even political affairs, especially in Turkish Islamic society.

Despite variations in climate and architectural heritage, private houses also had certain features in common which stemmed from the distinctive organization of Islamic family life. As a result houses tended to have little furniture and rooms were decorated with rugs, while walls might have wooden panelling, stucco, stone inlay or painted patterns. Another feature which still set Islamic civilization apart from that of most of western Europe was its deep-seated love of gardens. Those of the Ottoman state would eventually become world famous and would have a profound impact in terms of design, new species of flowering or scented plants, and of course in their use of water, upon European gardens. Above all they used running water and scent, with less emphasis as yet being placed upon coloured flowers; this tradition of gardens being deeply rooted in the Persian and Arab past where cool and well-watered gardens were regarded as a foretaste of Paradise. Gardens and the imagery of flowers were so central to medieval Islamic culture that the Persian poet Sa'di entitled his two greatest works the *Bustan* (Garden) and the *Gulistan* (Rose-garden). For their part the Ottoman Turks would take such ideas even further, both in the physical gardens themselves and in their use as literary images.

The *hamam* or 'Turkish bath' featured very prominently in the life of Ottoman cities, towns and even villages. It was particularly popular with women who would spend a great deal of time meeting their friends, exchanging news, eating sweets, having their hair cleaned and their body hair carefully removed with tweezers in carefully secluded *hamams*.

Like so many aspects of Islamic life, child rearing was strictly governed by religion, the circumcision of boys being celebrated with the biggest festivities a family could afford. Religious education started as soon as an infant could speak, but physical discipline was not normally imposed before the age of six. Unlike European children, a Muslim child had the same legal rights as an adult, so a smack which caused a persistent red mark theoretically made the parent liable to pay compensation, just as if the parent had struck an adult.

Reading and writing were taught in the local mosque, free or in return for such gifts as a family could afford. Mathematics, law, grammar and other subjects would be taught in another school attached to a larger mosque in the nearest town. Literacy remained the most important aspect of education, not merely for business or scholarship, but as an essential social skill. Girls from prosperous families were, meanwhile, taught music at home by their mothers or servants. University education was based upon the *madrasah*, a special form of 'collegiate mosque' which, by the later medieval period, provided access to higher education in almost all Islamic states. These *madrasahs* were maintained by the distinctive Islamic system of religious endowments, money, land or other forms of property known as the *waqf*, in Turkish *vakif*.

The medieval Islamic attitude towards sex differed considerably from that of medieval Christendom and, in many ways, had more in common with modern ideas. Marriage was regarded as the cement which bound society together and as a way of stopping sexual desires from becoming a public nuisance, but it remained a civil contract rather than a religious bond. A man could have up to four wives – if the first agreed, and if he was capable of maintaining them and carrying out his sexual obligations on a basis of strict equality. A first marriage was normally arranged by the parents, but subsequent partners were more freely chosen and divorce was common.

In contrast to the Christian Church's attitude towards sex, which was tolerated within marriage as a biological necessity, Islamic culture regarded it as an important part of human fulfilment, so much so that respected scholars wrote books on the subject. One such was *The Perfumed Garden* written by Shaykh Nefwazi in North Africa in the late-fifteenth century. Certainly no sin was attached to the sexual act itself, but only to relationships outside the accepted boundaries of marriage or concubinage which were regarded as a breakage of trust and a betrayal.

In contrast to the veil which was worn in public, elaborate and often revealing clothes were worn within the privacy of the *harim* or private 'women's rooms' where none but the closest family were allowed to enter. Even a husband could quite legally be excluded from the *harim*. Of course such social deals were not always reflected in reality, and when it came to illicit love-affairs, a highly developed language of flowers, fruit and other emblems developed, whereby messages could be sent without either party having to write anything down. Meanwhile homosexuality, though remaining totally illegal, flourished in a situation where the sexes tended to be strictly segregated.

Islamic culinary and dietary laws were similar to those of Judaism. Yet it was the climate of the Islamic heartlands which lay behind the different emphasis which was placed upon different meals. Breakfast, for example, was very important. A light lunch would be normally eaten in the heat of the day, while the main meal was in the evening. Food was only taken with the right hand, as the left was traditionally used for washing the private parts of the body.

The Muslim elites were, in fact, clearly very interested in food, which seems to have been similar in content, preparation and presentation to what might now be called 'nouvelle cuisine'. The result emphasized small quantities of the best and healthiest ingredients. Recipes tended to be quite simple, with a moderate use of spices and a great concern to bring out basic flavours. The ingredients, however, could be very varied because of the medieval Islamic world's 'green revolution' in agricultural techniques and the introduction of an astonishing array of new food crops from Asia.

Good cooks continued to form a highly paid elite, as they had during the Golden Age of the Caliphate in the eighth to twelfth centuries. This remained the case even if these cooks were slaves. In a large house the kitchen was by now a complex place with its own separate toilet and bathroom for kitchen staff. The main oven was normally charcoal-fired and was used for baking bread, pies, rice dishes and casseroles. There was often a second open fireplace for pots and pans, while separate knives cut meat and vegetables in another example of the Islamic concern for hygiene. Meanwhile, poor people who lacked full kitchens could use communal neighbourhood ovens, especially when making larger quantities for a family celebration. Kid, or young goat, was widely considered to be the finest meat, though mutton was eaten in greater quantities, followed by chicken and fish, with beef being regarded as suitable only for the poor.

Picnicking in the open air was another earlier Islamic tradition which the Ottoman Turks continued with enthusiasm, serving as an important form of family entertainment. Meanwhile the economic, military or political elites could also visit Christian monasteries, where they would enjoy the wine which Christians alone were supposed to drink. The Islamic religious elite of course abstained from such supposedly illegal consumption. Despite the widespread consumption of 'sherbets' made from fruit cordials, many people also brewed beer and wine at home. Traditional illegal alcoholic brews, having been fermented for four months, apparently needed to be strained before consumption. Rapidly fermented drinks made from raisins were, however, sometimes considered legal because their alcohol content was so small.

Public entertainment in all Islamic societies, including the Ottoman Empire, tended to be associated with religious or political celebrations, ranging from the end of the fasting month of Ramadan to the proclamation of military victories. Annual military displays provided a popular spectacle in a culture where most armies were made up of professional soldiers rather than by feudal levies. Shadow-puppet shows introduced from Central Asia were another form of entertainment that enabled ordinary people to poke fun at their supposed betters, while the latter had the same love of hunting as practically every other medieval political or military elite.

Cheetahs were used as hunting animals by some rulers who could afford them, and it was a small step from hawks and hunting dogs to more peaceful pets. Middle-Eastern rulers had long maintained menageries of exotic animals as a source of diplomatic gifts to other rulers. Of course the love of cats had an ancient history in the Middle East, with the long-haired Persian breed soon spreading to Turkey in the west and China in the east. Ordinary people generally made do with singing birds, but were also encouraged by their Muslim religion to look after wild creatures – the pigeons which swirled around the minarets of many mosques sometimes being fed from large seed trays on top of the buildings.

The art of dancing was almost as highly developed in the medieval Islamic world as it was in the Byzantine Empire and in India. However, dancing by women was supposedly confined to the *harim*, yet even here the traditional dancing which evolved into today's belly dancing was not necessarily erotic. It was also performed by women for women as a celebration of fertility and as exercise during pregnancy, though it would be naive to believe that such dancing was not also used to encourage a jaded husband or lover.

Strictly speaking Islamic culture had a matter-of-fact attitude towards death. Corpses had to be buried within a very brief period after death for reasons of public health and graves were not supposed to be ostentatious, except in the case of the Prophet and certain other religious figures. Nevertheless non-Islamic attitudes could not be so easily overturned, particularly in areas under Turkish rule where the tombs of rulers were sometimes very splendid in a clear continuation of pagan or shamanistic Central-Asian traditions. Even more unorthodox was the playing of music at funerals by some dervish sects, though this tended to be more characteristic of regions where Christian influence persisted.

Chapter 8

The Rise of Serbia & the
Decline of Byzantium

ver since its foundation, Serbia had looked south towards
Byzantium both as the source of its civilisation and as an area for
Serbian expansion. The first significant territorial advances came in
the reign of Stefan Uros II (1282-1321), but it was his son Stefan Uros III
who made a breakthrough by defeating Bulgaria at the Battle of Kyustendil,
also called the Battle of Velbuzd, in 1330. This victory not only made
Serbia the leading Balkan power. It also highlighted some significant
differences between a Bulgaria which was under strong eastern military and
political influence, and a Serbia which was already being influenced by
western and central Europe. At the Battle of Kyustendil the Bulgarians had,
in fact, been supported by numerous Mongol horse-archers. Wallachian
mounted-archers also fought for the Bulgarians, but they may have been
Turco-Mongol tribesmen from the Wallachian plain rather than Vlach or
'Romanian' warriors from the mountains. In contrast the Serbian army
apparently included around a thousand Spanish mercenaries, many of them
perhaps Catalan veterans who had previously fought for the Byzantines.

Despite his success, Stefan Uros III was overthrown by the Serbian
aristocracy which seemingly considered him too cautious and too peaceful.
In his place they installed his son, Stefan Duşan, who became the most
famous ruler of Serbia's Nemanja dynasty and the greatest conqueror in
Serbian history.

Stefan Duşan's reign was not a long one, lasting only from 1331 until
1355, but he had already ruled as 'sub-king' of the Zeta area while his father
Stefan Uros III was was overall King of Serbia. He first won a significant
military reputation at the Battle of Kyustendil, and after replacing his father
as king, Stefan Duşan tried to maintain good relations with Hungary in the

north, while following the traditional Serbian policy of southward expansion. This would be at the expense not only of Bulgaria, but also of the Albanians and the Byzantine Empire. One of the main reasons for his dramatic success was the lack of much real resistance. Indeed in many areas the existing Byzantine military aristocracy welcomed a strong new ruler after decades of Byzantine confusion and civil war. As a result Stefan Duşan became the most powerful ruler of medieval Serbia and was the first to address the Byzantine Emperor as an equal. Eventually he adopted the title of *Tsar* and proclaimed himself 'Emperor of the Serbs and Greeks', soon adding 'Bulgarians and Albanians' in 1346. Like many of his supporters he seems to have regarded Serbia as a natural and almost inevitable successor to the fast crumbling Byzantine Empire. Stefan Duşan certainly believed that his huge new kingdom would be a much more effective bulwark against the advancing Ottoman Turks. However, Stefan Duşan was still in his prime when he died and as a result his hastily constructed, heterogeneous Empire crumbled almost immediately.

This failure came as a surprise to most observers, perhaps even including the Ottomans themselves. International trade and above all mining had made Serbia rich, and Stefan Duşan had used this abundant wealth to recruit a large mercenary army which included substantial numbers of German knights, sergeants and others. His intention of replacing the clearly ailing Byzantine Empire with a new and vigorous Orthodox Christian Empire of his own eventually led him to start preparing for an assault upon the Byzantine imperial capital of Constantinople. It was, in fact, during these preparations that Stefan Duşan suddenly died in 1355, only three years after the Ottomans had taken control of Çinbe on the Gallipoli peninsula.

Under Stefan Duşan the turbulent Serbian aristocracy had accepted, or been forced to accept, the supremacy of royal authority. The king's own lands had similarly been expanded, as were those of the Serbian kingdom as a whole. By the time of the conqueror's death, his empire included not only Serbia, southern Bosnia and parts of Herzegovina but also Macedonia, Epirus and Thessaly in northern Greece, and – at least nominally – most of Albania. It was also under Stefan Duşan that a self-governing Serbian Orthodox Church fully emerged, with its own Patriarchate based at Peç in what is now Kosova. Duşan even transferred the capital of Serbia southwards to Skopje in what is now the Republic of Macedonia.

However, Stefan Duşan's successors as rulers of the hugely expanded Serbian state proved quite unable to continue his ambitions, although several of them are remembered as heroes of the epic Serbian resistance to

Ottoman Turkish conquest. Some wielded only nominal authority and Duşan's empire rapidly disintegrated into a series of local, occasionally-competing, principalities, some of which soon had to accept Hungarian and subsequently Ottoman suzerainty. Nevertheless these last Serbian rulers included some remarkable individuals. None strove harder to protect their people than Stefan Lazarevic, who is sometimes seen, most unjustly, as a traitor to the Christian cause.

Stefan Lazarevic was also the most loyal of the Ottoman ruler Bayezit I's Balkan vassals and would tip the balance at the Battle of Nikopol. Born around 1373, Stefan inherited his father's role as *Krales* or 'Prince of Serbia' following Lazar's death at the disastrous First Battle of Kosovo in 1389. Because he was still very young his mother Milica acted as regent and presumably helped arrange the marriage between Stefan's sister and Bayezit. Thereafter Stefan and the Ottoman ruler became genuine friends and comrades-in-arms. Stefan fought for the Ottomans as a vassal ruler at Rovine, Nikopol and Ankara, becoming renowned for his courage as well as the effectiveness of his army. When Bayezit was captured at the battle of Ankara in 1402 Stefan fled back to Serbia.

Bayezit died not long after, and on his way home the Serbian ruler visited the Byzantine Emperor in Constantinople where he was officially given the title of *Despot* of Serbia. With this Byzantine status Stefan now threw off his allegiance to the Ottoman state. Civil war amongst the rival Ottoman princes enabled him to consolidate and even extend Serbia territory but, like Mircea of Wallachia, Stefan Lazarevich tended to back the losing sides as the Ottomans painfully rebuilt their realm. However, he was more successful in his relations with his Christian neighbours, accepting Hungarian suzerainty and receiving Belgrade as a reward from King Sigismund around 1403. Two years later Stefan Lazarevich married Helena, the daughter of Francesco II Gattilusio the Genoese ruler of Mitylene (Lesbos). In his later years Stefan reestablished good relations with the Ottoman Sultan, and again received some southern territory as a reward. He also inherited lands towards the Adriatic coast from his uncle where, however, he was baulked by the Venetians. Stefan Lazarevic died childless in 1427 and was buried in the Manasya monastery he founded at Resava. The pious and scholarly Serbian ruler founded several such monasteries in his lifetime and had also translated several books from Greek into Serbo-Croat as well as writing original works.

Neighbouring Bulgaria was similarly fragmenting into three separate principalities. By the time the Ottoman threat became serious, the Balkans consisted of more than twenty separate states, all relatively small and some truly tiny. Many were also deadly rivals of one another and none were in a position to offer effective resistance to the approaching Ottoman armies. Meanwhile Byzantium was also in terminal decline, wracked by a civil war which opened up tempting possibilities for Ottoman interference. The Genoese had been allowed to take over the strategic trading island of Chios while on the Balkan mainland Thessaly and Epirus had been lost to the Serbs, leaving the Byzantine Empire of Constantinople with part of Thrace, some northern Aegean islands and most of the Peloponnese in southern Greece.

The sudden Serbian expansion had resulted in Serbian rule over several cities or large towns which had long been centres of Byzantine civilization. In such places many elements of ancient Romano-Greek urban life had survived for almost a thousand years since the decline of the old Roman Empire. It had been in such towns that, and after centuries of decline, a modest urban revival had began back in the tenth century. Yet the Byzantine world never witnessed the remarkable explosion of cities, trade and industry that was seen in medieval western Europe or indeed in the Islamic world. With the exception of Constantinople and perhaps one or two other major cities such as Thessaloniki, Byzantine towns tended to remain sleepy but pleasant places, with plenty of gardens and open spaces where men, though not women, could relax in public and meet their friends.

The wages of ordinary working people, the Byzantine 'urban proletariat', seem to have remained surprisingly low. Many worked for themselves as independent craftsmen or small merchants, while others were employed by the Church or the powerful monasteries, or worked in sometimes quite large government factories. Indeed there appears to have been considerably more state control of industry than in western Europe or the Islamic world. The Byzantine government was even able to prevent merchants or craftsmen leaving the Empire for fear that they might establish rival industries in neighbouring countries. Perhaps this was a wise move, since the Norman king of Sicily had been so keen to establish his own silk industry that his troops had kidnapped specialist weavers from the Greek city of Thebes in 1147. In contrast, the very poor or unemployed were constantly being moved on from the shanty towns they erected around the relatively prosperous cities of the Byzantine Empire.

In another major difference from western Europe, the Byzantine Empire was wholly dominated by its capital city, Constantinople, the 'Great City' to which the eyes of all Orthodox Christians turned. This even remained the case after the Fourth Crusade and the resulting fragmentation of the Byzantine world into rival 'empires' and *despotates*. Constantinople was certainly far larger than any other town in the Empire, although its vast walled enclosure would not be filled with buildings until long after Constantinople, now Istanbul, became capital of the Ottoman Empire. Instead its remarkable and highly impressive fortifications enclosed gardens, orchards and allotments as well as waste ground and several separate built-up areas. The only really dense habitation was at the easternmost end of the walled zone, around the Imperial Palace, the Cathedral of Santa Sophia and the Hippodrome. Elsewhere seven monastic and secular suburbs existed almost separately within Constantinople's walls, towers and gates.

Despite these open spaces the Great City constantly needed to import food, which was brought ashore under close government supervision at several small harbours in the sea walls. Meanwhile the Byzantine government was fully aware of the fact that any significant interruption in grain supplies from Russia, the Balkans or southern Italy could cause serious rioting. The government also tried to control the trade in salt fish, which was another basic foodstuff, and iron which was needed for military supplies and the nails needed for ship-building. Perhaps as a result, Constantinople was wholly dominated by the Byzantine Court and was not able to develop separate civic institutions. Nevertheless, here, as in most Byzantine towns, each quarter had its own recognized headman, while hospices were provided for the poor and elderly, each partially supported by charitable donations.

For centuries trade enabled the Byzantine Empire to maintain a stable currency which in turn underpinned its prosperity, but once this declined so did the Empire itself. The Empire's relative lack of mineral resources had always hampered its economic development. Instead the Byzantines became internationally renowned for fine craftsmanship in high-value goods such as silk, gold, silver, ivory and works of art, most of which were made in Constantinople itself. Less prestigious industries like pottery and leather-working were pushed outside the city walls altogether, as they were throughout most of the medieval world.

Other Byzantine cities did, of course, have their own specialized small-scale industries. Trebizond, for example, exported fine cloths and silk, as well as skins, furs and the produce of local mines. Perhaps for this reason it remained rich and quite strong until its final capture by the Ottoman Turks in 1461.

On the other hand it has been suggested that the primary role of Byzantine merchants and artisans was to provide luxury goods for the Byzantine Court, the Orthodox Church and the political or military aristocracy. Guilds had evolved out of the old Roman *collegia* and each industry had at least one such organization to control wages and the quality or workmanship. Every such guild had a president elected by its members and then approved by the local government. Although artisans were not forced to join the relevant guild, it does seem to have been difficult for individuals to alter their inherited 'family profession'.

Despite the Byzantine Empire's heritage of ancient Roman roads, the road system seems to have been surprisingly poor. Decorated carriages pulled by mules may have carried the wealthy or important around town, while noble women rode in litters carried by slaves, but beyond the city walls the old Roman road system had clearly collapsed. Here women as well as animals were now employed as 'beasts of burden' so, not surprisingly, maritime transport was preferred. Even so, by the fourteenth century Byzantine ships had largely lost out to their Italian rivals to such a degree that Italian sailors even dominated the Black Sea.

Although Byzantium was a vital link in the network of trade routes which linked China and India to Europe – the so-called Silk Routes – Constantinople did not really capitalize on its magnificent location until the late-twelfth century, by which time its foreign trade had largely been taken over by Italian merchants. Similarly Trebizond on the Black Sea coast, often called the 'gateway to Asia', depended on local commerce, possibly as a result of the high tolls they demanded from foreign merchants, who, as a result, preferred to use ports owned by Genoa or Venice.

Another field in which Byzantine influence spread beyond Byzantine frontiers and would to some degree outlast the fall of the Byzantine Empire was law. Byzantine law was based upon much earlier Roman law as formulated and rewritten in Greek for the Emperor Justinian back in the sixth century. It was, of course, also strongly influenced by Christian principles, while the period from the ninth to twelfth centuries had seen several attempts to make existing legal codes more workable. As a result, many legal treatises had been written around this time, but it was not until the eleventh century and after that law was taught to anyone other than the Corporation of Notaries or professional lawyers. Now Constantinople also had a third university to teach law to aspiring government officials.

As with most other aspects of Byzantine civilization, Byzantine law had a huge influence upon its Christian neighbours. The biggest and clearest Byzantine legal impact was on the Slavs to the west and north, many of whom translated Byzantine legal texts for their own use. In fact, one of the last Byzantine legal codes, dating from the fourteenth century, continued to be used by the Christian Balkan population after they fell under Ottoman Turkish rule because the Ottoman state had separate legal systems for each of its disparate religious communities or *millets*.

Law enforcement in the Byzantine Empire was nevertheless relatively straightforward, though not always very effective. Each city had an *eparch*, or prefect, who controlled trade and the quality of goods, supervised guilds and dealt with breaches of commercial law. He was assisted by a *symponos*, or assessor, who was responsible for law and order. In this he was supported by troops from the local garrison, as well as a *logothete* who was in charge of the law courts, and numerous more junior assistants. Since the *eparchs* controlled the judiciary, they were highly influential figures in local life, but legal affairs were less clear-cut where the rural population was concerned. Here in the countryside a sort of rural police force tried, with mixed success, to control banditry.

Byzantine trials also owed a great deal to Roman practice and included the right of appeal to other courts, with the Emperor as the final arbiter. As in western Europe, however, there was a clear distinction between secular and religious courts, at least until the Byzantine recapture of Constantinople from the Latin Crusaders in 1260. In fact the Byzantine legal system had become so corrupt by the late-thirteenth century that in 1296 the Emperor Andronicus II created a completely new High Court; yet even this failed to solve the problem. Eventually the distinctions between secular and church courts became so blurred that both systems were replaced by a single structure of regional courts. The resulting legal framework survived until the Byzantine states were finally obliterated by the Ottoman Empire.

Byzantine forms of punishment seem extremely cruel to modern eyes, and included cutting off noses, tongues or limbs. However, the Byzantines, like many medieval civilizations, regarded torture and mutilation as more humane than death or the destitution resulting from fines or imprisonment, probably because physical punishment only hurt the condemned offender, whereas execution, imprisonment or financial penalties also hurt his innocent family dependants.

Chapter 9

From Empire to Empire: Byzantine & Ottoman Government

*B*ecause the Byzantine Empire was the surviving eastern part of what had been the old Roman Empire, its people continued to call themselves 'Romans' right down to the fall of Constantinople in 1453. They were also known as such to their Muslim neighbours, who called the Byzantines *Rumi* or variations on that term, though they were generally known simply as Greeks to many later medieval western Europeans.

Having survived, though only just, the initial expansion of Islam in the seventh and eighth centuries, the Byzantine Empire coexisted with the Islamic Caliphates and their fragmented successor states, often at war but more commonly at peace. Then in the eleventh century another threat had appeared in the form of the Turks who overran the eastern provinces of the Byzantine Empire until they were partially driven back during the twelfth century.

Another, briefer, period of relative stability and prosperity had followed, but then the Byzantine Empire again began to weaken and fragment under pressure from both Muslim Turks and Latin Catholic western Europeans. Meanwhile other Orthodox and eastern Christian states survived and in some cases even for a while flourished, especially during the later-thirteenth and fourteenth centuries. Within the Byzantine Empire and its fragmented successor states, autocratic rule continued to be the norm and taxation was generally very high because of the need to maintain a large military structure. The traditional pomp of the Byzantine court also cost a great deal, as did Byzantium's elaborate but now failing bureaucracy.

The Byzantine economy had traditionally been a cash economy in which the state owned a great deal of rural land, urban property, mines and quarries. However, most of the government revenues needed to hire, pay and equip troops and fleets came from customs levies on imports and exports, inheritance, consumer goods and agriculture, where the rural village was the basic taxation unit. Here a man's neighbours had joint tax responsibility if an individual was unable to pay his dues. After the introduction of a quasi-feudal system, those who held *pronoias*, most of which were roughly the equivalent of military fiefs in western and central Europe, still had the right to raise some local taxes. Meanwhile the imperial government found it increasingly necessary to purchase the loyalty of political and military followers, either with a *pronoia* or with cash salaries in the late Roman manner. This became even more noticeable under the fragmented Byzantine statelets of the thirteenth to fifteenth centuries. Yet the rulers of these much reduced empires and *despotates* still tried to govern their little states in essentially the same manner, and with the same pomp, as their mighty predecessors.

Government was, at least in theoretical terms, very different within most Islamic states, including the Byzantines' immediate Turkish neighbours and rivals. Within these Islamic territories, rulers were theoretically autocrats who governed within strictly defined laws which themselves stemmed directly from Islamic Sharia law. This gave enormous power to any religious establishment which decided whether any particular policy was legal under Sharia law. As a result the *Ulema* or recognized religious scholars and the civilian bureaucracy together formed the 'Men of the Pen' who served as a counter-balance to the military who formed the 'Men of the Sword'. In theory, as the focus of popular discontent, an unjust government could be overthrown by the *Ulema*. It was also generally believed that an extortionate government would inevitably fail because its actions made its people unwilling to work and thus undermined its own financial foundation. Indeed the link between wealth, power and legitimacy was more openly recognized and discussed in Islam than it was in any other medieval civilization. On the other hand, violence always remained just beneath the surface and remained the normal way of settling both internal and external disputes.

Even as early as the eighth century, the Men of the Pen had emerged as a distinct and often highly educated class and would remain so in almost all medieval Islamic states. As such, they had clear parallels with the long-established bureaucracy of the Byzantine Empire but found fewer similarities within western Europe. By the eleventh century, the old Greek, Aramaic and Persian administrative elites of the Middle East had been largely Arabized, though not yet Islamized since Christians continued to play a major bureaucratic role in many regions. Together with their Muslim colleagues they were known as the *katibs*, or scribes, and were normally headed by a *vizir* (Arabic *wazir*) 'government minister'. Initially they had received regular monthly salaries but in later centuries, as the cash economy deteriorated, senior bureaucrats were given *iqta* fiefs comparable to those offered to military officers.

In reality, of course, there were considerable variations on this basic system between the eleventh and fifteenth centuries. This was particularly obvious of regions in those countries ruled by Turks, and even more so where Turkish or Turcified populations dominated, as they soon did within Anatolia.

For example, the Seljuk Turks and their successors in the eastern and central Islamic lands introduced new administrative features quite openly, sometimes without apparently trying to justify them with an Islamic theological veneer. These were, of course, primarily military states where the efficiency of the army remained paramount. Under the Great Seljuks of Iran, Iraq and some neighbouring regions (1037-1157), rule usually passed from a father to his eldest son, while younger brothers governed the provinces. The ruler himself was assisted by a senior *Vizir*, as well as by the newer figure of the *Pervane* or Lord Chancellor, and was advised by a *divan*, or council. These senior government officials were in turn supposedly supported by twenty-four secretaries, half of whom dealt with financial affairs whilst the others dealt with military matters. This idealized system was rarely reflected in everyday reality, yet it remained the theory at which subsequent government, including that of the early Ottoman state, constantly aimed.

The bureaucracies of these Islamic states were, meanwhile, real enough and their passion for paperwork left a heritage which can be seen across the Middle East to this day, including Turkey. Almost everything was written down, with paper – initially imported from China but soon being manufactured in bulk within most Islamic states – used for the most important documents. Within the Turco-Islamic realms records were usually kept in Persian, Arabic being used for religious law while Turkish was only used in everyday life. This sophisticated administrative structure would form the basis of subsequent Turkish states including the Ottoman Empire, and often included a feared 'secret police' to root out corruption amongst officials.

Friction between the Persian and Arabic speaking Men of the Sword and the generally less-educated Turkish Men of the Sword remained a problem in many such states, though each group recognized the importance of the other. The need to defend the state was obvious, but the soldiers similarly knew that trade and manufacture provided the taxation base which delivered their salaries and paid for their equipment. Both these elites also loved titles and display, the *Master of Ceremonies* being one of the most important officials at all Turkish courts, although the Turks' traditional concern for pure drinking water meant that the *Master of Water* was almost as significant. Next in seniority came the ruler's personal doctor, who was very often Jewish or Christian.

The Ottoman state did not, however, simply inherit its government and military traditions from earlier Seljuk government; neither the Great Seljuks of twelfth-century Iran nor the Seljuks of Rum (Anatolia) who had dominated thirteenth-century Turkey. They also owed much to the Mamluk Sultanate of Egypt and Syria, which itself inherited a government system from the Ayyubid realms established by Saladin. The latter, of course, had learned much from his predecessors, including both the Great Seljuks and the Fatimid Caliphate of Egypt. This was clearly a long, complex and highly sophisticated heritage.

Perhaps the single most important influence upon the early Ottomans was the Mamluk Sultanate, where there had been continuous and genuine efforts to keep the Men of the Pen separate from the Men of the Sword. In fact it could be argued that, despite a gradual decline in the status of the bureaucratic elite, Syrian and Egyptian *katibs* or scribes contributed as much to the prolonged survival of the Mamluk state as did the more famous Mamluk army. It is also worth noting that many such *katibs* were recruited from the descendants of Mamluk soldiers, since only first-generation slave-troops were considered worthy of elite military status.

Although the Ottoman state was supposedly modelled on that of the Mamluks, it nevertheless differed in several significant ways. In its early days, the Ottoman administration was largely tribal and relied on Turco-Mongol *yasa* laws rather than the Muslim *Sharia*. However, as it attracted refugees fleeing from Mongol oppression as well as defectors and converts from a crumbling Byzantium, the Ottoman state absorbed both Persian and Byzantine civil administrative concepts. The Byzantine impact became even more pronounced in the late-fourteenth and fifteenth centuries after the Ottomans had crossed the Dardanelles and gone on to conquer the Balkans. Here the Ottomans created the first European Islamic state since Muslim Andalusia had declined far to the west in the Iberian peninsula. Indeed, by the end of the fifteenth century the Ottoman Empire developed into what might be regarded as a new 'Islamic Byzantium' which gave considerably more freedom to its peasantry, was more open to new ideas and was considerably more favourable to commerce than the old Byzantium had been.

Ottoman expansion was carefully planned and was carried out with utter conviction. The first real Ottoman capital city had been Bursa in the foothills of the mountains of north-western Anatolia. Now, after perhaps using Didimotokon (Turkish Demotika) as their first or temporary

European regional capital, the Ottomans had settled upon Edirne as the base from which the greatest wave of Ottoman conquests was launched. Most of the fighting was done by armies operating on three frontier *uc* or marches. The first thrust was north-east through Thrace and was normally commanded by the Ottoman ruler himself. The second aimed north-westward through Bulgaria and its most famous commander was Kara Timürtash. The third was directed westward into Macedonia and Greece and its most famous commander was Gazi Evrenos.

Official Ottoman attitudes towards their Christian and Jewish subjects was almost as sympathetic and accommodating as that of the unorthodox *Bektaşi* dervishes who accompanied their armies. Previously persecuted minorities like the Bogomils of Bosnia soon converted to Islam in large numbers, while elsewhere in the Balkans Orthodox Christians often welcomed the Ottomans as liberators from Latin Catholic, western European, Crusader, Italian or Hungarian domination. The peasantry in particular appreciated the generally less-oppressive administration which characterized their new Turkish Muslim rulers. Certainly the Ottomans demanded fewer taxes than previous Byzantine, Bulgarian, Serbian and other ruling classes had done. The higher members of the Orthodox Church hierarchy, including senior monks and the cultural élite, generally bemoaned their change of masters, not only because Islam had seemingly triumphed over Christianity but because they themselves had much to lose.

On the other hand the Ottomans' insistence on clearly dividing the population into military and civilian classes enabled those of the existing Christian warrior élites who wished to remain to preserve their status without conversion to Islam. This, of course, applied more to the middle and lower ranks than to survivors of the higher aristocracy, most of whom either fled or accepted a significantly lower status than they had enjoyed before the Ottoman conquest. Where these existing Byzantine Greek, Bulgarian, Serbian and other Balkan military aristocracies were concerned, most of those families who came to terms with the Ottoman Sultanate converted to Islam after a few generations, though often remaining proud of their pre-Islamic origins. In the newly conquered Balkan provinces, known to the Ottomans as *Rumeli* or *Rumelia* (from the Turkish term *Rum Ili* or 'the Roman lands'), many of the existing feudal *pronoia* fiefs were simply changed into Ottoman *timar* fiefs. Some went to Turkish warriors while others were allocated to Christian soldiers who now fought for a new ruler.

During this early period of Ottoman expansion into Europe, the Ottomans retained a *gazi* or 'religiously motivated frontier warrior' outlook to which they increasingly added a sense of their own military and cultural superiority. In fact these early Ottoman conquerors sometimes seemed to see Europe in much the same light as nineteenth-century Americans saw their Western Frontier; namely as a land of opportunity and of destiny.

In more immediate military terms, Ottoman tactics were at first largely those of tribal Turcomans, harassing their foes with horse-archery and only closing when the enemy was sufficiently disorganised to make victory almost certain. Their earliest successes, even in the Balkans, had been against small and isolated garrisons, rarely against a large enemy field army. Land had been gained either by defeating local Byzantine noblemen, by buying both Muslim and Christian castles from those who despaired of their own ability to defend them, by absorbing existing landowners into Ottoman society, or occasionally by marriage alliances. To take a fortified town the Ottomans continued their traditional tactics of ravaging the surrounding countryside to intimidate the defenders and block their food supplies. Where necessary they apparently built their own small forts to strengthen such a blockade. Once in possession, however, the Ottoman rulers put great effort and perhaps expense into reviving a town's trade and bringing in settlers to increase its population.

Even in the second half of the fourteenth century, most Ottoman armies seem to have consisted of a large proportion of Turcoman cavalry supported by a smaller number of foot soldiers, but this emphasis was gradually changing. By the time the Ottomans first established a bridgehead on the Gallipoli peninsula they also had some sort of standing army capable of defending fixed positions as well as conducting offensive raids. The establishment of this first small 'regular' force led to the incorporation of Byzantine as well as classical Islamic elements into the Ottoman battle array, and in the military attitudes it thereafter displayed. Byzantine influence appeared, not surprisingly, strongest when it came to siege warfare.

Although the size of the Ottoman army was constantly and sometimes hugely exaggerated by its enemies, it was, at least by the mid-fourteenth century, substantial considering to the still small size of the Ottoman state. Large numbers of vassals and volunteers clearly followed the traditional Turkish horse-tail *tug* ensigns of the Ottoman *Emir* and his subordinate *beys*. Only later, when the Ottoman ruler Bayezit I claimed the title of *Sultan*, did any leader supposedly have any more than one horse-tail. Thereafter the Sultan would have four, his senior *vizirs* three, provincial *beylerbeyis* two and ordinary *beys* one.

Turcoman nomads, who formed the first element in the Ottoman armies, were generally known as *akincis* if they served for one campaign as volunteers receiving booty instead of pay, and as *yürüks* if they formed a tribal contingent. Such troops overwhelmingly fought as horse-archers, rarely owning more than leather lamellar armour and still using the Central Asian lasso as a weapon of war. These Turcomans could rarely capture a castle or even hold occupied territory. For this reason, as well as the near impossibility of actually governing such turbulent tribesmen, the Ottoman Emir Orhan soon relegated them to the frontiers as raiders.

Ex-Byzantine troops probably included both cavalry and infantry. Though they also often used the bow, their military traditions did not normally include nomad-style harassment horse-archery. Meanwhile most of the *gazi* volunteers seem to have fought in traditional Middle Eastern or Iranian Islamic styles as mixed cavalry and infantry. As such they would have been much more amenable to discipline than the tribal Turcomans, though their primarily religious motivation may sometimes have made them difficult to control. In contrast their moral and socio-religious code of *futuwa* provided a model for a virtuous life and formed a bond between a ruler, his *gazis*, and the Caliph or other senior Islamic spiritual leader. Though less clear-cut and certainly less class-based and military than the Western European code of chivalry, *futuwa* did include comparable ceremonies and inspired a similar sense of comradeship based upon shared ideals. From the late-thirteenth century onwards, Anatolian *gazis* were also said to have identified themselves by wearing tall felt caps, either red or white, which were clearly similar to those later adopted by some elite Ottoman military units, most notably the Janissaries.

Despite the existence of such highly motivated soldiers, Ottoman tradition maintains that the Emir Orhan Gazi (1324-1360) felt the need for a more disciplined and more easy controlled professional army. Here legend and fact are so intertwined that the truth is almost impossible to identify. Nevertheless, it does seem that a regularly-paid force of both Muslim and Christian horsemen and foot soldiers was established, supposedly by Orhan's *vizir* or chief minister, Ala' al-Din. The horsemen were known as *müsellems*, meaning 'tax-free', and were organised under the overall command of *sancak beys*. The men were theoretically divided into units of one hundred led by *subaşis*, and a thousand led by *binbaşis*. The foot soldiers, known as *yaya*, were similarly divided into tens, hundreds and thousands. They fought as infantry archers and were occasionally recorded in Byzantine service, where they were called *mourtatoi*. Both *müsellems* and *yaya* were at first paid regular wages, but by the time of Murat I (1360-1389) they were more normally allocated fiefs in return for military service, the *yaya* also having responsibility for the protection of local roads and bridges.

Being free Turkish landholders or farmers, the *yaya* again proved to be difficult to control and their loyalty also tended to be to their immediate commanders rather than to the Ottoman ruler. As a result *müsellems* and *yaya* were again gradually relegated to second-line duties by the late-fourteenth century and by the end of the sixteenth century they would either be abolished altogether or be reduced to a non-military status.

In a further attempt to create a completely reliable and loyal army, the Ottoman rulers adopted the centuries-old Islamic military tradition of recruiting soldiers of slave-origin. However, the Ottomans now added their own distinctive variations. The result was the famous *Kapi Kulu* corps whose name meant 'Slaves of the Gate (of the palace)'. Once again historical fact is almost entirely buried beneath heroic and pious legend. According to one mythical version of events, the *Kapi Kulu* corps was created by Kara Halil Çandarli, the supposed brother-in-law of the saintly Shaykh Edebali whose daughter Malkhatun was supposedly married to Osman, the founder of the Ottoman dynasty. Another story, which may contain some element of reality, maintained that the *Yeni Çeri* ('new troops') or Janissary infantry of this *Kapi Kulu* corps were founded in 1326 when the first recruits were supposedly blessed by Haci Bektaş. In reality Haci Bektaş would have been long dead by that date, even if he had really existed at all.

As his name indicated, the saintly and probably mythical founder of the Bektaşi dervish or *sufi* movement had been a *Haci*, meaning that he had been on Pilgrimage to Mecca. According to this legend of the creation of the Janissaries, his broad upraised sleeve is said to have draped down a recruit's back as he gave the younger his blessing, thus traditionally leading to the Janissaries' distinctive folded version of the tall white felt cap. In reality, however, it seems more likely that the first *Yeni Çeri* were prisoners of war, perhaps from the captured garrison of one or more Thracian towns, at least a generation later than the events described in these pious stories. On the other hand the *Bektaşi* dervishes did maintain a close and prolonged association with the Janissaries, and in the sixteenth century the *Shaykh* (Sheikh) or senior member of the sect was made the honorary Colonel of the Corps' 99th Regiment.

The *Kapi Kulu* corps also included a smaller number of cavalry units. Established at an earlier date than the *Yeni Çeri* infantry, they enjoyed higher status and wore upright or unfolded versions of the Janissary cap. These élite *Kapi Kulu* horsemen are, however, sometimes confused with Ottoman feudal, provincial fief-holding cavalry as both were called *sipahis*. Known more specifically as the *süvarileri* or *bölük halki* ('regiment men'), they eventually consisted of six units. The oldest were the Left and Right

Ulufeciyan ('salaried men'), founded in the fourteenth century by Kara Timürtash Paşa and the Emir Murat I who selected them from their own finest troopers. The Left and Right *Gureba* ('poor foreigners') had almost as long a history, having been recruited from *gazi* volunteers, while the *Silahtars* ('weapons carriers') were a very early bodyguard formation identified by the fact that their tall felt caps were red rather than white. These *Silahtars* were subsequently replaced as the Ottoman ruler's mounted bodyguard by a new unit, the *Sipahi Oğlan* ('Sipahis' children') early in the fifteenth century. Each unit of these *Kapi Kulu* cavalry was commanded by a *kethüda yeri* and was eventually recruited more broadly from the sons of *süvarileri* horsemen, as well as Arab, Persian and Kurdish Muslims and Janissaries who had distinguished themselves in battle. In later years the *Kapi Kulu* corps would also include artillery and engineer units.

Muslim settlers followed Ottoman conquerors and, together with the large numbers of local peoples who gradually converted to Islam, they steadily changed the appearance as well as the social structures of the conquered territories, especially the towns. At first the Ottomans displayed a limited or at best a localized interest in fortification (see Chapter 23). Nevertheless the presence of increasing numbers of Muslims in the Balkans, and of course in western Anatolia, had an impact upon the architecture of these regions.

Muslim domestic architecture emerged out of a variety of traditions and ranged from vast and splendid palaces to simple cave dwellings, yet in each case the Islamic religion dominated domestic arrangements so that all these 'homes' had features in common. Above all there was an emphasis on privacy and an almost modern concern for peace and quiet.

Despite the wealth and the military background of so many Muslim governments, Islamic palaces were rarely realistically fortified in a manner that could have withstood a serious attack. Most consisted of a palatial complex which included barracks, administrative offices, mosques, parade and training grounds, gardens, cisterns and sometimes an enclosed game reserve or even a horse-racing circuit. Later palaces tended to be smaller, but still followed the pattern established by the Abbasid Caliphs back in the eighth- and ninth-century golden-age of Islamic civilization. This resulted in a very clear separation of public reception halls and private residential quarters, together surrounded by lesser buildings and gardens. Almost nothing is known of the first Ottoman palace or palaces in Bursa, but the traditional pattern was clearly followed at Edirne in the later-fourteenth and first half of the fifteenth centuries. In contrast, the Ottoman palatial complexes in Istanbul, or conquered Constantinople, were smaller because they were built within the ancient city walls. Even so, the famous Topkapi Palace overlooking the Bosphoros and Golden Horn still covered a substantial area which is again subdivided along largely traditional lines.

Few ordinary Islamic domestic houses survive from the earlier part of the medieval period, though they are many more from the later centuries. Most are in places such as Damascus in Syria, though Turkey and parts of the Balkans also have a fair number.

The medieval architectural traditions from which these developed can be seen in a few illustrated manuscripts, such as those of the *Maqamat* of al-Hariri dating from thirteenth-century Iraq and Syria. These show various essential features in detail, though in a very stylized style. Several such aspects of traditional Islamic domestic architecture would be adopted within the expanding Ottoman Empire but this, of course, would eventually cover a huge variety of different climatic and geographical regions, resulting in many variations upon the basic theme. Amongst the basic features were internal courtyards, sometimes covered by a light fabric-covered wooden dome or pyramid which could be partially opened to let in light and air. In the hottest regions some houses had ventilation ducts which turned to catch the wind and channelled a cooling draught into the interior of the house. More common, especially in the houses of the wealthy or powerful, fountains and small water channels served as humidifiers in the courtyard and often also inside parts of the house itself.

Stairs tended to be external, though within the courtyards, and, like the many open verandas, provided space where semi-porous water containers used small amounts of evaporation to have a refrigerating effect on drinking water. As in most Islamic architecture, the decoration of houses and even palaces largely consisted of surface textures and colour rather than the basic structure of the building. An often harsh climate led to a love of idealized mini-landscapes such as gardens which aimed to be 'mirrors of Paradise', with an emphasis on greenery, shade and, again, flowing water. Unlike most modern European gardeners, or those of medieval Japan, Muslims did not try to accentuate a welcoming nature, but to replace an often hostile one. This tradition continued even in the gentler climates of Turkey and the Balkans. Everywhere water was an essential ingredient to create these mini-climates, or as a decoration, or to provide relaxing sounds.

In rural villages housing was of course much simpler. Written and illustrated evidence indicates that there were animals almost everywhere, though all but the most primitive hamlets had their own shops, pools of water and a mosque. Parts of south-eastern Turkey and northern Syria were noted for a distinctive form of 'beehive' house whose rounded shape, though looking odd from the outside, was efficient in reflecting heat in summer while retaining heat in winter. Elsewhere, some peasants lived in caves in central Anatolia, not because of backwardness but because rock dwellings were again cool in summer, warm in winter, while the local soft rock lent itself to such excavations.

Nevertheless, Turkish conquest and settlement resulted in several changes to more traditional Islamic domestic architecture. These not only reflected the Turks' own relatively-recent nomadic existence in Central Asia, but may even have included some distant Chinese influence. Palaces, for example, sometimes consisted of scattered pavilions rather than a single walled or otherwise enclosed complex. Some of these oriental features could be seen in ordinary Seljuk and Ottoman houses, at least those of the wealthy, and in parts of eastern Turkey some domestic architecture appeared more Central Asian than were the palaces of their rulers. On the other hand, the earlier Arab and Persian love of gardens and running water was enthusiastically inherited by the Turks, who took such ideas with them into the recently conquered provinces of south-eastern Europe.

Religious architecture of course remains one of the glories of Islamic civilization and this would certainly be true of the Ottoman Empire. Yet the mosque was basically a place of communal prayer, lacking the consecrated character of a Christian church or the sacred quality of an oriental temple. Early mosques had been based upon the traditional Arabian house rather than any earlier forms of religious architecture, and this unpretentious character meant that the basic mosque could easily develop into more specialized structures such as schools or a meeting place for dervish brotherhoods, or even, from the twelfth century onwards, into what was essentially a non-religious hospital.

At the same time it eventually became acceptable for the increasingly elaborate tombs of political or religious leaders to have mosques, or at least prayer-halls, attached to them. This was widely considered to be a Turkish or Persian addition to the basic Arab concept of the mosque being merely a place set aside for prayer, and was often criticized by more orthodox or conservative Arab Muslim scholars. The little that is known about the men who built these mosques and palaces sheds interesting light on medieval Islamic civilization. The use of slave labour was, for example, virtually unknown, while at the other end of the scale the best architects formed a highly paid elite who travelled huge distances from one patron to the next.

Chapter 10

Prelude to Disaster

The general background to the Crusade of Nicopolis, or Nikopol as it should more accurately be called, was the astonishingly rapid spread of Ottoman Turkish conquests in the southern Balkans during the second half of the fourteenth century. More specific was the Ottoman threat to Hungary following the failure of a Hungarian attempt to promote an uprising against Ottoman domination in Bulgaria, and the current Ottoman blockade of Constantinople, capital of what was left of the Byzantine Empire.

Several regional attempts to form a common front against the Ottomans failed, despite the fact that most local peoples were united by their Orthodox Christianity and shared Byzantine-style culture, while joining forces with European powers outside the Balkans remained very difficult. There was meanwhile religious friction between Orthodox Rumanian Wallachia and Moldavia and their nominal Catholic overlord Hungary. In contrast the Ottoman advance seemed inexorable following its victory over an alliance of local rulers at Çirmen on the River Marica in 1371. Nevertheless clashes with the declining Balkan Christian states were usually on a small scale, generally involving relatively low casualties, and in the 1380s Ottoman frontier armies actually suffered several setbacks, though none while their ruler was present.

Meanwhile those Christian states beyond the immediate zone of operations sometimes seemed unaware of the looming threat. In the 1380s the little Kingdom of Bosnia briefly rose to regional power as Serbia fell apart, the Bulgarian Kingdom of Vidin became an Ottoman vassal and Prince Vlad of Wallachia thought to use Ottoman help in winning his independence from Hungary. It did, in fact, appear that the Ottomans had their sights set on Serbia and eventually Hungary rather than Bosnia on the left flank of this primary thrust, and Wallachia on the right. Throughout Ottoman history the Rumanian principalities were seen as little more than a buffer on the Ottomans' right flank. Nevertheless Mircea, the new ruler of Wallachia, was wary. He took over the old Bulgarian Despotate of Dobruja to give his principality access to the Black Sea plus some territory south of the Danube, and made a treaty with Poland in 1389.

Mircea the Old of Wallachia ruled a far smaller area than did Sigismund of Hungary, and for many years did not even rule that. Nevertheless he earned the title of 'The Great' as well as 'The Old'. Wallachian history is far from clear in the fourteenth century, but Mircea certainly came to power as *Voivode* or prince in 1386 and soon set about extending Wallachian territory towards the Black Sea. According to one unsympathetic Byzantine source he 'stole' the throne 'like a robber'. He and his supporters had also formed part of the Balkan Christian alliance which was defeated by the Ottomans at the First Battle of Kosovo in 1389. Like almost all medieval Wallachian rulers, Mircea changed alliances and switched suzerainty from Hungary to the rising Ottoman Empire and back again in a skilful but necessarily devious effort to preserving Wallachian autonomy if not full independence. He had to fight rival leaders who, like himself, were similarly used as political pawns by Wallachia's larger neighbours.

Consequently Mircea had to fight several limited guerrilla-style wars and he had little choice but to take part in the disastrous Crusade of Nikopol in 1396. After the massive Ottoman defeat by Timur-i Lenk in 1402, Mircea, like Sigismund of Hungary and Stefan Lazarevic of Serbia, supported various rival Ottoman princes as they struggled for control of the shattered Ottoman state. More often than not Mircea chose the unsuccessful side and once the Ottomans regained their stability Wallachia could not avoid becoming an Ottoman vassal state. Even so this probably only took place the year after Mircea died in 1418. Mircea's reputation outside Wallachia varied considerably. Amongst the Crusaders at Nikopol only Enguerrand de Coucy seems to have admired him, but the Byzantine chronicler Dukas called Mircea 'the profligate voivode of Wallachia' who had 'many bastard sons'. In contrast Ottoman sources generally regarded him as 'the most courageous and shrewd among the Christian princes'.

The moves by Mircea of Wallachia in 1389 prompted a rapid Ottoman reaction. Ali Paşa Çandarlı seized Nikopol on the other side the Danube and in 1391 the Ottomans launched their first raid north of the river. This in turn led Mircea to abandon his alliance with distant Poland in favour of an alliance with a nearer and more traditional source of support, Hungary. King Sigismund of Hungary and *Voivod* Mircea of Wallachia may next have launched their own raid deep into Ottoman-ruled Bulgaria in 1392, though the dates are somewhat confused. Bayezit was currently busy in Anatolia as the Hungarians and Wallachians retook Nikopol with ease. A new and more effective Balkan Christian coalition seemed to be in the making, but the following year the Ottoman ruler returned to Europe and reimposed Ottoman hegemony in a lightning campaign, as a result of which the rump Bulgarian Kingdom of Tarnovo was fully incorporated into the Ottoman state while Vidin and Serbia returned to their previous status as Ottoman vassals.

Far to the south the Crusading Order of the Hospitallers based on the Greek island of Rhodes tried to negotiate a truce with the Ottomans but their refusal to grant freedom of navigation to Turkish merchants led to failure. Now they in turn expected an Ottoman attack at any time, but were uncertain whether it would be against Rhodes itself or against the Hospitallers' vulnerable enclave at Smyrna (Izmir). Many Hospitaller knights on Rhodes had also died in a recent plague, so all the Order could do was to send reinforcements east.

For his part, Bayezit set about cultivating Serbian friendship in the hope of using Serbia as a buffer against Hungary. This resulted in Serb forces being given a privileged position amongst Ottoman vassal contingents. The status of the Serbian Orthodox Church was similarly enhanced, while the Bulgarian Church officially disappeared as a separate Orthodox entity.

The significance of Italian colonial or merchant outposts in the Black Sea during the forthcoming Nikopol campaign has only recently been recognized. This was one of the world's major hubs of international trade, both east-west and north-south. At the centre of this network of communications was the Crimean peninsula, where the Mongol Golden Horde, the Venetians, Genoese and still even the Byzantines competed for dominance. The Golden Horde, however, had no fleet while that of Byzantine Trebizond was tiny. As a result, Italians ruled the seas and although they frequently fought each other this meant that Latin Crusader expeditions enjoyed naval superiority in both the Aegean and Black Seas well into the fifteenth century. Of course Italian outposts around the Black Sea had to deal with very powerful neighbours, particularly on the northern coast where the Golden Horde was not yet in serious decline.

By the late-fourteenth century Genoa was the major maritime power in the Black Sea and could almost deal with the Golden Horde on terms of equality. Genoese outposts were, nevertheless, more of a commonwealth than an overseas empire. Their merchants, sometimes in company with unofficial adventurers, penetrated far up the great rivers which poured into the Black Sea, including the Danube, and efforts by such Italian merchant communes to keep on good terms with Islamic neighbours could scandalize other Europeans. Nevertheless Genoese Kaffa in the Crimea fought its own war with the Golden Horde in 1385-86 and also had to keep an eye on the little known Greek Crimean principality of Theodore Mangoup. The Genoese had similarly established a colony at Kilia near the mouth of the Danube and this felt threatened not only by the Ottomans but by local Balkan rulers. A fort on an island near Giurgiu, far up the Danube and only a hundred kilometres from Nikopol, may also have been of Genoese origin while Genoese merchant ships may have regularly sailed up river as far as the Iron Gate or Derdap Gorge on the border of Hungary.

The Kingdom of Hungary would be a major participant in the Nikopol Crusade. Yet it was still suffering the effects of a period of bitter civil war. Cultural differences between various regions within the kingdom remained huge, ranging from the Catholic Magyars (Hungarians) in the centre and west, the Catholic Slovakian Slavs in the north, assorted Slav peoples both Catholic and Orthodox in the south, and the mixed Catholic and Orthodox region of Transylvania in the east. Furthermore, Hungary, Poland and the western Ukrainian principality of Galich-Lodomeria had been under one crown until recently, this fragile union only having collapsed with the death of King Louis the Great in 1382.

Transylvania retained its semi-autonomous status within Hungary but this was under increasing threat as growing numbers of German miners, merchants and others settled in its fast expanding towns. Tension was also increased by the activities of Catholic friars who tried to impose Catholic Christianity on the Orthodox population. The status of local Transylvanian *voidodes*, governors or princes, was also declining, some choosing to accept Hungarian culture and Catholicism while others migrated with their military followers over the Carpathians to Moldavia and Wallachia. These were confused and troubled times even without the approaching Ottomans.

Meanwhile the southern border of the Hungarian kingdom remained fluid and the status of the Slav provinces varied. Hungarian rule in Croatia, Dalmatia and Macsó in what is now Serbia was usually effective, but Hungarian authority in Bosnia was rarely stable, particularly in the southern hills where local *bans* held sway. Once again, as in Transylvania, the missionary activities of Catholic friars caused deep resentment and tended to weaken Hungarian prestige rather than to enhance it.

Beyond the Carpathians, Moldavia and Wallachia occasionally accepted Hungarian suzerainty while Hungarian rulers always regarded these Rumanian principalities as vassals. In the mountains and foothills Rumanian speaking peoples and their local leaders held sway, but on the adjoining plains nomadic peoples of Turkish origin had only recently accepted Moldavian or Wallachian rule as the Mongol Golden Horde lost control of these westernmost parts of its sprawling steppe empire. The same was true of Slav communities living along some of the great rivers.

Moldavia, though a more recent political entity than Wallachia, had reached the Black Sea and in the 1380s and 1390s. Its prince may even have ruled Podolia north of the Dniester before this fell to an even more astonishing new arrival on the scene, namely the Principality of Lithuania. Meanwhile Wallachia was the Rumanian state most concerned with the rising power of the Ottomans. The Mongols had abandoned the lowlands between the Danube and the Carpathians decades ago and instead various steppe peoples had converted to Christianity while their leaders either become, or were absorbed into, regional ruling and military elites.

Like Moldavia, Wallachia had grown rich by lying astride important trade routes. Even though its separate status nevertheless remained insecure, and its political and military structures fragile, the *voivode* of Curtea de Argeş gradually rose to become the *Grand Voivode* and eventually Prince of Wallachia. With Mongol help the Wallachians defeated a large Hungarian army in 1330 to win autonomy, though not as yet independence. Meanwhile this new state pressed steadily eastward along the north side of the Danube towards the Black Sea where Mircea the Old's temporary occupation of the Dobruja may even have provided him with a small Black Sea fleet, inherited from the previous Byzantino-Bulgarian rulers of the area.

When Louis the Great of Hungary died in 1382 he left his formidable widow Elisabeth and two daughters, Maria aged eleven and Hedwig aged nine. Maria was crowned the day after Louis was buried but the Poles refused to recognize her as their queen though, after some argument, they accepted Hedwig two years later. This ended the 'personal union' between Hungary and Poland which, after Queen Hedwig of Poland married Prince Jagiello of Lithuania, was replaced by a new 'personal union' between the latter two countries.

Unfortunately Maria was already engaged to Sigismund of Luxembourg, the Margrave of Brandenburg and son of Emperor Charles IV of Germany. He in turn never really accepted the loss of Poland which he had hoped to rule along with Hungary. Nor did he and Maria seem in a hurry to marry. As a result Hungary was ruled, somewhat ineffectively, by the queen-mother Elisabeth. To further complicate the issue King Charles of Naples, ruler of southern Italy and adopted son of Louis the Great, maintained that he should have become King of Hungary. Charles of Naples found support amongst much of the Hungarian nobility and in 1385 he invaded Dalmatia. Maria was forced to abdicate in favour of Charles who was then assassinated by followers of the queen-mother Elisabeth. Charles' supporters next joined Tvartko the *ban* of Bosnia in rebellion, helped by the Venetians, leading to civil war, the capture of Maria and the poisoning of Elisabeth. Finally Sigismund entered the fray, freed Maria and had himself crowned king in 1387. Meanwhile his younger brother Wenceslas had been King of Bohemia since 1378.

As if these convoluted events were not debilitating enough in the face of single-minded Ottoman expansion, Queen Maria died in 1395 after which many people thought that Sigismund had lost his right to the throne. Though Sigismund ruthlessly crushed all rebellions he always seems to have had more interest in Central European affairs than those of the Balkans. His reign of fifty years was actually the second longest in Hungarian history, but during the latter part of it Sigismund was also Emperor of Germany. Generally speaking he was regarded as a German foreigner by most Hungarians and it took many years, long after the disastrous Nikopol Crusade, for Sigismund to be grudgingly accepted by the majority of his people.

As the Ottomans drew closer, the Hungarians tried to improve relations with the Orthodox communities in Transylvania, rewarding Mircea of Wallachia's shift from his previous Polish alliance by giving him the strategic mountain Duchy of Fagaraş and the County of Severin in 1391. Amongst various legends from this time, which may contain grains of truth, Sigismund sent an ambassador to Bayezit demanding why the Ottomans were raiding territory the Hungarians regarded as their own. Bayezit reportedly said nothing but pointed to some weapons hanging on a wall of his tent, this being interpreted as a challenge to battle. Also on his way home from an unsuccessful raid into Ottoman held Bulgaria, Sigismund is said to have slept with a certain Elisabeth Morsinay in the county of Hunyadi, their illegitimate son supposedly being the great hero of the next phase of Hungarian-Ottoman warfare, Janos Hunyadi.

Whatever the truth, the events of 1391 and 1392 convinced Sigismund that Hungary needed help from Western Europe while similarly convincing Bayezit that the Bulgarian vassal Kingdom of Tarnovo was unreliable. So Sigismund set in motion the summoning of a Crusade and Bayezit sent his son Sülayman to crush Tarnovo and execute its king, Sisman. Most of the Ottoman army which actually took Tarnovo consisted of Balkan Christian troops, but elsewhere the Danubian frontier castles at Silistria, Nikopol and Vidin were strengthened, while Muslim immigrants were encouraged to settle this strategic region. Another legend maintains that Sisman's son, the last of the Bulgarian royal dynasty, converted to Islam, became governor of

Samsun in Anatolia and died fighting for the Ottoman Sultan in 1420. In 1393, however, a combined Hungarian-Wallachian army regained the outpost of Nicopolis Minor, opposite Nikopol on the north side of the Danube and confirmed their suzerainty over the rest of Wallachia.

Bayezit clearly did not feel that the Ottoman position in the Balkans was secure, so in the winter of 1393-4 he virtually tricked his Christian vassals into attending a conference at Serres in northern Greece. They feared he might take the opportunity to execute them all at a single stroke, but in fact Bayezit merely wanted to confirm his authority, decide who was and who was not loyal, and convince the Byzantines to hand over several key ports before these fell into Venetian hands. The man whom Bayezit selected as his most trusted vassal was Stefan Lazarevic of Serbia. On the other hand, this meeting convinced Emperor Manuel II that Byzantium was doomed unless he won help from the west.

As soon as he got home to Constantinople Manuel threw off Ottoman suzerainty and prepared to endure a new siege. This was not long in coming and it would last, on and off, for eight years. Sometimes the Ottoman siege was little more than a blockade and the main problem for the inhabitants of Constantinople seems to have been a lack of grain, wine and cooking oil. The city was already half empty and full of derelict buildings, many of which were now torn down so that their beams could be burned as fuel.

However, the situation was not a desperate as might be thought. The Ottomans did not yet have the great cannon which would blast down the walls of Constantinople half a century later, and their first assault was beaten back. A letter written by Emperor Manuel to his teacher Cydones in late 1394 or early 1395 sounded confident enough, even when preparing to venture beyond his capital's massive fortifications; 'But, for the moment, I am going forth to give aid to a certain fortress that is being besieged – small, to be sure, and little able to profit our enemies if it should be taken, though it would provide them with honour and delight.'

What the Emperor Manuel most wanted was naval help from Venice, to guarantee continued food supplies. Unfortunately the Venetians wanted to maintain good trading relations with the Ottomans and even refused to buy the Byzantine island of Limnos when it was offered to them. For his part Bayezit could use a rival claimant to the Byzantine crown, John VII son of John V, to make trouble for Emperor Manuel. This John was based in the Byzantine town of Selymbria (Silivri) and, with his own followers backed up by Ottoman soldiers, he himself unsuccessfully attacked Constantinople in September 1395. Thereafter the pressure on Manuel eased, though an Ottoman blockade continued.

Even as the Ottomans besieged Constantinople, clashes increased along the Danube frontier and, in the face of the common Ottoman threat, the barons of Hungary put aside their quarrels with Sigismund. There were several major confrontations in 1395. Though there is still some debate about the precise date of the Battle of Rovine, and of its true outcome, it seems likely that it resulted from a major Ottoman raid into Transylvania and Wallachia early that year. The raiding force was led by Bayezit himself, accompanied by several of his most important Balkan Christian vassals. Gazi Evrenos may have been present, though other sources put him in charge of another Ottoman force which raided southern Greece. Bayezit apparently attacked seven Hungarian fortified towns and castles before a bloody battle with Mircea's troops at Rovine, near the river Argeş, probably on 17 May. The Wallachians claimed a victory and the Ottomans certainly suffered heavy casualties, including the Serbian nobleman Konstantin Dejanovic and the famous Marko Kraljevic who is remembered in Balkan legend as a great hero against the Turks. Nevertheless the Ottomans held the field and were briefly able to place Mircea's rival Vlad on the Wallachian throne. They also installed or strengthened garrisons at Giurgiu and Nicopolis Minor north of the Danube.

An interesting but garbled account of this battle survived in an anonymous seventeenth-century Greek chronicle which seems to have drawn upon lost Turkish sources. It stated that;

> ... Mircea was the lord of Wallachia, had received troops from Moldavia, and was a brave man. The Moldavians were stout fighters ... He [Mircea] made regular stops in forests and oak groves. Whenever the Turks reached these regions, Mircea's Wallachians emerged, captured or killed the Turks, and vanished into the forests. One day Mircea marched out onto the plains openly, sought an engagement and butchered many of them. When Bayezit saw this turn of events he became frightened, held a meeting with Evrenos Paşa and decided to discontinue the present campaign against Mircea.

In reality Mircea of Wallachia lost control of most of the territory he held south of the Danube while Sigismund redoubled his efforts to get help from Western Europe.

It is impossible to state just when the idea of the Crusade League was born. It is also easy to overestimate the role of Emperor Manuel II of Byzantium, since King Sigismund of Hungary was clearly more significant. Nevertheless Manuel did reach an agreement with the Genoese and sent a high ranking embassy to France in 1395, asking for help. Sigismund also realized that leadership of a Crusade could bolster his shaky prestige, not only within Hungary but in his rivalry with other neighbours, not least his own brother Wenceslas of Bohemia. His ambassadors toured the major European powers, eventually concluding treaties with France, Venice and various German princes as well as Emperor Manuel of Byzantium and Mircea of Wallachia. They also received a favourable response from England, the Hospitallers and the Kingdom of Aragon, which currently ruled Sicily and part of Greece.

Sigismund is not, however, believed to have wanted a full-scale Crusading invasion of the Ottoman Empire. Rather he seems to have envisaged a defensive or preemptive campaign within Hungarian territory and its vassals. All this took time and effort. For example Nicholas of Kanizsay the Archbishop of Gran had arrived in Venice in March 1395. There he got promises of naval transport before travelling to Lyon where he and his followers were lavishly entertained by Duke Philip of Burgundy. After paying his respects to the Duchess of Burgundy in Dijon, Nicholas of Kanizsay rode to Bordeaux to meet Henry of Lancaster, the future King Henry IV, who abandoned his own Crusading dream and promised English help. This never materialized, but the Hungarians pressed on to Paris where Charles VI 'The Mad' was enjoying a period of sanity. He in turn sent a letter to King Richard II of England in May stating; 'Then, fair brother, it will be fair moment... that you and I, for the propitiation of the sins of our ancestors, should undertake a crusade to succour our fellow Christians and to liberate the Holy Land'.

The Regents of France, who held real authority in the kingdom, also assured the Hungarians that the French nobility would help their cause. One of the most immediate results of these agreements was the raising of special taxes for a Crusade, the Duke of Burgundy pulling in the huge sum of 700,000 gold francs while Count Guy VI de la Trémoille alone raised no less than 24,000. The Hungarians, it seems, returned home bearing good news, and were encouraged on their way by further promises from various leading German rulers.

It was certainly remarkable that Sigismund's representatives got agreement from both the Duke of Burgundy and the Duke of Orléans, bitter rivals for the domination of France, particularly as both seemed to place the interests of their Duchies ahead of that of France, let alone Hungary. On the other hand the Hungarians were lucky in arriving after a four year truce had been agreed between France and England, leading to a pause in the seemingly endless Hundred Years War. Germany was similarly enjoying a period of peace, while Milan's domination of northern Italy had also imposed some sort of stability there.

Help was being promised from all sides, yet it was the Burgundians who took the lead and would bear the main burden. There were several reasons, none of them seemingly concerned with Crusading ideals or indeed the welfare of Hungary and the Balkans. Duke Philip was eager to avoid involvement in any renewed Anglo-French hostilities and saw the Crusade as a way of demonstrating Burgundy's newfound power. He had already raised men and money to fight for the Crusading Teutonic Knights against the Lithuanians but his close advisor Pierre de la Trémoille now convinced Philip that fighting the Turks was more glorious. Duke Philip had previously sent an armed delegation under Guillaume de la Trémoille and Regnier Pot in April 1394, to assess the situation in Hungary. Their followers may have been amongst the French troops who helped Sigismund in Wallachia.

Certainly the Burgundian delegation returned a year later in time for detailed military discussions which took place in Dijon. There, in the presence of the Admiral De Vienne, Guillaume de la Trémoille and his brother Guy, Duke Philip's son John of Nevers promised to dedicate his youth and his first feat of arms to the service of God. He also volunteered to lead the Crusade and, despite his inexperience, this was agreed. Other more qualified men were available and the young John had also broken his shoulder in a recent fall from his horse. Several senior barons were doubtful about his appointment but eventually accepted the appointment in August 1395, presumably because John of Nevers' role was nominal and essentially political while real command was placed in the hands of the Count d'Eu. Other senior men and advisors were to include the Admiral De Vienne, Marshal Boucicault, the two Sires de Bar and the Count de la Marche, who were cousins of the French King, plus the Sires de Saimpy, de Roye and de la Trémoille.

Enthusiasm for the Crusade was widespread and genuine, so much so that only the elite were actually allowed to join the army. A huge celebratory mass was held in the Cathedral of St. Dénis in Paris but even now Count John of Nevers was not knighted. This, they said, was because 'He was to receive the accolade like a knight of Jesus Christ at the first battle against the infidels'.

Though only the nobility was permitted to 'take the Cross' and join the Crusading army, the leaders did recruit a relatively small number of professional archers and crossbowmen. Meanwhile the Burgundian chamberlains put almost more effort into arraying the Crusaders in brocade clothing, gilded and silvered harness and supplying the Count of Nevers' units with green satin tents. His two hundred servants were also all dressed in the same green. Armour and tableware was the most magnificent available and, perhaps not surprisingly, the Duke of Burgundy found it necessary to raise additional taxes. These were of two types; those to equip his son John in a suitable manner and those to finance a 'voyage overseas'. Since town and country could not provide enough money, a special tax was also imposed on those members of the knightly elite, including women and children, who were not taking part in the expedition.

Compared to such an effort, the contributions of Venice, Genoa, the Crusading Orders and the two rival Popes seemed rather small. The Hospitallers were undoubtedly keen on the Crusade, since their garrisons at Rhodes, Smyrna and other part of the Aegean felt threatened by the Ottomans. In April, Philibert de Naillac, Grand Prior of the Hospitallers in Aquitaine, agreed to support the Crusade and left for Rhodes with reinforcements later that year. The De Naillac family were one of the oldest and most important in the Berry area of central France, being lords of Le Blanc, Châteaubrun, Gargilesse and Bridier. Philibert became the most famous but as a younger son he had to seek his fortune elsewhere. He chose to enter the Military Order of the Hospitallers and by 1383 he had risen to become Grand Prior of the Order in the Aquitaine province of south-western France. Meanwhile his senior brother Guy II de Naillac, called 'The Valliant', became Seneschal of Guyenne, fighting the English on behalf of the French King. In 1395 and 1396 Philibert de Naillac was quietly helping distribute the family estates amongst his brothers as well as helping his brother Hélion draw up his will when the call came for a Crusade. He was sent to the main Hospitaller headquarters on the island of Rhodes where, in March, the Grand Master Ferdinand de Hérédia suddenly died. Philibert de Naillac was elected as the thirty-third Grand Master and almost immediately led a squadron of Hospitaller war-galleys with the rest of the Crusader fleet to the mouth of the Danube. Following the Crusader defeat at Nikopol, De Naillac escaped downriver with Sigismund of Hungary. After his return to Rhodes, the Hospitallers bought Sparta and Corinth fro the Byzantine Despot Theodore and when this sale was annulled they took the fortress of Salona and another castle instead. Thereafter Philibert de Naillac commanded a small Hospitaller fleet which continued to give the Ottomans trouble in the Aegean as well as joining the French nobleman Boucicault in ravaging the coasts of Mamluk-ruled Lebanon in 1399. He died in 1421 at what was then considered a remarkably great age.

Even the Grand Master of the Teutonic Knights in Prussia supported a Crusade against the Turks, if only because he remembered the trouble caused by overenthusiastic Crusaders in the Baltic. The Pope in Rome, Boniface IX, was enthusiastic, preaching the crusade in those regions loyal to him, as well as a second Crusade against his rival's supporters in southern Italy. Meanwhile the Pope in Avignon, Benedict XIII, similarly granted indulgences to Crusaders marching against the Turks, despite the Crusade in question having been authorized by his rival.

The Venetian Senate agreed to join the Crusading League in 1395, though only at sea, while Venetian ambassadors secretly continued to try and mediate between the Ottomans and Byzantines because hostilities endangered trade. As yet the outlying Latin Kingdom of Cyprus played no role, though it would eventually have to contribute handsomely to the ransoming of prisoners. In February 1396 the Crusading alliance between Hungary and the Byzantines was formally signed in Buda, the western half of the modern Hungarian capital of Budapest. Under this agreement the Byzantines would apparently supply ten war galleys, built in Venice but paid for by Sigismund, to be used in the Danube area. In the event these do not seem to have taken part, probably because Constantinople was too closely blockaded by the Ottomans.

This was a new kind of Crusade, emerging at a time when the old Crusading ideals were virtually dead amongst the majority of Western Europeans. Now Kings and other great secular rulers promoted and organized a Crusade, while the Popes followed their lead. The previously almost antagonistic ideals of Crusading and Chivalry had finally merged into one, and the expedition itself was now considered a 'voyage' or adventure rather than an armed pilgrimage. As the famous Burgundian poet Eustace Deschamps wrote around 1395;

> Princes mondain, je vous requier et proy
>   Que vous m'aidiez les Sarrasins conquerre:
> Je suis la loy, soiex avecques moy
>   Pour conquerir de cuer de Sainte Terre.

The medieval Ottoman command structure was so totally under the control of the ruler that only occasionally do subordinate leaders emerge from the shadows. The Nikopol campaign was one such occasion. It clearly involved some remarkably talented and successful Ottoman figures. The most senior was the *Grand Vizir* or 'prime minister' Qara Timurtaş, the son of Qara Ali Bey who had been a famous warrior under the Emir Orhan earlier in the fourteenth century. The origins of his family nevertheless remain obscure, though Timurtaş himself was first mentioned during the reign of Murad, advancing the Ottoman frontier up the Tunca river in Thrace. Over the next years he led the Ottoman armies which conquered much of eastern Bulgaria, and rose to become the *Beylerbeyi*, military commander of

Ottoman territory within Europe. In this role he reorganized the Rumelian or Balkan forces under his command, established two new elite cavalry regiments called the *Ulufeciyan* regular or salaried troops, while also recruiting local *Voynuks* or Christian soldiers.

During the early 1380s Qara Timurtaş conquered more territory in Macedonia, western Bulgaria, as well as raiding Albania and Bosnia. Of course Timurtaş and his men took part in campaigns on the eastern front in Anatolia, his courage winning him the right to have a standard with three horse-tails, the first *Beylerbeyi* to do so, as he was promoted to the status of *Vizir*. In 1388 Timurtaş was, however, defeated by the Serbs and it was this victory over a minor regional force which encouraged Lazar of Serbia to assemble a large coalition army which was then crushed at Kosovo a year later. Not long afterwards Qara Timurtaş probably earned Bayezit's unspoken gratitude by executing a dangerous rival, the Qaramanid ruler of Konya, who was also Bayezit's brother-in-law, though supposedly without Bayezit's authorization. Now an old man, Timurtaş continued to lead conquering armies in both central Turkey and central Greece, but would be captured alongside Bayezit at the battle of Ankara. Murdered in 1405 by one of his own servants during the anarchic civil wars which wracked the Ottoman state after Bayezit's death, he was buried in a mosque he himself founded in Bursa.

The career of Gazi Evrenos Bey was even more dramatic and longer. According to some sources, mainly Greek, Evrenos son of Isa (Jesus) Bey Prangi came from a family of Byzantine origin which transferred its allegiance to the Turkish Karasi rulers of western Anatolia and had converted to Islam early in the fourteenth century. Other scholars, generally Turkish, claim that the family was of ancient Turkish origin. Certainly Gazi Evrenos was first mentioned as a middle ranking *bey* officer in an area which the Ottomans had recently annexed from the Karasi Oğullari, and was amongst those troops sent by Orhan to help the Byzantine Emperor Cantacuzenos during a civil war against the rival Emperor John V.

After the Ottomans won a foothold on the European side of the Dardanelles in 1354, Gazi Evrenos rapidly became one of their most successful commanders. He remained so under no less than five Ottoman rulers, taking part in virtually all the critical campaigns within Europe and several in Asia. He became *Uc Bey*, governor of the 'Left March' or that section of the frontier whose task was to extend Ottoman control along the Aegean coast of Greece to Thessaloniki, Macedonia, Albania and finally down into the heartlands of Greece. This he did with astonishing success before his death on 17 November 1417. By that time Gazi Evrenos Bey was not only old, highly experienced and highly respected, but was one of the biggest landowners in the Ottoman Empire. Indeed Gazi Evrenos Bey was clearly more than merely a soldier. Unlike most other leading Ottomans of that time he was a relatively orthodox Muslim, making the *Haj* pilgrimage to Mecca and promoting the establishment of mosques, *madrasah* religious schools, *imaret* hostels for the poor, dervish convents, *hamam* public baths and *caravanserai* hostels for merchants. In this he was encouraged by several Ottoman rulers, a letter from Murad in 1386 instructing Evrenos that; 'Your representatives should look after the poor. They should provide enough for them. Our God holds the poor dear to him.'

Under his governorship Komotini, in what is now north-eastern Greece, changed from a sleepy Byzantine backwater to a flourishing centre of Turkish-Islamic cultural life, one of the first in Europe. As the Ottoman frontier was pushed forwards, so Serres and finally the new town of Yeneci Vardar (now called Yenitsa) became the centres of the *Uc* frontier march. Gazi Evrenos Bey's tomb still exists at Yenitsa, along with a dedicatory inscription which includes;

> Transported from this Transient World to the Realm of Permanence, the receiver of God's mercy and forgiveness, the blessed, the martyr, the king of the gazis [religiously motivated warriors] and the fighters of jihad, slayer of the infidels and the polytheists,... Hajji Evrenos son of Isa, may God illuminate his grave and may his dust be fragrant, to the mercy of Almighty God and His approval.

A third Ottoman commander during the Nikopol campaign came from a very different background. He was Ali Paşa Çandarlı Zade. Like his father the *Grand Vizir*, Çandarlı Halil Hayr al-Din Paşa, he was a *qadi* or qualified religious judge before becoming *Qadi'l-Askar* or 'Judge of the Army' and a military commander in his own right. His mother was a daughter of the most important religious teacher at Iznik (Nicea) while his father was sometimes credited with creating the famous *Yeni Çeri* 'Janissary' infantry corps.

The Çandarlı family was, however, of Turcoman nomadic Turkish origin and enjoyed enormous prestige amongst Ottoman troops of Turkish origin, no less than five members of the family serving as *Grand Vizirs*. Though Ali Paşa Çandarlı's military career was less dramatic than that of Gazi Evrenos, it was he who had first conquered the citadel of Nikopol for the Ottomans, as well as conducting various successful campaigns in the Balkans, Anatolia and playing a decisive role during the battle of Kosovo. As *Grand Vizir* during Bayezit's reign he was both head of administration and finance, as well as commander of the whole army beneath Bayezit himself. Nevertheless he is best remembered for his legal and administrative contributions rather than his military ones, and for his love of the pleasures of this world, much like Bayezit, in fact. Ali Paşa Çandarlı died in 1407 and was buried at Iznik, in his father's tomb-mosque.

The idea that the Crusaders who came to grief at Nikopol, or at least their leaders, really intended to march all the way to Jerusalem and conquer the Holy Land is almost certainly a myth. Even under the best circumstances this would have been impossible, and in fact the ultimate intentions of this Crusading army were never made clear, except in largely meaningless rhetorical statements. Similarly Sigismund is very unlikely to have wanted an entirely defensive, passive and static campaign, as it was virtually impossible to maintain a large medieval army in one spot for any length of time. He probably wanted a pre-emptive invasion of Bulgaria, similar but on a larger scale to operations the Hungarians had themselves already carried out earlier, to forestall an anticipated Ottoman attack on Hungarian territory.

Sigismund also seems to have wanted the main army to march through Transylvania, across the Carpathians, and into Wallachia. This would have confirmed the shaky allegiance of both the Transylvanians and of Mircea of Wallachia who, it was feared, was still negotiating with the ruler of Poland. The French and Burgundian commanders, however, feared being held up in the difficult mountain passes. They wanted to stay close to their Danubian supply route and may furthermore have hoped to separate Serbia from the Ottomans. Hence they insisted upon following the main river.

Thereafter the French and Burgundian commanders probably envisaged a march across Bulgaria to capture the Ottoman capital of Edirne, then raising the Ottoman siege of Constantinople, saving or perhaps taking over what was left of the Byzantine Empire and forcing the Ottoman Turks back into Anatolia. This was ambitious but not beyond the realm of possibility. If it was their plan, then their preparations made sense. A Crusader supporting fleet in the Black Sea and Danube met the Crusading army outside Nikopol within a day or so of its arrival, which indicated careful preplanning and probable communications along the northern or Wallachian side of the river. Nikopol was also ideally located, and sufficiently strong, to serve as a base for subsequent operations southwards into Bulgaria, towards Edirne and Constantinople.

Bayezit's campaigns before the Crusade of Nikopol were a continuation of the long term strategic plan instigated by his predecessors, both in the Balkans and in Anatolia. The Ottomans had already shown that they could defeat the armies of the Balkan states either individually or together. Bayezit's own strategy had been to consolidate his control over Bulgaria, without which the Ottoman position in Europe would have been untenable. Most fortified places in Bulgaria were in the south of the country, though there were several strongly walled cities in the central plain. The only large fortified city on the northern or Danube frontier was Vidin, which was also a major river port through which Bulgaria had traditionally traded with Central Europe. The other strongpoints along the river were smaller, though some, like Nikopol, were also very strong and their primary role seems to have been to command various crossing points over the river.

Ottoman control of northern Bulgaria also gave them potential command of the lower Danube. Not surprisingly, therefore, Bayezit had already made Nikopol the centre of Ottoman power in this region, entrusting it to Doğan Bey, an experienced veteran. Nevertheless Ottoman methods of conquest avoided tying down their best troops in garrison duties and so made considerable use of the forces of their Balkan vassals to hold fortified places, stiffened with a small number of Ottomans to ensure loyalty. This meant that the bulk of the Ottoman army was always available for major campaigns, even at short notice.

Once the Crusader army invaded Ottoman territory, Bayezit dedicated everything to defeating it while Doğan Bey, commander of the Ottoman garrison in Nikopol, was ordered to resist to the last. Bayezit may also have feared that the Venetians would take this opportunity to expand their coastal possessions in Albania, seize Thessaloniki and threaten the Ottomans' recent hold on Macedonia. On the other hand the campaign took place during a good period for the Ottomans. Their traditional campaigning season ran from August to October and their horses had been fattened by the recent harvest. A large part of the Ottoman army was already gathered for the siege of Constantinople, the bloody conqueror Timur-i Lenk was busy elsewhere and even the Ottomans' main rival in Anatolia, Burhan al-Din of Sivas, was engrossed in a frontier squabble with the rulers of Karaman.

Bayezit clearly had excellent intelligence about the Crusader army and its movement. The importance he gave to the Nikopol garrison even hints at the possibility that he knew their intentions. Furthermore Bayezit and his commanders well understood Western European tactics and how to deal with them. This is not as surprising as it might sound because the Ottomans could draw upon the long Islamic heritage of military theory and writings, much of it focused on the threat posed by European armies since the Crusades of the twelfth century.

The result would be a complete success which was summarized a generation later by Bertandon de la Brocquière, a Burgundian who had studied the Ottoman army at first hand. As he wrote around 1433;

> Even when they defeated Emperor Sigismund [at Nikopol] and my lord Duke John [of Nevers], God rest his soul, they were as diligent as I have said earlier... When they arrive at the fields and stronghold where they want to fight, this is what they do. They divide into several battalions according to how many they are and whether they are in wooded or mountainous country... They set up a kind of ambush by their experienced people. They are well mounted, for they are light, and when they have found the Christians in a bad situation they recognize their advantage and know how to use it. If they find the Christians in good order they come galloping along the army, far enough away so their arrows will carry into the Christian army, aiming either at the men or the horses. This they do as long and as tenaciously as necessary to create disorder. As soon as there is any sign that the Christians are going to chase them, even if there is only a quarter as many chasing as retreating, they flee immediately.... Also each of them carries a little drum attached to his saddle horn, and if they see that those who follow are in disarray, whoever is in command begins to beat his drum three times. Then they all beat theirs and suddenly assemble like a group of little pigs that cry to one another. If they can keep them [the enemy] in disarray they know how to meet them. If by chance the pursuers are in good order and all together, and reach the emplacement of the main army which is divided into several battallions, they [the Ottomans] charge from all directions. If in this way they cannot throw the Christians into disorder, I was told that they have another tactic. The whole army faces the Christians head on. They have several ways of throwing fire to frighten the horses, or they bring up a great number of camels which are fierce and brave. They drive them forward and get them as close as possible to the Christians' horses to frighten them and throw them into disorder.

A Burgundian Ordnance or official proclamation dated 28 March 1396 fixed Dijon as the place where the Franco-Burgundian Crusaders should assemble by 20 April that year. Other Ordnances set out the rules by which the army would be organized, supplied and discipline maintained. Many of these documents survive and they give a far more accurate impression of what the army was really like than high-flown literary chronicles do. The core of the expedition was the military household or *Hôtel* of the Count of Nevers. It was an army within an army and mirrored that of the Duke of

Burgundy's own *Hôtel* which only recently included archers. At the start of the campaign the Count of Nevers' *Hôtel* consisted of one hundred and eight knights, one hundred and seven squires, a mere twelve archers and twenty-two crossbowmen. It nevertheless formed a coherent and structure fighting force of two hundred and forty-nine fighting men. Much less is known in detail about the rest of the Franco-Burgundian army, which probably consisted of other military households or *hotels* led by senior noblemen. Boucicault, for example, brought along fifteen knights and seventy other 'gentlemen'.

Regulations designed to impose discipline had been drawn up by the War Council on 28 March and though they failed dismally they shed light on prevailing social attitudes. For example a nobleman causing disruption could lose his horse and harness, a non-noble drawing a knife in a quarrel would lose a hand while anyone caught stealing would lose an ear. All were expected to obey military commands but in battle '*The Count* [of Nevers] *and his company always claim the avant garde*'. This would lead to disaster at Nikopol.

This was undoubtedly a very aristocratic army, but it included some men who had experience of Crusading warfare. The Count of Nevers' own *Hôtel* included thirty-five such veterans but all except one had campaigned in the Baltic or North Africa or had only been on peaceful Pilgrimage to the Holy Land. One man who had personal experience of the Ottoman Turks was Jean de Vienne, who had been with the Count of Savoy's expedition back in 1366. Other men outside this elite *Hôtel* had not only fought against the Ottomans but had in some cases even served as mercenaries in Ottoman service.

Meanwhile other small Crusading contingents were assembling in Germany, the Low Countries and England, the latter perhaps led by John Holand the Earl of Huntingdon and younger brother of King Richard II, though this remains doubtful. A small contingent did arrive in Hungary from Spain, as did several Polish knights. By now, however, voices were being raised in criticism of the forthcoming campaign. They even included the Crusading propagandist Philippe de Mézières who complained that things were being done in completely the wrong way. Aged almost seventy and living in the Convent of the Celestines in Paris where he was probably already a sick man, Philippe fulminated against the organizers of the new Crusade, who were not only morally unprepared and insufficiently penitent, but had ignored his advice concerning a new 'Crusading Order of the Passion'. He also maintained that by planning to travel overland across the Balkans they were going the wrong way. The knights, he proclaimed, were being drawn east by '*Vain Madame Ambition, one of the Mightiest Ladies in the World*'. It would, he proclaimed, end in disaster.

Chapter 11

Humbling the Crusaders

The first stage of the Crusaders' march against the Ottomans in 1396 was well organized and the main army reached Vienna without significant problems. On May 11 the city council of Regensburg had received a letter from the Count of Nevers requesting river transports to carry Crusader supplies down the Danube. Here at Regensburg the French and Burgundians were now joined by German forces under Count Palatine Ruprecht and the Count of Katznellenbogen. Amongst them, in the retinue of Lord Leinhart Richartingen, was a young squire named Johann Schiltberger whose account of his adventures across much of western Asia following his capture by the Ottomans remains one of the most extraordinary books from this period. In Vienna, the commanders were royally entertained by the Duke of Austria, but it seems that some of the priests who accompanied the Crusading army were already complaining about immorality amongst the troops.

A massive river fleet of seventy ships and barges now sailed down the Danube from Vienna to Buda, followed by the main Crusader army which reached the Hungarian capital late in July. The size of the army which eventually encamped outside Budapest led King Sigismund to write that; '*Their lances could have upheld the sky from falling.*' Nevertheless their true numbers have been the subject of prolonged and often unrealistic debate. Most earlier scholars have greatly exaggerated the size of the Crusader army, and even more so that of the Ottomans. In fact the young squire Schiltberger was probably closest the mark when he wrote that the Crusaders numbered some 16,000 men. Traditional Turkish sources give the number of Ottoman troops as 10,000 though, with their Balkans vassal contingents, they may have been around 15,000. One thing remains clear, and that is the numerical similarity of forces which eventually faced each other outside Nikopol.

Sigismund had been expecting an Ottoman invasion for which he had envisaged a defensive campaign but the anticipated Ottoman assault never materialized. Instead Hungarian reconnaissance parties ranged deep into the Balkans and found no evidence of major Ottoman forces. This led the French and Burgundian leaders to declare that Bayezit feared to face them so they insisted on taking the offensive, supposedly against Sigismund's wishes. On the other hand some sort of expedition into the Balkans must have been envisaged all along because a Crusader fleet was already assembling in the Black Sea.

Quite when the Crusader army set out from Budapest is unknown. Nicolas de Gara, the Constable of Hungary, led the vanguard down the left bank of the Danube, followed by the French and Burgundians. The Count of Nevers, however, seems to have marched with King Sigismund in the rearguard, which consisted of the main Hungarian force and probably the Germans. Perhaps they were still discussing future moves. Meanwhile a huge convoy of supply vessels sailed down the river. At Orşova the army assembled to cross to the southern side of the Danube. Downstream was the formidable Derdap Gorge, or Iron Gates, which not only formed a natural frontier between the Balkans and Central Europe, between the Orthodox and Catholic worlds, but was also a formidable though not entirely impassable barrier to navigation.

It took eight days to ferry the army across the Danube and almost at once the Crusaders started behaving with great barbarity to the local Orthodox Christian population who were subjects of the Bulgarian ruler Stratsimir, who was himself a vassal of the Ottomans. To the Hungarians, however, this was territory which should rightly have been their vassal. Franco-Burgundian overconfidence perhaps also accounted for the fact that no precautions are said to have been taken during the march along the southern side of the Danube to Vidin.

It is again unclear whether the river supply fleet sailed beyond the Derdap Gorge, though the number of small vessels later reported at Nikopol suggests that some did so. A part of the Hungarian army had also taken a different route from Budapest, through Transylvania to Braşov and across the Carpathian Mountains into Wallachia. Apart from gathering the perhaps unwilling Transylvanian contingents they also may have had the task of expelling Mircea's pro-Ottoman rival Vlad before driving the small Ottoman garrison from Nicopolis Minor (now Turnu Magurele) on the northern side of the river.

The main Crusader fleet which left Rhodes in August had sailed past Constantinople to the Danube Delta. It consisted of forty-four vessels under the overall command of the famous Venetian admiral Thomas Mocenigo. On the twenty-ninth or thirtieth of August all or part of this armada began sailing up the Danube towards Nikopol.

According to the French chronicler Froissart the Crusaders attacked several small outposts after crossing the Danube but at least one castle held out until the Crusader army continued its marched towards Nikopol, whereupon one of its commanders hurried to warn Bayezit of the invasion. This may well be true, though the Ottoman ruler would have had other warnings as well. Nearby Vidin had been a minor fortress in Roman times. Subsequently it became a Bulgarian provincial capital, a Byzantine frontier post and was held by the Hungarians in the 1360s. Thereafter Vidin was the capital of a small Bulgarian principality, currently a vassal of the Ottoman state. When the Crusader army arrived early in September 1396 the Bulgarian vassal king John Stratsimir opened his city gates.

The tiny Ottoman garrison, which was said to be commanded by a 'Greek Christian', probably a *voynuq* auxiliary leader, presumably surrendered, since there was little if any fighting. Nevertheless, they were promptly massacred before the Crusaders marching on to Orjahovo, which was another strongly fortified town overlooking the Danube. It guarded an important ferry point and was strongly garrisoned because this, since the incorporation of the Bulgarian Kingdom of Tarnovo into the Ottoman state, was now Ottoman rather than vassal territory. An initial attack by around five hundred French and Burgundian soldiers was foiled. A brisk siege then followed and several further assaults being thrown back before the arrival of the Hungarians convinced the defenders that they should surrender.

The Ottoman commander sent a delegation of local Orthodox Christians to the Crusader camp, offering to lay down their arms in return for their lives. Sigismund, it seems, would have granted this request but the other Crusaders claimed that their men had already scaled the walls and that they therefore had the right to treat the place as they wished. The result was another and larger massacre of Muslims and Orthodox Christians alike, men, women and children, though the Crusaders took many of the leading citizens and perhaps part of the garrison prisoner in the hope of exchanging them for ransoms. As a result the Hungarians felt that their initial acceptance of the surrender terms had been betrayed while their king had been insulted.

Part of the Crusader fleet probably arrived near Nikopol on the tenth of September and is likely to have anchored near the Wallachian northern bank until the main army arrived two days later. Nikopol itself was much stronger than the places the invaders had faced so far, apparently having been one of Tsar Sisman's royal residences before his kingdom was overthrown by the Ottomans. Thereafter its fortifications had been strengthened by the Ottomans and a large, well-supplied garrison installed under an experienced officer named Doğan Bey. The first Crusader assault failed and so the Crusaders settled down for a prolonged siege. This went on for fourteen days, the army attempting to scale and undermine the walls of Nikopol while their fleet blockaded the Ottomans from the river. These efforts failed and the defenders, now aware of the fate of their colleagues in Vidin and Orjahovo, had no intention of surrendering.

Foiled in their attempts to storm the town, the Crusaders settled down to a prolonged blockade to starve the defenders into submission. Meanwhile there was no news of Bayezit coming to relieve Nikopol. The idea that the Crusaders were so overconfident that they neglected to send scouting parties southwards is almost certainly a later myth, put about by chroniclers seeking to explain the defeat of this Christian army as a result of its own sins. Nevertheless the fact that the Crusaders could so easily be resupplied from Wallachia must have limited the need for foraging parties to venture far into unfriendly territory.

Pious chroniclers are also likely to have exaggerated the decline of morale and morals within the Crusader camp. However, enthusiasm may have waned and tension between the Hungarians and the Franco-Burgundians clearly increased. Crusader behaviour towards the local Orthodox Christians Bulgarians, who were treated almost as if they were enemies and who therefore rarely offered information about the Ottomans, also led to worsening friction with the Orthodox Christian Wallachians.

For its part the Ottoman garrison defended itself fiercely and effectively, so that once the siege was lifted their commander Doğan Beg was given the title of *Şuja al-Din* or 'Hero of the Faith'. The Crusaders may have believed that Bayezit was thousands of miles to the east. In reality he and the best part of his army had been besieging Constantinople when the Crusader army crossed the frontier. Ottoman intelligence services were seemingly as good as those of their Islamic predecessors because Bayezit promptly had lifted the siege and burned those siege machines which could not be easily moved as soon as the Crusader army left Budapest – long before it reached Ottoman territory. The fact that the Crusader fleet of forty-four warships and transports which passed through the Dardanelles and Bosporus on their way to the Danube made no attempt to stop Ottoman troops from Anatolia crossing over into the Balkans suggests that most were already there. Bayezit is also said to have been gathering his forces near Edirne when a spy brought him a copy of a letter the Byzantine Emperor Manuel to

Sigismund of Hungary, declaring; 'Why do you delay? The Turks are preparing for you, prepare yourself!

Information from the Ottoman side of the campaign is relatively limited though the Byzantine chronicler Dukas stated that; 'Bayazid, who had been informed many days earlier of the gathering of the nations from the west, assembled his entire army from the east and west and, further augmented by troops who were laying siege to the City [of Constantinople], led them in person.' Ottoman chroniclers add that as soon as Bayezit knew that the invaders had entered his territory he sent Gazi Evrenos Bey with an advance guard of light troops ahead of the main Ottoman army. Meanwhile the garrison of the Byzantine capital was too small to take advantage of Bayezit's departure and the lack of Byzantine ships in the Crusader fleet which eventually sailed up the Danube suggests that the Byzantines were unable even to contribute to the naval campaign.

Bayezit ordered Ottoman forces in the Balkans not to attack the Crusaders but to assemble between Edirne and Plovdiv while vassal contingents apparently assembled around Plovdiv itself, with the Serbs under Stefan Lazarevic arriving via Sofia. The speed of the Ottoman mobilization eventually caught the Crusaders by surprise. In fact Bayazid was fortunate in having the nucleus of his army already assembled for the siege of Constantinople, after which he summoned all the contingents that were immediately available and then marched northwards. The main Ottoman army almost certainly headed directly from Edirne to Tarnovo while Stefan Lazarevic probably marched from Plovdiv. Both forces had to cross the Balkan range which, though not particularly high, was very rugged. Bayezid went across the Shipka Pass on the twentieth of September, Stefan Lazarevic's Serbs probably a day later, both forces linking up at Tarnovo on the twenty-first or twenty-second.

Like the Western European knightly class, the Ottoman military elite were keen on winning fame in this world as well as Paradise in the next. Their attitude to warfare is reflected in the *Iskandername*, an epic poem written only a few years after the battle of Nikopol;

> Those who've left a famous name never died,
> > Those who've left no trace never lived.
> Surely this is why you came to earth,
> > That men should recall your worth.
> May I not die! say you of noble birth?
> > Strive then, that you leave a blessed name.

The Ottoman army was finally found at Tarnova by a Hungarian reconnaissance force under John of Maroth, the experienced *ban* or governor of the Hungarian frontier province around Belgrade. He was one of Sigismund's most loyal supporters and may have been sent to confirm earlier rumours brought back by foraging parties, rumours which the Franco-Burgundian Crusaders refused to believe.

The remainder of the Ottoman march to Nikopol was through easier country, where the Ottomans met no obstacles nor were they apparently challenged by enemy outposts. On 24 September Bayezit established his camp on a hill, several kilometres south of the Crusader camp. The morale of his men was high, since the Ottomans had twice before been victorious outside Nikopol. Ottoman sources even maintain that Bayezit was able to reach the walls of Nikopol, probably at night, and speak with the garrison commander who recognized his voice, though it seems unlikely that he was able to deliver additional supplies. In fact, according to the Ottoman chronicler Neşri, these were not needed, Doğan Bey telling Bayezit that; 'Our supplies are plentiful, and now that the Sultan is here we shall not be defeated.' To which Bayazid supposedly replied; 'Hang on bravely, I will look after you. You shall see that I will be here like a flash of lightning!'

Clearly Bayazid decided to follow traditional Islamic tactics and make the enemy attack him rather than making the first move. Equally clearly the idea that the Crusaders were surprised in their camp by the Ottomans is false. As a result the Ottomans established field fortifications on a battlefield of their own choosing. European accounts of the battle clearly describe a hedge of sharpened stakes forming the equivalent of a palisade, but they make no mention of a ditch. Later Ottoman armies clearly did use entrenchments and ditches, but Bayezit probably had no time for such elaborate field fortifications. For their part the Crusaders now found themselves with a formidable enemy army on one side, a still vigorous enemy garrison on the other, and with no strong base to fall back upon. A broad river without a bridge also lay between them and the nearest friendly territory in Wallachia. If defeated they would be trapped and this, as well as the traditionally offensive tactics of the French and Burgundians, necessitated the Crusaders taking the offensive.

On 24 September the Crusaders, perhaps fearing a rescue sortie by the garrison in Nikopol, had massacred the prisoners taken at Orjahovo. Such drastic action was common enough on Western European battlefields, but it was new to the Ottomans and, as the Crusaders clearly had no time to bury the dead, it would cost them dear two days later.

The Battle of Nikopol was fought in Monday 25 September 1396 on open ground not far from the walls of the town, though its precise location

1. The main gate of the Byzantine castle in Trikala, central Greece. Overlooking the horse-raising Plain of Thessaly, Trikala was a major military centre during the later medieval period. (David Nicolle photograph)

2. Byzantine carved marble relief of a warrior fighting a dragon, 13-14 century. He wears a short mail shirt and carries the typical Byzantine or Balkan triangular shield of this period. (Byzantine Museum, Athens; David Nicolle photograph)

3. The decision by Greek Orthodox monks to built monasteries on the extraordinary rock pinnacles at Meteora is often thought to reflect fear of the Turks. In fact this process began during the lawless period before the Ottoman conquest of Greece. (Monastery of Ayion Panton, Meteora; David Nicolle photograph)

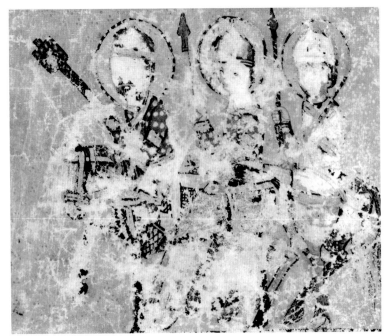

4. Alexander the Great leading his army, in the *Iskandername* by Ahmedi. His status is shown by the fact that he carries a mace. Made in 1416, this damaged manuscript is an exceptionally rare example of Turkish Anatolian art from this period. (Bibliothèque Nationale, Ms. Turc 309, f. 290v, Paris)

5. A Kuman horse-archer on a fragment of ceramic tile from Margaret Island, Budapest, 14th century. The Turkish Kumans or Kipchaks ruled the steppes north of the Black Sea before the Mongol invasions. Many then fled into Hungary and the Balkans where they played a significant role until the Ottoman conquest. (Lost during the Second World War, Magyar Nemzeti Múzeum photograph)

6. An early-14th century wall-painting of Saint Theodore Tiro, showing light-infantry equipment mixed with the archaic elements traditionally given to warrior saints in Byzantine and Balkan art. (*in situ* Kariye Camii [Church of Theodore Metochites], Istanbul; David Nicolle photograph)

7. St. Demetrius or St. Merkurios on a wall-painting made between 1338 and 1350. The style reflects strong Italian influence and this archer-saint has a typically Italian bascinet helmet with a raised visor. (*in situ* Monastery Church, Decani, Kosovo; David Nicolle photograph)

8. A detail from the first page of the late-15th century Ottoman *Sulaymanname* manuscript, showing a ruler, a general and soldiers in typical Turco-Islamic military gear. (Chester Beatty Lib., Ms. 406, f.1v, Dublin)

9. The Martyrdom of St. Demetrius, on a 15th-century Byzantine icon. Again there is the typical late Byzantine mixture of realistic elements, such as the helmets and swords, and unrealistic archaic armour which recalls Roman or even Hellenistic Greek forms. (Benaki Museum, inv. 2980, Athens; David Nicolle photograph)

10. The Rumanian principalities of Wallachia and Moldavia accepted Ottoman suzerainty but retained a large degree of independence. Many of their monasteries were not only strongly fortified but became major centres of post-Byzantine civilization. Late-15th and early-16th century Sucevitsa, seen here, was one of the most flourishing. (David Nicolle photograph)

11. The recently restored fortifications of the Hisar fortified area, on the eastern side of the Tophane district of Bursa. This was the Ottoman state's first real capital and the Turks are known to have carefully maintained its existing Byzantine walls and towers. (David Nicolle photograph)

12. The Genoese Gattilusi family ruled several Aegean islands and coastal enclaves during the later middle ages, and was closely linked to the Byzantine imperial ruling dynasty. This was emphasised in carvings which showed the Gattilusi and Byzantine imperial arms next to each other, this example being on the harbour tower at Enez. (David Nicolle photograph)

13. Enez, at the mouth of the River Marica, was an important fortified port in medieval times, and was held by the Genoese Gattilusi rulers of Lesvos under Ottoman suzerainty until 1460 when the Sultan transferred it to the deposed Byzantine ruler of southern Greece. (David Nicolle photograph)

14. The fortified inner harbour at Gallipoli. Cut from the hillside, with a single narrow entrance defended by a tower which was originally taller than it is today, this harbour provided a secure refuge for the first Ottoman galley fleet from the late-14th century onwards. (David Nicolle photograph)

15. The Ottomans proclaimed their conquests by religious and charitable buildings rather than fortresses. One example is the Eski Dzhamiya [Old Mosque] at Stara Zagora in eastern Bulgaria which is one of the earliest surviving Ottoman Turkish buildings in Europe, dating from 1408-9. (David Nicolle photograph)

16. The Kilidülbahir fortress, on the European shore of the Dardanelles has a 'clover-leaf' plan which was clearly designed to both house and resist gunpowder artillery. Like Kale-i Sultaniye [Canakkale] on the Asian shore, it was built for Sultan Mehmet 'the Conqueror' to protect the Dardanelles in the mid-15th century. (David Nicolle photograph)

17. Although Anadolu Hisari has been considerably altered, part of the original keep remains. This was the first significant Ottoman castle on the Bosphorus and although it could not close the Straits, it dominated the mouth of a small river which could serve as a harbour.
(David Nicolle photograph)

18. The Baba Vida castle in north-western Bulgaria was one of the most important fortresses on the Lower Danube. It dates from several periods, much of the existing fortifications being Ottoman Turkish. However, this tower is regarded as a 13th- or 14th-century Bulgarian construction.
(David Nicolle photograph)

19. A shield and sword, crudely carved on a 14th- or 15th-century Bogomil tomb from Bosnia. The Bogomils followed a dualist faith related to that of the Albigensian 'heretics' of 13th century southern France. (Archaeological Museum, Sarajevo; David Nicolle photograph)

20. The carvings on the best-preserved and most highly decorated of 15th century Bogomil tombs found in Bosnia included these horsemen, dressed in European style but apparently almost unarmoured in a Balkan or even Middle Eastern light cavalry tradition. (Archaeological Museum, Sarajevo; David Nicolle photograph)

21. The southern circuit walls Tarnovo, the fortified capital of the Kingdom of Bulgaria during the 13th and 14th centuries. (David Nicolle photograph)

22. This illustration comes from an Ottoman *Kulliyat* or 'anthology manuscript' made around 1480. The two figures on the left wear distinctive folded hats which identify them as members of the elite *Kapi Kulu* corps, probably being Janissary soldiers. (Topkapi Library, Ms.Revan 989, f.230r, Istanbul)

23. Khusrau hunting, in an Ottoman version by Hatifi, of the traditional Persian tale of *Khusrau and Shirin*, painted around 1498. One of the horsemen in the background, picking up a bird shot by the hero, has the tall, unfolded version of so-called 'Janissary hat' worn by senior officers or cavalrymen. (private collection, New York)

24. One of the illustrations in an Ottoman *Kulliyat* or 'anthology manuscript' includes two members of the elite *Kapi Kulu* corps. The man standing on the left has the unfolded felt hat of a Janissary officer, while the kneeling man on the left has the folded version of the same hat which identifies him as a Janissary soldier. The manuscript was made around 1480.
(Topkapi Library, Ms.Revan 989, f.230r, Istanbul)

25. A fully armoured knight accompanied by two 'figures of death' on a wall-painting made around 1475 when Croatia was at the frontline in the struggle against a still-expanding Ottoman Empire. (*in situ* Church of St. Mary, Beram; David Nicolle photograph)

26. After they conquered the Serbian fortress of Smederovo at the end of the 15th century, the Ottomans added three polygonal artillery towers or bastions. These were much lower than the medieval fortress and reflected the new concerns of gunpowder warfare. (David Nicolle photograph)

27. The massive land-defences of Constantinople [Istanbul] are well-known. However, their strength did not rely solely on three lines of increasing strong walls and towers. They was also a complex defensive system making subtle use of small postern gates which enabled defenders to counter-attack attackers in their flank or rear. (David Nicolle photograph)

28. The Adriatic coast of the Balkans had close cultural, economic and political links with Italy. This is clearly seen in the armour, weapons and heraldry on a mid-15th century carving on a medieval house in Sibenik. (*in situ* no. 18, Ulica Jurja Barokovica, Sibenik; David Nicolle photograph)

29. Golubac fortress stands next to a modern reservoir where the Danube flows through the Derdap Gorge. With the exception of the now partly-flooded polygonal artillery bastion, which was added by the Ottomans after they captured the castle in 1458, the fortifications are Serbian, dating from the 14th and 15th centuries. (David Nicolle photograph)

30. Bodrum Castle was built by the Crusading Order of Hospitallers in the early-15th century, at the end of an easily-defensible peninsula in south-western Turkey. It made use of the latest styles of European fortification and resisted the Ottomans for over a century. (David Nicolle photograph)

31. While Rhodes was ruled by Western European Knights Hospitaller for several centuries, the local Orthodox Christian population continued their own flourishing culture. Warrior saints were still painted in a very traditional style, though the realism of this late-14th century saint's face suggests some Western artistic influence. (*in situ* church of Ayios Nikolaos, Fountoukli, Rhodes; David Nicolle photograph)

32. Turkish nomads in a manuscript illustration by Siyah Qalam [Black Pen]. It was almost certainly painted in the late-14th or early-15th century, probably in eastern Anatolia or western Iran. (Fatih Album, Topkapi Library, Ms. Haz. 2153, f.8v, Istanbul)

33. One of the earliest attempts to illustrate the fall of the Byzantine imperial capital of Constantinople to the Ottoman Turks with any degree of accuracy was a wall-painting on the outside of the church in the Moldavian monastery of Moldovitsa. It was made half a century after the event and carefully emphasized key events ranging from the displaying of St. Veronica's Veil imprinted with the picture of Christ's face, in an attempt to get Divine intervention, to the key role played by cannon on both sides during the siege. (David Nicolle photograph)

remains a matter of debate. What is clear is that Bayezit used natural features to secure his position, his left flank being close to a wood while his right flank was protected by very broken ground beyond which were steep slopes leading down to broad marshes along the southern shore of the Danube. He was also on slightly higher ground than the plateau south and east of Nikopol. Most importantly there was a deep and narrow wooden ravine to his front.

The actual Ottoman battle array at Nikopol is relatively straightforward and was fully within Anatolian Turkish military traditions as seen throughout the fourteenth century, not only amongst the Ottoman army itself but also in other Anatolian Turkish forces. This habitually placed infantry archers ahead of the main cavalry element, which was itself divided into a larger centre and smaller wings which could also be thrust forwards, giving the whole array the appearance of a crescent. As was also traditional, the Balkan or Rumelian provincial cavalry were placed on the right wing because the battle was fought on European soil. The Anatolians would have had this place had the battle been in Asia, but at Nikopol they were on the left.

Infantry were placed in the centre protected by a dense thicket of sharpened wooden stakes. The small numbers of Janissary *ortas* which so far existed are likely to have been placed with the ordinary *azap* foot soldiers rather than held back with Bayezit's household corps, which almost entirely consisted of cavalry. In front of the thicket of stakes were the light cavalry *akincis*, operating as skirmishers or to draw the enemy forward against the main field defences and thus exposing them to flank attacks by the provincial *sipahi* cavalry. Meanwhile Bayezit himself was some distance to the rear, out of sight of the enemy behind the brow of a hill. Normally the ruler would be surrounded by his personal guard, with household cavalry to right and left, and this as probably the case at Nikopol. To one side of the Ottoman household division, probably the left, was the Serbian vassal contingent under Stefan Lazarevic.

Bayezit clearly planned to draw the Crusaders into an assault and then hit them in the flanks while they were fighting his infantry. Two things, however, did not go as anticipated. The Franco-Burgundians attacked so precipitously that the Crusader army was effectively divided into two parts, and then the Franco-Burgundians broke through the Ottoman infantry more quickly than expected.

With the exception of King Sigismund's largely Orthodox Christian Wallachian and Transylvanian vassals, the morale of both armies was very high, but when it came to discipline things were very different. Like most

Western European armies, the Crusaders were not specifically trained what to do in case of a reversal. In contrast the Ottomans were so trained, and as a result they did not run away when beaten but reformed, usually behind their original positions.

However, the Crusader army did not rush headlong into battle 'hot with wine and courage', as has been suggested by some historians. Its leaders may have hurried from their evening banquet to a somewhat acrimonious discussion the previous evening, but the morning's array had at least been agreed. Sigismund had advised caution and suggested that they should first discover if Bayezit was actually moving to attack. If so, the Crusaders should send the relatively light cavalry of Transylvania and Wallachia to clear the field of Ottoman *akincis*. Mircea agreed with this tactic and may even have volunteered to open the assault, since he had some claim to the territory on which the battle would be fought. The French and Burgundian men-at-arms would then attack the Ottoman main force, supported by the Hungarian cavalry with perhaps minor Crusader contingents defending their flanks.

The reaction of the Germans, Poles and other smaller contingents is unknown, but many of the Franco-Burgundian leaders were furious at the idea of entering battle behind those they regarded as peasants. The hot-headed Count d'Eu is even said to have declared; 'Yes, yes, the King of Hungary wants to have the flowers of the day and honour!' He also maintained that to place the French 'in the rear' would deny the Count of Nevers his agreed place in the van and 'expose us to the contempt of all'. Sigismund gave way and the following morning the Franco-Burgundians took up their position at the front of the Crusader army. Behind them, spread along a broader front, were the Hungarians plus Germans, Hospitallers, and probably Bohemians and Poles. On the right flank were Sigismund's Transylvanians led by Laczkovic while on the right flank were the Wallachians led by Mircea. This array may have had the additional advantage that the Transylvanians, who mostly came from an area of broad plains, were placed on a level plateau, though one dotted with woodland. The Wallachians, most of whom came from a land of forested mountains, faced broken and wooded terrain where a small stream tumbled down towards the Danube. In fact the Crusaders' left flank probably rested on the top of the slope leading down to the Danube while their right flank is likely to have been close to the head of two ravines which ran down beneath the western wall of Nikopol itself.

Early on the morning of the battle Sigismund sent his own *Grand Marshal* to try to convince his allies not to advance too hastily from what was quite a good defensive position. The Count of Nevers now summoned his own advisors. Some agreed with Sigismund's advise but D'Eu seized one of the banners of the Virgin and shouted; 'Forward in the name of God and St. George, today you shall see me a valourous knight.' The battle-hardened Admiral de Vienne was clearly not impressed and replied; 'When truth and reason cannot be heard, then must arrogance rule.' When doubts concerning various individual's courage started to be bandied about no one wanted to be shamed, so the attack was launched. D'Eu commanded the van, with the Count of Nevers and the main body close behind. Knights, squires and their relatively small number of mounted infantry moved forward together. Some German and other Crusaders may have been with them, perhaps even some Wallachians with their friend the French Sire de Coucy since several were subsequently captured.

As the sun rose the only Ottoman troops visible to Crusader scouting parties were a swarm of light cavalry *akincis* on the slope of a hill beyond a deep, narrow and thickly wooded ravine. Even these Ottomans would not have been visible to the main Crusader formations. The *akincis* are also said to have obscured the thicket of sharpened stakes and Ottoman infantry beyond, though given the nature of the ground this seems unlikely. What probably happened was that mounted Crusader scouts skirmished with the *akincis*, either on the plateau or in the wooded ravine, without being able to break through onto the hillside beyond. Bayezit's household division and the Serbs would also have been obscured by the shape of the hill beyond the ravine.

Seeing only *akincis*, and perhaps believing the usual European myth that Turkish armies consisted of such lightly equipped skirmishers, the Franco-Burgundian contingent moved forward across the level plateau towards the edge of the plateau without giving Sigismund any forewarning. They would now have found the ground sloping steeply downwards towards a narrow but probably dry stream bed with dense undergrowth and trees on both sides.

It was not the function of *akinci* light cavalry to confront a close mass of heavily-armoured horsemen and the fighting which did take place at this point would have been little more than skirmishing as the nimble *akincis* tried to take advantage of the steep wooden ground. European chronicles maintain that the Crusaders broke through the ill-equipped Ottoman light cavalry who scattered and thus exposed the Ottoman infantry behind their thicket of sharpened stakes. In reality, the *akincis* would have done what they were supposed to do; namely, shoot a few volleys of arrows, skirmish in an effort to draw the enemy forward and then break away around the flanks to reform behind their own foot soldiers.

At this point the French and Burgundians seem to have paused, perhaps taken aback by seeing the steep slope topped by a forest of sharpened stakes and great numbers of infantry. It is easy to imagine that the Crusaders, as they emerged from the woods, now presented the Ottoman infantry archers with a magnificent target. Crusader chronicles make it abundantly clear that arrows poured down upon the Franco-Burgundians. According to the epic *Deeds of Marshal Boucicault*, he subsequently recalled that 'Hail nor rain does not come down in closer shower than did their shafts'.

Military historians have argued over whether the Crusaders now dismounted to climb the slope and uproot the sharpened stakes by hand or whether they largely broke through on horseback. This discussion is probably misleading for several reasons, and also assumes much too much control by the commanders over their men. The slope was steep and in places almost precipitous. Many horses would have been wounded by the arrows or would have thrown their riders in the confusion. On the other hand, Ottoman composite bows, though they had greater range, accuracy and a higher rate of shooting than Western European longbows or crossbows, shot notably lighter arrows. On that morning of 25 September 1396 many Crusader knights and squires would have lost their horses and have clambered up the slope on foot, while many others would still have been mounted. Those on foot would have wrenched at the sharpened stakes, helped perhaps by those on horseback, while the Ottoman archers poured volley after volley into their ranks but were probably appalled to find that the arrows had less effect than anticipated.

Within a short time the Crusaders broke through the stakes and got amongst the virtually-unarmoured infantry. Carnage ensued and offers of surrender were denied. Since the French and Burgundians had attacked on a relatively narrow front, the surviving Ottoman foot soldiers were probably forced to the flanks rather than fleeing along the ridge behind them. Traditional Ottoman histories describe this as a trap into which the Crusaders fell, but if so it was a trap which nearly failed.

The Franco-Burgundian corps is also said to have dispersed Ottoman cavalry immediately behind the infantry. This is usually taken to mean the *akincis*, who had reformed here, but it may have included *sipahis* guarding the gap between two infantry corps. After defeating the Ottoman infantry, Coucy and De Vienne, who were both quite elderly, recommended that the Crusaders pause for a rest, but the younger men *'boiling with ardour'* insisted on pressing ahead. Presumably they expected to find the Ottoman camp and pillage it. Instead they were struck in the flanks by the provincial *sipahis*, this again being a standard Ottoman tactic. A desperate mêlée ensued in which many Crusaders were obliged to fight on foot. Heavy casualties were suffered by both sides before the *sipahis* withdrew towards the flanks. All this happened on a steep slope in the blazing sun and by the time it was over the Crusaders, young and old, were almost exhausted. They may also have realized that the Hungarians were still too far back to give immediate support while the Ottomans were proving far tougher foes than anticipated. Nevertheless they seem to have continued up the hill.

At this critical point Bayezit's household division came into sight over the brow. It must have been a severe shock for the Crusaders who, though tired, also believed that they had won the battle. Bayezit's cavalry elite now crashed into the somewhat disorganized French and Burgundians. According to the Monk of St. Denis; 'The lion in them turned into a timid hare.' Many fled or tumbled back down the steep hill, some escaped back to the plateau, others down the ravine towards the Danube where, however, they found broad marshes rather than the clear river's edge they had seen only five kilometres upstream.

The rest, including most of the French and Burgundian leaders, stood and fought. Not surprisingly Crusader chroniclers stress the prowess of their own men. Less colourful Turkish sources merely state that the Ottomans closed in on the Crusaders from three sides, which suggests that the provincial *sipahis* rejoined the fight from the flanks. Perhaps basing his work on the recollections of Ottoman troops who took part in the battle, the Byzantine chronicler Dukas maintains that Bayezit's household troops emerged from a wooded area to attack the Crusaders. The Ottoman chronicler Neşri, who specifically based his account on statements by the sons of those who took part, stated that one part of the Crusader army panicked, shouting 'The Turks are behind us! The Turks have got behind us!'

The brave old Admiral de Vienne tried to rally the Crusaders but only ten companions stood by him. Six times, it was said, the Banner of the Virgin was struck down but was raised again until finally the Admiral, covered in wounds, was beaten to the ground, the sacred banner still in his lifeless hand. The Count John of Nevers' bodyguard eventually persuaded him to surrender, though they also had to convince the Ottomans that the young man was indeed a great nobleman worth a considerable ransom. Thereupon the other surviving knights lay down their weapon, as did several Wallachian noblemen who had been with the Franco-Burgundian vanguard.

Western and Ottoman sources agree that the battle of Nikopol was, in effect, two battles in which the Ottoman army destroyed the Franco-

Burgundian and Hungarian Crusaders separately. The precise sequence of events is nevertheless unclear. The main question is whether the French had already been defeated before the Hungarians came into contact, or whether the two combats overlapped. Sigismund would not have been able to see the fate of his allies and it seems unlikely that his patrols could have crossed the ravine once the *akincis* reformed. The Hungarian king's famous remark to Philibert de Naillac, Grand Master of the Hospitallers, that; 'We lost the battle by the pride and vanity of those French. If they had believed my advice, we had enough men to fight our enemies, was probably made later when the battle had indeed been lost. On the other hand, the stream of wounded and riderless horses, cantering back from the ravine does seem to have shaken Hungarian morale.

Quite what Sigismund, the Hungarians, Germans and other smaller Crusader contingents did next is unclear, though most evidence suggests that they moved forwards in a vain attempt to support the Franco-Burgundians. If so they probably did so before the latter had surrendered. The Wallachians and Transylvanian were probably still with Sigismund and it was probably only when Ottoman troops emerged from the trees along the ravine that Mircea and Steven Laczkovic decided that the day was lost. Neither man felt particular affection for Sigismund and, more importantly, they knew that their home territories would soon be raided by the victorious Ottomans. Mircea in particular wanted to keep his none too numerous forces intact to defend Wallachia. Their withdrawal was, of course, seen as desertion by the Hungarians. Mircea's men crossed the Danube, perhaps using the small boats which had been ferrying supplies from Wallachia rather than the larger Crusader vessels moored in the river. The Transylvanians may have gone the same way, though it is more likely they retraced their steps along the southern side of the river, back to Transylvania via Orşova.

Meanwhile Sigismund and his central corps seem to have continued to move forwards. This was still a considerable force and seems to have cut its way through at least one division of Ottoman infantry who can only have been the *azaps* and perhaps Janissaries previously broken by the Franco-Burgundians. The fact that they had reformed confirmed the superior discipline of the Ottoman army but there is no evidence that Sigismund reached the Ottoman field fortifications.

This would suggest that the Ottoman infantry had moved forwards, either to attack the Hungarians or in the hope of taking the Crusader camp and relieving the garrison in Nikopol. The chronicler Neşri maintained that the 'front line' of the Ottoman army was on the offensive and, according to squire Schiltberger, who was present; 'They were all trampled and destroyed and in this engagement an arrow killed the horse of my lord Lienhart Richartingen, and I Hans Schiltberger, his runner, when I saw this ... , rode up to him in the crowd and assisted him to mount my own horse, and then I mounted another which belonged to the Turks, and rode back to the other runners.' This also strongly suggests that the Ottoman infantry were caught in the open, probably on the plateau but still close to the wooded ravine. According to a little known Greek chronicle, written in the seventeenth century but drawing upon now lost Turkish sources; 'the archbishop of Vienna [by which the author probably meant the Archbishop Nicholas Kaniszay of Gran] saw the rout of the [French] army, he led his soldiers to the centre of the struggle, launched a counterattack against the Turks and slew many. The Christians were shouting, Victory! Victory is ours! and the archbishop was able to put the Turkish troops to flight.'

After this success the Hungarians took on a body of Ottoman cavalry, probably one or both wings of provincial *sipahis*, who would have moved forward with their foot soldiers. Several Crusader contingents were engaged at this point, including the Hungarians under Nicolas de Gara and the Germans and Bohemians under the Count of Cilly. Bayezit's own household division was probably not involved and the outcome was still in the balance when the Ottoman ruler ordered Stefan Lazarevic and his Serbs into the fray. They charged towards the main Hungarian banner held by Nicolas de Gara's standard-bearer and overthrew it. Aiming for the enemy leader's banner had, of course, been an essential feature of Byzantine and Islamic warfare for centuries.

Some sources suggest that the Serbian attack was a form of ambush and it may well have been launched from a wooded area, probably from Stefan Lazarevic's position to the left of Bayezit's own banner. If so it is likely to have hit the Hungarians in the flank or even rear. Its impact was decisive, as Schiltberger made clear; 'When all the [Turkish] foot soldiers were killed, the king advanced upon another corps which was of horse. When the Turkish king saw the king advancing, he was about to fly, but the Duke of Rascia [Serbia] known as the Despot, seeing this, went to the assistance of the Turkish king with fifteen thousand chosen men and many other bannerets. And the Despot threw himself with his people upon the King's banner and overturned it.'

Once the banner had fallen, and the Hungarians commanders realized that they were on the verge of defeat, they convinced Sigismund that he must quit the field. At first the Hungarian withdrawal towards the river seems to have been in relatively good order, most of the senior men getting on board ships anchored offshore with little difficulty. According to Bertrandon de la Brocquière, drawing upon Burgundian recollections; 'Two hundred Lombard and Genoese crossbowmen held off the Turks until the Emperor [Sigismund] had boarded his galleys on the Danube.' Whether this took place on the eastern or western side of Nikopol itself is unknown, though references to some groups making a final stand on small hilltops while others were hunted amongst the hills rather suggests that it was downriver from the fortified town. The Ottomans who shot arrows at the ships as they passed had probably taken control of the high bluff overlooking the river east of Nikopol.

A larger part of the ordinary soldiers were less fortunate. According to De La Brocquière; 'Six thousand Wallachians, with the Knight of Poland, had placed themselves on a rise a little way off from the Emperor and were cut to pieces.' Squire Schiltberger saw the catastrophe first hand; 'When the cavalry and foot soldiers saw that the King had fled, many escaped to the Danube and went on board the shipping. But the vessels were so full that they could not all remain, and when they tried to get on board they [the crew] struck them on the hands so that they were drowned in the river. Many were killed in the mountains as they were going to the Danube.' Dukas probably based his version on Ottoman recollections, writing that; 'The survivors fled to the Danube where the majority threw themselves into the river and drowned.' It was clearly a case of every man for himself and in fact a remarkable number of Crusaders escaped, including survivors of the Franco-Burgundian vanguard amongst whom were several quite senior men.

Bayezit was astonished by the luxury found in the Crusader camp where he and his commanders celebrated their victory in one of the finest tents. More grimly, however, the Ottoman ruler also saw the massacred prisoners from Orjahovo and Vidin, and resolved to revenge then by executing his own Crusader captives next day. The following morning Bayezit's anger had not subsided and he ordered all those who held prisoners to bring them before him. According to Islamic law these were the property of those who had captured them, though, like all other booty, one fifth was to go to the ruler.

No Ottoman sources describe what happened next, so we only have the accounts of survivors. They maintained that Bayezit ordered all captives to be executed, saving a few who were selected for ransom, but that after a period of slaughter the Ottoman ruler either grew sickened and ordered the killing to stop, or was persuaded to do so by his advisors on the grounds that such a massacre would anger God.

Some Crusaders who escaped overland endured terrible privation and many succumbed to their wounds. The people of Wallachia and even Transylvania were far from friendly and the Carpathian mountains were amongst the wildest parts of Europe, full of wild animals which also took their toll. Winter descended before the fugitives reached home and even then weakened men continued to die of disease, including the Count Palatine Ruprecht Pipan, who succumbed after arriving at his father's town of Amberg.

Meanwhile those who escaped down the Danube in the Crusader fleet reached the Black Sea, perhaps stopping at Genoese Kilia to get provisions, and then turned south towards Constantinople. The Venetian galley carrying Sigismund and his party reached the Byzantine capital where he discussed the situation with Emperor Manuel. Sigismund seems to have promised to launch another Crusading expedition the following spring, but this never took place. Thereupon the Hungarian party set sail again in two galleys, travelling via various Venetian colonial outposts until they arrived at the Adriatic port of Dubrovnik on 21 December. On the way King Sigismund and his companions had to endure the humiliation of seeing Bayezit's Crusader captives paraded along the shore at Gallipoli as his ship sailed through the narrow Dardanelles.

Captivity amongst the Ottoman Turks was not new for many of the western European military elite and the prisoners taken for ransom at Nikopol were reasonably well treated. Some idea of the fate of the younger prisoners can be found in the recollections of squire Schiltberger. Nothing, however, is known about those humbler prisoners who, escaping execution on the day after the battle, simply disappeared. The majority would have become slaves both in the Ottoman state and sold further east. Some presumably converted to Islam, earned their freedom and were eventually integrated into Islamic society.

Those senior men held for ransom spent most of their captivity in the original Ottoman capital of Bursa. They were given bread and meat, had some freedom of movement and were even allowed to hunt. Nevertheless their health suffered and after a while the Count of Nevers was separated from his companions. The Count d'Eu, who may already have been wounded, soon died at Mihaliç near modern Karacabey. He was buried in the Monastery of St. Francis in Galata, across the Golden Horn from Constantinople, which suggests that his body was handed over to the Genoese authorities. Here, or in a neighbouring monastery, other knights who either died in captivity or during their escape by ship from Nikopol were also buried. The aged Sire de Coucy was now a broken spirit. Though described as a tall, heavy man of great strength he eventually sickened and died, while the younger De la Trémoille withstood his incarceration best.

It took a long time to arrange ransoms for the surviving noble prisoners. Jacques de Heilly, having been selected by both the Count of Nevers and Bayezit, had been sent via Milan to Paris with official news of the Crusader defeat and a demand for ransoms. He arrived on Christmas Day 1396 and immediately went to see King Charles in the Hôtel Saint-Paul. Still wearing his riding boots and spurs he knelt before the King and assembled barons to tell the whole appalling story. He then handed over letters from the Count of Nevers to his parents, the Duke and Duchess of Burgundy, plus letters from other prisoners. In return the King awarded him a pension of two hundred *ecus* but as Jacques de Heilly was still on parole he had to return to Bayezit. With him went three senior Burgundian knights whose task was to negotiate the amount of ransom and the release of prisoners.

Some of these ransoms were so huge that they had an impact on the economies of several countries, resulting in higher taxation in France and especially Burgundy. By January 1397 begging letters were already circulating amongst the noble families, written by the wives or families of those held captive. Some of the proudest nobility in France asked the *Doge* or ruler of immensely-wealthy Venice for help. Meanwhile Marshal Boucicault and the Sire de la Trémoille were allowed, on parole, to visit the Genoese Lord of Mitilene (Lesbos) to speed the transfer of money. Both men fell ill and De la Trémoille died. Though Boucicault's own ransom was now paid, he would not abandon the Count of Nevers and continued to urge the payment of the vast sum demanded.

One of the few men in France who had not been shocked by the news of Nikopol was Philippe de Mézières. Instead he promptly announced that he had a vision in which he saw; 'A big man with a pale face, haggard and disfigured, bare feet, bare head, a pilgrim's staff in his hand on which he leaned, dressed in an old Turkish robe, off white and torn, a cord rope around his waist, a large wound in his left side all covered in blood.' It was the ghost of Jean de Blaisy who knelt beside Philippe, giving him news of the terrible Crusader defeat. The ghost also told of strange visions seen during the battle and said that he was a messenger from the dead and the captives, calling on all Catholic rulers to remedy the situation. This in turn led to Philippe to write his *Desconfiture de Hongrie and Epistre Lamentable* in 1397.

While De Mezieres blamed the sinfulness of the Crusaders, other French writers blamed the Hungarians. Amongst them was the poet Eustace Deschamps who, even before the end of 1396, wrote;

Nicopolis, city of pagan lands,
   In these days saw a great siege,
Abandoned through arrogance and folly;
   Because of the Hungarians who fled the field.

This was, of course, entirely unfair, though the myth persisted. The notoriety of the battle of Nikopol also reflected the fact that the best Crusading army that western Christendom could muster had been utterly defeated at its first real battle. It was supposed to have been the vanguard of much larger efforts, perhaps led by King Charles of France and King Richard of England. However, these never materialized and the 'Crusade of Nicopolis', as it is usually known, has been described as 'the last great international enterprise of feudal chivalry.' The Crusade became the 'impossible dream' of the fifteenth century.

Not surprisingly, the Nikopol campaign had a significant impact on Hungary. It had not only been the defeat of a major Christian alliance, but it severely damaged King Sigismund's reputation, undermining his already weak authority. In 1401 Sigismund was even imprisoned by rebel barons, but they had to release him after seven weeks because they could agree on no better ruler. More positively, the Hungarian king started a vigorous and prolonged programme of military reform. The Diet or 'parliament' at Temeşvar in 1397 proposed several significant changes, regulating the military obligations of senior churchmen as well as barons, both of which groups had to provide *banderia* feudal levies to defend the kingdom. More importantly, perhaps, a *militia portalis* was established in which every landowner had to provide one light cavalryman from every twenty tenant holdings, later raised to thirty-five. Whether the majority of these light cavalrymen were drawn from the peasants themselves, or were hired soldiers, remains unclear but they were paid and equipped by the local nobility, probably as mounted archers. Clearly such a force was designed to face the growing Ottoman threat.

Fortifications along Hungary's southern frontier were similarly modernized with the help of Italian *condottieri* mercenaries and architects. At the same time fifteenth-century Hungarian chroniclers tended to be less prejudiced against their Ottoman foes than were their western neighbours. In fact the Ottoman were not described as being particularly cruel or wicked. Instead the greatest fear was reserved for their supposed '*false kindness*' which '*worked against the soul*' and encouraged Christians to convert to Islam.

For the Ottoman army the battle of Nikopol had been a total if expensive victory. To publicize his triumph across the Islamic world Bayezit sent batches of prisoners to various other Muslim rulers. Most are believed to have been from the younger captives, but not all. The German squire Johannes Schiltberger was to have been amongst a group of sixteen youngsters sent to the Mamluk Sultan in Cairo. They were led by an older man, a Hungarian knight, but in the event Schiltberger's wounds were too bad for him to travel. Almost twenty-four years later the Venetian traveller Emmanuel Piloti visited Egypt, where he heard of two hundred French and Italian prisoners of war who had converted to Islam, risen to some prominence in the Mamluk military system and were currently based in Cairo's Citadel. Perhaps they also included some of Schiltberger's comrades.

Instead of going to Egypt, Schiltberger spent six years as a 'foot page' to Bayezit and then six years as a 'mounted page' to his successors. He was again captured and recaptured, this time by other Islamic armies, spending further years in the service of various rulers and travelling through the Middle East, southern Russia, Transoxania and perhaps even northern India. Though technically still a slave, Johannes Schiltberger was treated much the same as other Christian mercenaries in Islamic service. He retained his Christian faith, no attempt being made to force him to convert to Islam, and he met fellow Christians of what were to him strange denominations in the Caucasus and Central Asia before eventually returning to Rome in 1427.

Chapter 12

The Ottomans Face Catastrophe

*T*he Battle of Nikopol had been an overwhelming victory for Bayezit and the Ottoman army, but it would soon be overshadowed by greater and far more dangerous events. After Nikopol, Bayezit decided against another major campaign in Europe, though he did send raiders deep into Hungarian territory. Instead he consolidated Ottoman authority within those parts of the Balkans already taken. The little Bulgarian Principality of Vidin, previously a vassal, was placed under direct Ottoman rule and the entire southern bank of the lower Danube river became a frontier zone or *uc*. Here colonisation by those considered reliable was encouraged and as a result the majority of the population soon became Muslim. Elsewhere Ottoman troops penetrated central Greece while Bayezit himself returned to his previous desultory blockade of the Byzantine capital of Constantinople.

Bayezit I was born in 1354, the son of the Ottoman ruler Murad I and 'Rose Flower' Khatun who is sometimes said to have been of Greek origin. The boy reportedly grew up at Didimotokon in what is now the north-eastern tip of Greece. As one of the ruler's sons Bayezit was appointed governor of the recently conquered Germiyanid *beylik* around 1381. Within a few years he was responsible for Ottoman affairs throughout the east, while his father Murad focussed on conquering large swathes of the Balkans in the west. Bayezit meanwhile earned a reputation as a brave though impetuous young soldier, probably earning his nickname of *Yildirim* 'The Thunderbolt' after defeating the Karamanids in 1386.

When Murad lay mortally wounded at the Battle of Kosovo he asked his civilian and military leaders to recognise Bayezit as their next ruler, and as a result Bayezit's only surviving brother was assassinated to avoid a civil war. Nevertheless Bayezit still had to quell an uprising by various vassal princes, after which he concluded an agreement with the powerful Serbs by marrying Maria, also known as Despina and Olvera, a daughter of King Lazar of Serbia, who had himself been killed at the Battle of Kosovo. In return Stefan Lazarevich, the new Serbian ruler, remained a loyal vassal and friend until Bayezit's death. A large part of Bayezit's life would be spent on campaign, usually on the offensive, but also resisting invasions from east and west, of which the Nikopol Crusade was merely one.

The only significant war that Bayezit lost was his last, when he was defeated and captured by Timur-i Lenk at Ankara in 1402. He died in captivity the following year. Not surprisingly the Byzantines feared Bayezit greatly, the historian Dukas describing him as; 'a persecutor of Christians as no other around him, and in the religion of the Arabs a most ardent disciple of Muhammad whose unlawful commands he observed to the utmost, never sleeping, spending his night contriving intrigues and machinations against the rational flock of Christ.' From the Turkish perspective Bayezit was a great conqueror and one of the first Ottoman rulers to be a patron of poets. One of the few surviving fragments of Ottoman poetry from this time was by Niyazi and was written in praise of Bayezit himself: 'The shy deer of heaven is safe from the leopard-sun, since it has made the shadow of your lion-banner its refuge.' Bayezit was also a supporter of some unorthodox *sufi* mystical Islamic groups, one of his daughters – Nilüfer, 'Water-lily' – reportedly marrying the leader of the Suhrawardi dervishes.

Some scholars had already been attracted to Bayezit's entourage, but victory over a massive and abundantly-financed European Crusade further enhanced Ottoman prestige. Consequently, large numbers of sometimes highly-educated administrators, religiously motivated soldiers, talented craftsmen and renowned scholars started to appear in the Ottoman court. This had previously been regarded as brave and warlike but hardly yet a significant centre of Islamic civilisation. In fact there were plenty of such people now available because the eastern Islamic lands had been thrown into near anarchy as a result of Timur-i Lenk's savage campaigns of conquest.

Timur-i Lenk, better known in Europe as Tamerlane or Tamberlane, claimed to be descended from Genghis Khan and although this was probably false, his activities were certainly within Mongol traditions. Timur not only overran large areas of Russia, Iran, India and Central Asia and was only prevented from attempting the conquest of China by his own death. Indeed his campaigns were marked by savage massacres and cruelties that exceeded in number and viciousness those committed by his Mongol predecessors.

Not entirely because of his atrocities, Timur-i Lenk became a legend within his own lifetime, his deeds and his brutality holding the attention of many chroniclers. The *Zafarnama* was a sycophantic account of the conqueror's exploits by Sharif al-Din 'Ali Yazdi, probably written before Timur died. The bitterly critical *Aja'ibi'l-Maqdur* by Ahmad ibn Arabshah was penned after its author fled to Ottoman territory, where he served as a secretary to Sultan Mehmet I. Tamerlane's deeds also came to be well known in Europe by the early sixteenth century when Europe was threatened by the advancing Ottoman Turks. So the exploits of a warrior who had not only defeated the Ottomans in battle but had captured their Sultan was bound to receive a sympathetic hearing. Yet Europeans also knew about Timur's many massacres and his blood-curdling reputation, all of which were woven into Christopher Marlowe's play, *Tamburlaine the Great*, which was written and performed before 1587.

Though by both medieval Islamic and modern standards Timur-i Lenk was a monster of cruelty, he was undoubtedly intelligent. Illiterate, though by no means ignorant, he spoke three languages, loved listening to history but not poetry, admired artists and craftsmen, and had a passion for sumptuously decorated tents. He was also one of the best chess players of his day. Timur played not only the game similar to that played today, but other versions that have fallen out of fashion, including the 'greater game' played on a board ten squares by eleven and with additional pieces, such as two camels, two giraffes, two sentries, two siege engines, and a prime minister.

Though he assumed an air of piety, Timur-i Lenk seems to have cared only for the good opinion of his soldiers, who in turn adored him. He certainly showed great personal courage in battle, often sharing the dangers of frontline combat. Whereas Genghis Khan and his sons had carried out massacres, these were usually done dispassionately for the calculated purpose of terrorizing their foes into submission. Timur's massacres were more frequent, more obviously sadistic and often served no apparent purpose. Yet the visiting Spanish ambassador Clavijo could still report that Timur was admired for his justice. Even a mortal enemy like Ahmad Arabshah, who described Timur as a 'mad dog', also admitted that he; 'did not love jest or falsehood. Nor did wit or sport please him while truth, though troublesome to him, did please him. He was not downcast by adversity nor joyful in prosperity ... He was spirited and brave, inspiring awe and obedience.'

Many of those regions which Timur-i Lenk invaded were already in a state of some confusion if not chaos. Iran, for example, had fragmented into a series of small states after the fall of the Mongol Il-Khans during the fourteenth century. Further to the west two Turcoman tribal states, those of the *Aq Qoyunlu* ('White Sheep') and *Qara Qoyunlu* ('Black Sheep'), ruled eastern Anatolia and Armenia, competing with each other and with the rising power of the Ottoman Turks. Meanwhile Kurds and Armenians squabbled for land in this same area. Even the Armenians and Georgians, both of whom were Christians, mistrusted each other. In fact the Georgians had even been expanding from their lush Caucasus valleys before Timur arrived on the scene, whereas the Armenians were no longer masters of their ancestral homeland.

The whole area, along with Europe and China, had also recently witnessed a terror worse even than the Mongols; namely, the Black Death and the recurrent waves of plague that followed. Almost entire populations had died, although the effects varied from one area to another. The total loss of human life is, of course, impossible to calculate but modern research in those areas where records survive, as well as archaeological study of settlement patterns, show that in some regions up to a third of the inhabitants died – which is roughly what medieval chroniclers themselves believed.

The western Mongol Khanate of the Golden Horde appears to have been particularly badly hit, at least as far as its military potential was concerned. Perhaps this was because, in such a nomadic society, the loss of a third of all males meant the loss of a third of the army. In settled areas of the Middle East, where armies were often smaller professional forces, the ranks could be filled with slaves or volunteers eager for the privileges that went with a military career. These factors would all have their impact upon Timur's forthcoming career of conquest.

Islamic reaction to the catastrophic Black Death appears to have been different from that seen in Europe. Whereas Christian Europeans tended to see the Black Death as divine punishment for their sins and thus turned to religious hysteria and the persecution of Jewish minorities, the typical Middle Eastern reaction was a return to the security of family and tribe. Instead of mass hysteria there seems to have been an increasing use of birth control, which was sanctioned by Islam but not by the Christian church. Indeed the medieval Arab attitude towards love and sex was already summed up in the saying; 'Love is kissing and the touching of hands – Going beyond that is asking for a child.' So, as life got harder, children were seen as an added burden. In fact the population of the Middle East never fully recovered from the effect of the plagues until modern times; a vicious spiral being created which linked drastic population reduction to economic decline and contracting agriculture.

Timur's army was a permanent force in an almost constant state of mobilization and in 1385-6 it was the turn of western Iran, Iraq and Georgia to feel its fury. Tabriz, capital of the Jalayrid dynasty, fell and the Jalayrid ruler, Ahmad ibn Uwais, retreated to Baghdad. In the summer of 1386 Timur's army turned against the Christian kingdom of Georgia. Their attack was irresistible, Timur himself taking part in the final assault on the Georgian capital of Tbilisi. The Georgian king, Bagrat, was captured, dragged off in chains and persuaded to convert to Islam before being permitted to return to Georgia to repair the damage.

Timur's army now rested on the grassy steppes of Azerbayjan before turning on the Qara Qoyunlu who ruled eastern Anatolia. The Qara Qoyunlu, who were warlike and still nomadic Turcomans, beat off the first raids until Timur himself seized their capital of Van in the summer of 1387. Huge numbers of Armenian inhabitants were bound and thrown from the surrounding cliffs but here, as an Armenian chronicler tells us, a few survived because their fall was broken by the piled corpses of those who went before. Such massacres were repeated across southern Iran in 1387 where, at Shiraz, Timur came close to killing Hafiz, one of the greatest Persian poets. The bloodthirsty conqueror had apparently taken exception to his verses and raged at the poet; 'With blows of my bright sword I have conquered most of the world and devastated thousands of towns and countries to beautify my cities of Samarqand and Bukhara. And you, miserable wretch, would sell them both for the mole on a Turkish girl's cheek.' Bowing low Hafiz replied; 'Alas, Sire, it is because of such extravagance that I have fallen on evil days.' Fortunately Timur showed an unexpected sense of humour and, instead of killing the poet, showered him with gifts.

In the forbidding uplands of eastern Anatolia, a region that even today has a wider selection of ferocious wild animals than any other part of western Asia or Europe, Timur came up against remarkably successful resistance by the Qara Qoyunlu. In fact, these fierce Turcoman nomads never really accepted Timur's domination and they also held a series of virtually inaccessible castles. Timur's army nevertheless captured the city of Mardin, where the defeated garrison was unexpectedly spared because the conqueror had received news of the birth of a grandson, Ulughbeğ, the future 'astronomer king' of Samarqand. Van was also taken for the second time before Timur's host again moved north into Christian Georgia.

This time Timur did little more than pass through on his way to settle final accounts with Toqtamish, who was once more threatening Timur's northern frontier. On 15 April 1395 the armies of Timur and Toqtamish met near the River Terek, a strategic point where so many battles had been fought. This time Timur's victory was complete and the shattered remnants of Toqtamish's army plus that of his Russian vassals were pursued as far as the Principality of Moscow. There Timur turned back not, as the terrified Muscovites believed, because of the miraculous intervention of the Virgin Mary, and still less through fear of Moscow's military might, but because he had no interest in conquering the poor and backward Russian principalities. Instead he turned south, sacked the European trading post of Tana (modern Azov) at the mouth of the river Don and then headed for Sarai, capital of the Golden Horde.

The destruction of Tana was hardly more than an excursion for Timur-i Lenk, yet it was a carefully calculated one that indicated considerable understanding of international trade and its economic implications. Less is known about the organization and defence of Tana than about those of Kaffa on the Crimean coast to the south, but all these trading posts were dominated by the Genoese. They formed the lynch-pins of immensely rich trade routes across the steppes to China, for it was from them that Genoese, Venetian and other ships took the exports of the Orient to Europe. It was also from them that Russian and Turkish slaves were exported to Egypt, to be trained as professional warriors, the original *mamluks* upon whom the power of the Mamluk Sultanate was built. The destruction of Tana did not cut these trade routes but did them terrible damage and thereafter most trade between China and Europe used a more southerly route through Timur's own empire, with all the profit from tolls and taxes which that entailed.

For two years it appeared that Timur-i Lenk, the now aged conqueror, was finally settling down to enjoy the spoils of victory. He was not, and after a particularly bloody invasion of northern India, he prepared for further wars against his western foes. Here the Jalayrid ruler Ahmad ibn Uwais had retaken Baghdad but, of all Timur's western rivals, the Ottoman and Mamluk Sultanates were the most formidable. Timur's undoubted grasp of strategy may have meant that he intended his first invasion of eastern Anatolia to frighten the Ottoman Sultan Bayezit before he abruptly turned south to deal with the Jalayrids and Mamluks before these could threaten his rear and flank. Thereupon Timur returned to settle accounts with the Ottomans. It was by any standards an amazing expedition, which took Timur's army back and forth across half the Middle East, winning victories at every turn.

In August 1400 Timur marched against Sivas in the heart of Anatolia, a city that had only recently been incorporated into the Ottoman Empire.

Here prisoners were forced to work as pioneers, undermining the walls and erecting earth platforms from which Timur's siege machines could hurl rocks and fire-pots into the town. The garrison, largely consisting of Armenian *sipahi* feudal cavalry, put up a stout resistance but eventually had to capitulate. They were buried alive in the city's moat although the Muslim inhabitants were spared. One Armenian chronicler, Thomas of Medzoph, even maintained that a choir of children came out of the city singing in hope of softening the conqueror's heart, but that Timur ordered his horsemen to ride them down. Certainly, Timur-i Lenk's treatment of Christians in eastern Anatolia was particularly savage and probably contributed to the loyalty these communities developed for the mild rule of the Ottomans.

Thousands of other Armenian captives were transported to Iran and central Asia, where their descendants survived for many generations. Captured Turks, including those from the warlike Qara Qoyunlu, were also sent east to be held ready for Timur's proposed invasion of China. Meanwhile the Qara Qoyunlu continued to resist. Their indomitable ruler, Qara Yusuf, was several times driven into exile but always returned. In contrast the second main Turcoman tribe in this area, the Aq Qoyunlu, came to terms with Timur and even sent troops to help him fight the Ottomans.

First, however, Timur had to deal with his southern flank. Though the Mamluks refused an offer of alliance with the Ottoman Sultan Bayezit they also refused to accept Timur's suzerainty. Such, in fact, was the political confusion in Cairo that the Mamluks were unable to organize a defence until Timur actually invaded their territory. The frontier city of Malatya fell in September 1400, as did a number of north Syrian castles, though not without a fight. In one siege, at Bahasna, the defenders hurled a huge stone right into Timur's tent, but the only result was that no quarter was shown to the brave garrison when it surrendered. Timur's army next reached the great city of Aleppo where, on 30 October, the Mamluk garrison marched out to give battle.

The struggle was brief and one-sided, with Timur using war elephants captured in India. Among the defeated Mamluks was a young Syrian who fought on though he had received over thirty sabre cuts to his head and other wounds in his body. Found later among the dead and dying he was brought before Timur who, according to the Mamluk historian Ibn Taghri Birdi; 'marvelled extremely at his bravery and endurance and, it is said, ordered that he be given medical treatment.' Aleppo was not so fortunate. The city was taken by assault and the usual massacre and piling of severed heads followed, while Timur engaged in a theological debate with some of the city's terrified religious leaders.

Timur next marched south. Hama was sacked and its people slaughtered. Damascus was bypassed and Timur's men came face to face with the main Mamluk army at Qatrana, east of Mount Hermon. There the two forces remained until 8 January 1401, when the Mamluks suddenly withdrew on hearing of a threatened coup d'état in Cairo. Damascus was thus left virtually defenceless, its garrison having been decimated in a previous unsuccessful sortie. The city surrendered, but the governor decided to resist in the citadel. When, after a bitter month-long siege the citadel finally fell it was found to have been defended by hardly more than forty Mamluk warriors. The survivors were enslaved. Damascus itself had already been sacked while its inhabitants suffered some of the cruellest tortures yet recorded even in Timur's sadistic career. Others were enslaved and sent off to central Asia, among whom was a twelve-year old boy named Ahmad ibn Arabshah who was later to write a savage biography of the man who had enslaved him.

The Jalayrid capital of Baghdad was the next to suffer, so much so that by 1437 the Egyptian historian al-Maqrizi recorded that Baghdad could hardly be called a city at all. Now Timur turned to face his most powerful foe, the Ottoman Sultan Bayezit. Both men were successful conquerors, Bayezit having crushed a European Crusade at Nikopol in 1396. His army enjoyed the same record of success as did Timur's and, not surprisingly, the two warrior rulers were wary of each other, initially first limiting themselves to an exchange of flowery threats.

Timur also appears to have hoped for an anti-Ottoman alliance with various Christian powers and in the winter of 1401-2 he tried to draw in local Christian rulers but they, recalling Timur's all too recent massacres, declined. The Byzantine 'Empire of Trebizond' was already Timur's vassal but they were not in a position to supply the twenty galleys he now demanded. The Byzantines of Istanbul and the Genoese of Pera (the modern Galata suburb of Istanbul) may have promised naval support against Bayezit but nothing came of it. Meanwhile both sides prepared for war. Timur's first action was to seize Erzinjan, where he demolished the Armenian Cathedral of St. Sergius. From there his army moved to Sivas, where it held a full-scale military review that showed just how modern and sophisticated its organization and uniforms had become. Such reviews not only checked an army's equipment and readiness but also boosted morale before a coming battle.

Timur now completely outmanoeuvred Bayezit, despite the latter's formidable military reputation. Nevertheless, Bayezit's men were obliged to do most of the marching while Timur besieged Ankara. Finally, on 20

July 1402, tired and thirsty, the Ottomans were thrown into what has been described as one of the first modern battles in Middle Eastern history.

Although Timur's armies often included infantry, they were still dominated by horse-archers who fought in the old Turco-Mongol tradition of the steppes. Meanwhile, at least a third of the Ottoman troops who faced Timur in 1402 were infantry, either Ottoman Turks or Slav vassals from the Balkans. The rest were quasi-feudal *sipahi* regular cavalry and Tatar or Turcoman auxiliary horsemen. Timur's force may also have been one hundred and forty thousand strong, compared to Bayezit's Ottoman army of only eighty-five thousand.

Bayezit, having been strategically outmanoeuvred, had a long march behind him whereas Timur's men were fresh from besieging the nearby city of Ankara. Both took up defensive positions before the battle, Timur establishing a camp fortified with a ditch, piled rocks and a palisade. He had also taken the precaution of poisoning the wells along Bayezit's line of march so that the Ottoman troops and their horses were probably very thirsty by the time battle was joined. Sultan Bayezit formed his army behind the small Kizilçaköy stream and along a low spur of hills that ran from the flank of Mount Mire. These hills were held by elite Janissary and other infantry with the *sipahi* cavalry from Anatolia on their right flank and the *sipahis* of Rumelia on their left. Much of the Ottoman infantry, in particular the Serbian vassals, were clad in heavy mail hauberks and fought with axes.

Timur-i Lenk divided his army into seven divisions, as he had done when he defeated the Golden Horde at the Battle of Kunduzcha eleven years earlier, but here they were arranged in a different manner. Timur's son Shah Rukh led the left flank, Mir 'Ali the vanguard, Timur himself the centre, with his guards forming a separate division slightly to the rear. Abu Bakr led the right flank, which, together with a right flank reserve, took up positions on the far side of the small river Çubuk. The main reserve stood between Timur's guards and the citadel of Ankara which was still held by an Ottoman garrison.

The sequence of events in the Battle of Ankara is open to dispute. Bayezit may have made the first move, sending the cavalry on his left to attack Timur's right flank. Or it could have been Timur who took the initiative, attacking the Ottoman left. One thing is clear. The Rumelian *sipahis* on this wing were either repulsed or began to waver, many fleeing the field. Timur's other wing then outflanked the Ottoman right and attacked the Serbian vassal contingents who formed the second line of the Ottoman right. Here Timur's men were either forced back by the Serbs or retreated in order to draw the enemy after them. Whatever the cause, the Serbs did pursue Timur's cavalry but lost their own cohesion and fell back beyond their original position.

At this point Bayezit's Tatar auxiliaries changed sides, presumably having previously arranged this with Timur. They suddenly attacked the Ottoman left wing, where the Rumelian *sipahis* were already wavering. An Ottoman reserve force under Mehmet Çelebi charged the Tatars in an effort to retrieve the situation but Bayezit's left still gave ground. Turcoman contingents from regions of Anatolia that had only recently come under Ottoman rule formed the bulk of Bayezit's cavalry on the right flank. They now deserted as well, though it is unclear whether such a betrayal had been arranged beforehand.

With their cavalry falling back on both wings, the Ottoman infantry in the centre found their flanks exposed. The battle was clearly lost and while the Ottoman reserves now retreated to safety with the heir to the Ottoman throne, the Serbian cavalry also withdrew in good order. Meanwhile Sultan Bayezit led his own infantry guards to join the Serbian infantry and thus cover his son's escape. Six squadrons of cavalry from the shattered Ottoman right were already making a stand on a nearby hill known as Catal Tepe so it was to here that Bayezit and the remainder of his army retired. Timur's forces made repeated attacks upon this hill, though all were beaten back. As night fell Bayezit broke eastwards with about three hundred cavalry but his horse fell and he was captured, to be bound and dragged before Timur who was by now playing chess in his tent with his son Shah Rukh.

Later sources stated that Bayezit was held captive in an iron-barred cage, but this is probably a legend which grew out of Ahmad Arabshah's poetic description of the Ottoman Sultan having 'fallen into the hunter's snare and been confined like a bird in a cage'. Bayezit does, however, seem to have attempted an escape and was thereafter chained by night, travelling by day in a wagon or litter surrounded by a stout grille. Christopher Marlowe took the story a stage further by having Bayezit use these same bars to end the misery of his defeat; 'Now, Bajazeth, abridge thy baneful days, and beat thy brains out of thy conquered head, since other means are all forbidden me, that may be ministers of my decay.'

The shattered Ottoman army had meanwhile fled westward, many of its survivors being ferried across the Dardanelles to Europe in Genoese and Venetian ships. Meanwhile Genoa thought the time ripe for an alliance with Timur, though the Venetians kept the conqueror at arm's length. The defeat and subsequent death of Sultan Bayezit of course threw the Ottoman

Sultanate into turmoil, but their Empire was already as much a Balkan-European state as an Anatolian-Asian one. In the short term, however, Timur's invasion strengthened the nomadic Turcoman element in Anatolia against that of the peasants and towns, a factor that would eventually help the Ottomans revive their fortunes.

After the Battle of Ankara, Timur ravaged right up to the Aegean Sea, using the citadel of Kütahya as his base. Down on the coast the city of Smyrna (Izmir) had been in European Crusader hands since 1344, though the westerners never took the citadel or much surrounding territory. Many different people had contributed to this extraordinary Christian outpost, including Venetians, Genoese, the remaining Crusader principalities in Greece and Cyprus, a French army under the Dauphin of Vienne and above all the Order of Hospitallers based at Rhodes. Now the garrison consisted of two hundred knights and their followers under the Spaniard, Inigo d'Alfaro.

Timur demanded that they surrender and either accept Islam or pay tribute, but d'Alfaro refused and on 2 December 1402 the siege began. Izmir harbour was partially blocked by causeways built out into the sea and Timur's engineers constructed huge mobile wooden towers manned by up to two hundred soldiers. These were wheeled against the walls, which Timur's sappers meanwhile undermined. After less than fifteen days the city fell, the population being slaughtered while the surviving defenders fled to the neighbouring island of Chios.

Chapter 13

The Ottomans Survive

The defeat of Sultan Bayezit I by Timur-i Lenk (Tamerlane) in 1402 could have spelled the end of the Ottoman state, but the fact that it did not do so says a great deal for the inherent strength of early Ottoman government and military systems. Though the evidence is not entirely clear, it seems that Bayezit's sons Musa and Mustafa had also been taken prisoner by Timur-i Lenk after the battle of Ankara, though they were later released, perhaps in the hope of stirring up rivalries and further confusion within the Ottoman state. Bayezit himself died at Akşehir in March 1403, after which Timur returned to Central Asia to prepare for his proposed invasion of China. In fact Tamerlane or Tamberlane the bloodstained conqueror died in 1404 while actually leading his army towards the Chinese frontier.

Timur-i Lenk left Anatolia in a situation similar to that which had existed before Bayezit conquered so many of the rival Turkish *beyliks* in the final years of fourteenth century, several of these *beyliks* having been given back their independence by Timur. The greatest of these was once again Karaman, which Timur apparently hoped would serve as a strong buffer and vassal state between himself and what remained of the Ottoman Sultanate. Meanwhile the Ottomans were diverted by a civil war between Bayezit's four sons, each of whom wanted to be ruler. An extraordinary feature of their long struggle was that it remained almost entirely confined within the now reduced Ottoman state. Clearly loyalty to the descendants of Osman, the first real Ottoman ruler, remained strong amongst the Ottoman Turks and there were hardly any attempts to break away from Ottoman rule, although many vassal regions did regain their independence. For the military and political elite of the Sultanate it remained a question of which Ottoman prince to support. Meanwhile the deep-seated *gazi* tradition remained so strong that raids were sent deep into central Europe even while rival Ottoman forces were fighting each other on behalf of the four Ottoman brothers.

At one time Bayezit's eldest son Sülayman seemed likely to emerge victorious, as he was proving himself the most effective battlefield commander. He initially controlled the capital, Edirne, along with most of the European provinces and he was also supported by some powerful Christian vassals. Meanwhile his brother Isa controlled the old capital Bursa plus some Anatolian provinces. Another brother, called Çelebi Mehmet, governed Amasya, while the fourth brother Musa was being held virtually as a prisoner in Kütahya, capital of the revived *beylik* of Germiyan. This was a highly unstable state of affairs and even as early as 1403 Mehmet marched west at the head of his supporters to defeat Isa and overrun most of north-western Anatolia. The following year saw Isa on the European side of the straits, then returning to Anatolia where he was again defeated by Mehmet. Meanwhile a revolt erupted in and around the devastated city of Izmir (Smyrna) where an adventurer named Cüneyt Bey had taken control of the briefly revived *beylik* of Aydın.

Cüneyt remains an interesting figure. After seizing Aydın, he was removed by Süleyman who instead put him in command of Ottoman forces at Ohrid in Macedonia. By 1412 Cüneyt Bey was back at Ayasoluk (Selçuk, ancient Ephesus, now known as Efes) on the Aegean coast of Anatolia where he declared himself independent. This time Prince Mehmet brought Cüneyt Bey to heel but nevertheless left him in charge of the town and its citadel. In return for fighting an ally of Mehmet, Cüneyt was next given command of the strategic frontier *sancak* or province of Niğbolu (now Nikopol) overlooking the lower Danube river in northern Bulgaria. However, a few years later this restless adventurer gave his support to 'The False Mustafa', an unsuccessful pretender to the Ottoman throne, but eventually deserted him as well. After this brief support for the False Mustafa, Cüneyt Bey rebuilt an autonomous province around Izmir, back in western Anatolia, and then took control of the neighbouring islands, only to be defeated by the new Sultan's Genoese allies. Cüneyt Bey was finally captured and executed in 1426.

By then the Ottoman civil war was over, having lasted until 1413. Isa's final attempt to win the throne came eight years earlier when he formed an alliance with the *beyliks* of Aydın, Saruhan, Menteşe and Teke, which had themselves only regained their independence as a 'gift' from Timur-i Lenk. Isa was nevertheless defeated and thereafter disappeared from the scene. In 1406 the eldest of the competing brothers, Sülayman, invaded his brothers' territories, along with those of their *beylik* allies in Anatolia. Although his campaign was successful, Mehmet formed an alliance with the *beylik* of Karaman and sent his brother Musa by sea to the vassal state of Wallachia, from where he in turn invaded Rumelia, the directly-ruled Ottoman provinces of the Balkans. This obliged Süleyman to return across the straits from Asia to Europe, after which he defeated Musa in Thrace.

From 1406 to 1413 the Ottoman Sultanate remained divided, with Mehmet ruling Anatolia and Süleyman ruling Rumelia. In 1410 Musa again invaded the European provinces, defeating and killing his brother Süleyman near Edirne. Now Mehmet invaded Rumelia, but was defeated by Musa and had to withdraw back to Anatolia, leaving the Ottoman state again divided, this time between Musa and Mehmet. The climax finally came in 1413 when Mehmet forged an alliance with Byzantine Constantinople and Serbia in the west, and the *beylik* of Dulkadir in the east. Assembling a more-than-usually formidable army Mehmet crossed the straits and defeated his brother near Samakov, Musa being killed not long after.

Mehmet, the surviving brother, was now the undisputed Ottoman Sultan. His first priority was to restore Ottoman power in Anatolia and in the Balkans, tasks which had still not been fully completed by the time of his death in 1420. Fortunately for the Ottoman Sultanate, Mehmet I was succeeded by an even greater son, Sultan Murat II. He continued building upon his father's work, improving the Ottoman civil administration and military structures to such an extent that his son, Mehmet II, was able to make the Ottoman Sultanate into an empire which covered huge regions of both south-eastern Europe and western Asia. Furthermore, Sultan Mehmet II would subsequently come to be known in history as Mehmet Fatih, 'Mehmet the Conqueror', because it was he who finally conquered the Byzantine imperial capital of Constantinople.

The strength of Ottoman institutions, which had been demonstrated during this prolonged civil war, did not depend only upon military and political power. They were now also firmly based upon Islamic Law, or *Sharia*, though this had not always been the case. Ever since the mid-seventh century there had been tension at the heart of Islamic civilization between the ideal of a society built upon Divine Law as revealed in the Koran and clarified by *Hadith*, the traditional saying of the Prophet Muhammad, and the efforts of mortal men to build such a society. As a result there tended to be little argument about what was wanted, but plenty of disagreement about how to put Islamic law into practice. In the early centuries everything focussed upon this attempt to build directly upon the foundation provided by *Sharia*. Since the coming of the Turks in the eleventh century, however, and more particularly since the Mongol invasions of the thirteenth century, another element had entered the discussion. This was the *Yasa*, or traditional Turco-Mongol customary law, which crept into various aspects of Islamic society in various parts of the Middle East, most notably of course in those states inhabited or governed by Turks or Mongols and their descendants.

Another characteristic of traditional Islamic society had been that *Sharia* Law did not really recognize corporate bodies, but fundamentally only accepted the rights of the individual, even in what might now be called family law. In the final analysis this meant that everyone, male, female, young or old, was theoretically equal. The arrival of the Seljuk Turks in the mid-eleventh century began a process of deep-seated but often deeply contentious change as the new Turkish authorities started to separate spiritual and temporal powers. This was where the *Yasa* came in. At first it only affected the ruling and military elites, while the bulk of the existing Arab or Persian population still lived under *Sharia* law. Nevertheless the Turco-Mongol *Yasa*, like the Islamic *Sharia*, was considered to be above any ruler, however powerful, and consequently such rulers were expected to enforce its provisions, just as they were expected to enforce *Sharia* where it was deemed appropriate.

The Turks, having conquered a large part of the Byzantine Empire following their victory at Manzikert in 1071, adopted a tolerant approach which attempted to accommodate existing Byzantine and other non-Islamic legal systems. The same approach was subsequently taken by the Ottoman Turks, especially as their vast and expanding empire incorporated different legal codes for each of its main religious groups.

Even where the dominant Muslim population was concerned, the Ottoman state recognized two separate legal structures: the religious *Şeriat* (Arabic *Sharia*) and the secular *Kanun*. The latter arose from Sultan Mehmet II's (1451-1481) efforts to unify the varied secular laws of his huge realm, including elements of the old Turco-Mongol *Yasa*. It also made official an earlier Seljuk idea that the Sultan was secular co-ruler, with the Caliph as 'religious ruler'. The Caliph in question was still the Abbasid Caliph, who was a virtually powerless and indeed shadowy figure living in Cairo as a puppet of the Mamluk Sultanate. This ancient Abbasid religious dynasty, which dated back to the mid-eighth century, would finally come to an end in the early-sixteenth century when the Mamluk Sultanate itself fell to Ottoman conquest. What precisely happened remains unclear, but it seems that the last of these puppet Caliphs was taken to the Ottoman capital of Istanbul (Constantinople) where he spent the rest of his life, supposedly 'donating' the Caliphate to the Ottoman Sultan on his death-bed. Thereafter the Ottoman ruler had the status Sultan-Caliph. In fact this Ottoman Caliphate continued to exist for a further six years after the overthrow of Sultan Muhammad VI in 1918, until abolished by the Turkish republic in 1924.

As a result, the Ottoman Sultan's secular laws covered administration, trade, land holding and taxation, while the Caliph retained authority over religious matters and moral behaviour. Medieval Islamic civilization had a remarkably uniform legal structure built upon two pillars; the *qadis* or judges, with their staff of the 'judgement system', and various essentially separate enforcement authorities. But whereas the 'judgement system' hardly changed over the centuries, the enforcement agencies altered according to the political climate at the time and place.

In most of the larger or more formally organized states such as the Ottoman Sultanate, there was at least one *qadi* for each city or region, plus another for the army. In *Sunni* Islamic realms, each *qadi* belonged to one of four recognized *Sunni* Schools of Law and had studied in a *madrasah* or mosque-based religious college. The *qadi's* independence from local political pressure was supposedly guaranteed by a regular salary from the central government, while the head of the system was the *Grand Qadi*, who had to be a man of recognized knowledge, piety and energy. Though paid by the state, he also had authority over the government's actions and could usually rely on popular support when criticizing irreligious or excessive behaviour on the part of the authorities – even sometimes of a ruler himself. The authority of *Sharia* law was, in fact, so strong that it remained notably free of corruption, but in many places also tended to become very conservative and resistant to change.

Meanwhile the *muhtasib* and his staff had a foot in both law enforcement and judgement. Their role was to supervise markets, *esnaf* craft associations, business life, and general behaviour in public places. On the other hand, their authority was far less than that of the *qadi* and his staff. Whereas the *muhtasib* was an almost permanent feature of Islamic cities, other law enforcement agencies changed over the years. In many areas, for example, every urban quarter, tribal community and village had its own chief, often known by the Arabic term *ra'is* meaning 'head'. Such individuals could be powerful figures who not only defended the interests of their own people, but were also held responsible for any serious or persistent breaches of law and order amongst them. In fact the *ra'is* could be an amalgamation of sheriff, militia commander, mayor and leader of local merchants. Another traditional law officer was the *Shihna* who had originally been a Seljuk Turkish military governor but soon evolved into a local police chief commanding the a local garrison and *Shurta*. The latter had first emerged many centuries earlier as an elite bodyguard, but eventually evolved into a mixture of local police and firemen who could also be summoned to fight as soldiers.

Although all people within the Ottoman Empire were subject to the Sultan's law or *Kanun*, each *millet* or religious community was also governed according to its own laws. The two pillars of judgement and enforcement were also brought closer together, especially where Muslims were concerned. Naturally, the *qadis* still interpreted *Sharia* law and pronounced judgements. In practical terms, however, it was the *qadi's* employees who investigated criminal cases, arrested and interrogated suspects, summoned witnesses and punished the guilty after the *qadi* had made his final judgement.

In this they were helped by the local *Sancak Bey*, or military governor, but because he was so often away on campaign, it was frequently the local *Subaşi* or police chief who played a more important role in finding and arresting suspects. The *Subaşi* also had authority to detain suspects on his own initiative, though not to try them. Judgement always had to be carried out in the presence of local witnesses to ensure fairness, while the trials themselves relied on the testimony of witnesses, both to the litigant's character and the facts of the case.

The legal profession had similarly developed very early on in Islamic history. At its heart were the *Ulema*, a corps of recognized religious scholars qualified to interpret *Sharia* law in practical terms. They advised the *qadis* or judges, who were also recruited from their ranks. The science of *Fiqh*, or jurisprudence, was studied at a *madrasah* or religious college. *Fatwas* were legal pronouncements on the basis of *Sharia* law, while those qualified to serve as legal consultants were called *Faqihs* (*Fakihs*) or *Muftis*, of whom there was at least one in every town or district. A less common institution was the *Dar al-'Adl* or 'Palace of Justice', staffed by *Mazalim* or those knowledgeable in law, whose task was to control abuses of power and serve as a Supreme Court.

Different 'schools' of *Sharia* law demanded different degrees of evidence before a guilty verdict was reached. So for example, a condemned person had to be of sound mind before he or she could be considered responsible for his or her actions. The punishments accepted by Islamic *Sharia* law were also varied and occasionally ruthless. Nevertheless, the concept of compensation rather than vengeance was central to *Sharia*, though the ancient concept of 'an eye for an eye' remained. Consequently murder could be punished by death or by a very substantial fine.

Persistent theft could result in the amputation of part of a hand but in practice physical mutilation was noticeably less frequent in the Ottoman Sultanate than it was, or had been, in the Byzantine Empire. Adultery was theoretically punished by stoning to death, but could only be proved if there were four eyewitnesses, which made such judgements extremely rare. Fornication was punishable by one hundred lashes and banishment for a year while drunkenness in a public place deserved eighty lashes. All such physical punishments had to be carried out in public to demonstrate that justice was being done and to ensure that nothing further was inflicted.

One of the most important *Hadiths*, or sayings, of the Prophet Muhammad stated, 'Let there be neither injury nor vengeance for that injury', and this, along with Koranic verses which advocated mercy, ensured that the maximum penalty was usually exacted only in the most serious cases. While the ancient Persian tradition that a ruler should do all in his power to win loyalty contributed to the generally quite benign attitude of the Ottoman rulers to low-level disobedience, the Turks had also introduced other punishments based upon more ruthless Central Asian traditions. In practice, however, these normally only applied only to political crimes, especially those by the political elite. Nevertheless they included strangling, hanging or, in the worst cases of treason, impaling or skinning alive.

Chapter 14

An Islamic Empire in Europe

*T*he Byzantine city of Adrianople, now Edirne, may have fallen to the Turks as early as 1361. It has even been suggested that the first Turks to take control of Edirne were not actually Ottomans, but this major city was certainly under Ottoman control by 1366 following a small but historically significant Turkish victory over a combined Byzantine Greek and Bulgarian army somewhere between Babaeski and Pinarhisar. The following year the Ottoman *Emir* Murat I made Edirne the administrative capital of his expanding *Rumelian* or Balkan provinces, though Bursa continued to serve as the administrative capital of the Ottoman state's Anatolian provinces. This move to a new location on European soil was very significant for the future history of the Ottoman state. Thereafter the Ottoman Turkish capital would remain on European soil, even when transferred to Istanbul (Constantinople) after the conquest of that city in 1453. In contrast the shifting of the capital of the Turkish Republic back to Asia, to the central Anatolia city Ankara after the First World War, would be a similarly significant act.

Known as Edirne to the Turks, who always tended to simplify the sometimes convoluted Greek names of the cities they seized, ex-Byzantine Adrianopolis now became the focal point from which Ottoman campaigns thrust in four directions. These lines of advance were: westward along the coast of the Aegean Sea through western Thrace to Macedonia; north-westward up the Marica (Turkish Mariç or Greek Evros) River into the heart of the medieval kingdom of Bulgaria around what are now Plovdiv and Sofia; northwards towards the eastern end of the Balkan Range and the lower course of the river Danube; and eastward across eastern Thrace towards Constantinople (Istanbul) itself.

Ottoman successes attracted scholars as well as soldiers, and Bayezit I, who ruled from 1389 until 1402, had several famous people in his new court at Edirne, even before his remarkable victory over the invading Crusaders at Nicopolis in 1396. They included the historian Ibn al-Jazari, who actually finished his epic poetic verse *History of the Prophet and Caliphs* three days after the battle of Nicopolis, while still living in the Ottoman army camp.

Prior to that remarkable victory, Ottoman rulers had been addressed merely as *Emirs*, but after it Bayezit persuaded the titular Abbasid Caliph in Cairo to grant him and his successors the more senior title of *Sultan*. The fact that the Mamluk Sultan of Cairo, who ruled the biggest and most prestigious Islamic state in the Middle East, allowed this suggests that the Mamluks did not yet see the Ottomans as significant rivals. If so, they were very wrong.

The Ottoman Sultan's new status now encouraged yet more scholars to make their way to the increasingly wealthy and cultured Ottoman court. Not surprisingly, perhaps, the city of Edirne was soon graced with some fine new Islamic buildings. The *Eski Cami* or 'Old Mosque' dates from the start of the fifteenth century, but remained rather stern and old-fashioned in design. This was also true of the Mosque of Murat II, which was not completed until 1435/6. In contrast there is the beautiful *Üç Serefli Cami* or 'Three Balconies Mosque' which was built for the same ruler. Though this *Üç Serefli Cami* was finished only a few years later than the Mosque of Murat II, architectural historians regard it as the first significant building in a new and truly Ottoman architectural mode. Its great dome is almost twenty-five metres across and would not be surpassed until Sultan Mehmet the Conqueror built his victory mosque in Istanbul a generation later. Each of the four minarets of the Üç Serefli Mosque is also decorated in a different manner, one having a remarkable multiple spiral pattern in red and white, while the tallest has the three balconies which give the mosque its name.

Meanwhile senior military leaders often paid for the construction of secular buildings as acts of patriotism, loyalty and piety. These include the bridge of Gazi Mihail, a convert from Christianity, which dates from 1420, and the *Orta Imaret* which was a soup kitchen providing food for the poor. Sadly very little remains of the great Ottoman palaces built in Edirne during the fifteenth century, but a huge *bedestan* or covered bazaar constructed at the start of that century survives largely intact in the middle of the city. The transfer of the Ottoman capital to Istanbul after the fall of Constantinople in 1453 had little impact on the importance of Edirne which remained the administrative centre of the Rumelian or European provinces, as well as being the site of the Sultans' favourite country retreat until the nineteenth century.

The city would similarly continue to serve as the main strategic military base for the conquest of south-eastern Europe and, in much later years, for the defence of what remained of these Ottoman possessions. Its magnificent monuments would suffer severe damage during the Russian invasions of 1829 and 1878, while a long siege and brief occupation by the Bulgarians in 1913 did further damage. During the rest of the twentieth century Edirne's location on the very edge of Turkey's remaining European land frontier meant that it was cut off from much of its economic hinterland, and consequently would not be as modernised as Istanbul had become. As a result Edirne could, until very recently, be described as the only remaining truly 'Ottoman' city in Europe.

The role of art and artists in the medieval Islamic world was different from that in western or even eastern Europe. The iconoclasm, or deep-seated dislike of representational religious images which had convulsed Christianity in the early Middle Ages, remained a feature of Islamic art though it was never as emphatic in Turkish or Iranian art as it was in the Arab lands. This is very clear in Ottoman art, which produced a remarkable form of manuscript illustration developed from earlier Turkish, Central Asian and Persian forms. In fact the Muslim fear of realistic representation on the grounds that it could lead to idolatry was never as pervasive as is often thought. There was plenty of representational secular art, even a certain amount of three-dimensional sculpture, and in some unorthodox or ultra-Shi'a parts of the Muslim world there would always be a small amount of realistic religious illustration, though this was strongly frowned upon by the more orthodox Sunnis.

Instead, during the medieval period Islamic religious art developed a sophisticated repertoire of decorative motifs based on abstract patterns and stylized plant life, as well as the Arabic script. In fact the latter was often used in such a stylized manner that it was almost impossible to read. This varied decorative repertoire of motifs was then used on surfaces ranging from the margins of book pages to the domes of mosques. Meanwhile secular patrons continued to demand illustrated books of heroic or humorous stories, superbly carved ivory panels, huge wooden doors covered with scenes of courtly life, and assorted forms of ceramic, glass and metal-work where little human figures often seemed lost amongst a mass of floral or abstract decoration.

Like that of all other cultures, Islamic art evolved over the centuries and reflected the tastes of new political or military elites. For example, the Seljuk Turks, who took control of most Muslim lands from the eleventh to thirteenth centuries, brought with them from Central Asia a love of human sculpture dating from a time before they converted to Islam. As a result people, animals and mythical monsters were carved on buildings, even including a handful of religious ones. A few almost life-size statues of Seljuk rulers or court officials survive in direct contradiction to the belief that there was no realistic sculpture in Islamic art. The Turks and Mongols similarly stimulated textile design with new ideas for rugs and wall-hangings brought from as far away as China. In fact the Seljuk period saw a remarkable degree of similarity between realistic illustration on widely different scales. Thus the ancient eastern Iranian and Central Asian school of wall painting was now mirrored in often tiny book pages, as well as in new forms of ceramic decoration.

The more orthodox elements of the Islamic religious establishment are said to have been almost as suspicious of music as they were of 'idolatrous' representational art, on the grounds that music was so powerful that it could lead people away from religion. Certainly Arabic, Persian and Turkish literature is certainly full of references to men and women going into raptures over some particularly effective performance, while talented musicians, poets and singing girls clearly had a power and influence to be envied by modern pop stars.

By the eleventh century, what might be described as a new 'art music' had emerged from a blending of the musical heritages of the Arabs, Turks, Persians, Berbers and European Andalusians. Performers came from every corner of Islamic civilization to find patrons amongst the wealthy political and mercantile elites of the Middle East, but, although the Middle Ages were a golden age in Middle Eastern music, little is known about how it actually sounded. This is because music was learned by ear, not by written notation, despite the writing of numerous books on musical theory. The basic modes were different to those in European music, having more in common with the music of India, Iran and Byzantine Greece. On the other hand, the musical instruments used in the Islamic and western European worlds during the middle ages were not so different, even though they were tuned differently. Many of these instruments are still used today and include the plucked harp, zither, *oud*, *sahin* and later the Turkish *saz*, the bowed *nabab* and *rabab*, various woodwind instruments, the distinctive stringed *qanun* played with small hammers, and assorted drums.

In general, Islamic music tended to be soft and plaintive to western ears, with singers being famed for trilling sounds and vocal gymnastics as found in modern opera, while words tended to be simple and repetitive, though sung in innumerable different ways. Although *Shi'a* Muslims developed an emotional form of religious 'passion play', it seems to have been under

Turkish rule that music was more widely introduced into unorthodox forms of Muslim worship. This was particularly apparent in Anatolia, even before the rise of the Ottomans, and almost certainly reflected continuing Christian influence, which prompted various *sufi* or mystical religious brotherhoods to introduce music and even dance into their celebrations. The most famous of all these brotherhoods was, of course, that of the *Mevlavi* or 'Whirling Dervishes'.

There was virtually no concept of 'literature' in medieval Islamic civilization because writings to the highest literary standards were involved in almost every aspect of culture and a great deal of everyday life. As the untainted and direct word of God, Islam's holy book, the *Koran*, was regarded as being far above mere literature, but it was also the fountainhead of perfect language. The Arabs' ancient poetry came second, and although this was rooted in an epic desert tradition it evolved considerably during the Middle Ages, with new poetic forms and new themes such as verses on love, wine and war. Each form was strictly governed by its own conventions and the poet was admired not so much for what he said as the way he said it. Meanwhile the ruling elites were expected to support poets and writers, and literary skill was so highly regarded that a rather tedious form of rhymed prose was often used, even in official government documents.

Medieval Persian literature had followed a different path. Beyond the Persian-speaking lands themselves, Persian would soon serve as the language of government and culture in most of the Turkish or Turkish-ruled realms – including the Ottoman Sultanate. This process really began in eastern Iran during the tenth and eleventh centuries as a reaction against two centuries of Arabic cultural domination. Like other aspects of this Persian revival, literature harked back to the glories of the ancient Persian empires, most obviously in Firdawsi's great *Shahnamah* poetic epic, completed around 1010. This recounted the seemingly-eternal struggle between Iranians and Turks, yet it would became a favourite amongst the Turks themselves, again including the Ottomans.

From the later-eleventh to the thirteenth centuries, Persian literature continued to flourish under Seljuk Turkish rule, producing a series of political and military treatises, including those known as 'Mirrors for Princes' which provided advice for the ruling class. Persian became, in fact, the language of administration, while Arabic remained that of religion, even in areas where Turks formed the bulk of the population. It would remain so in the Ottoman Turkish Empire almost up to modern times.

Turkish literature has rarely been given the status extended to that of

Arabic or Persian, but the later medieval period did see the writing of exciting warlike tales and perhaps the funniest stories in Islamic literature. Those concerning the escapades of Nasraddin Hoja were typically Turkish, often rude and disrespectful, but at the same time deeply moral. The *sufi* religious brotherhoods, which had become a characteristic feature of Turkish Anatolia, were largely responsible for the survival of Turkish during the disastrous Mongol invasions, and from then on Turkish literature began to flourish in its own right.

The contrast between the attitudes and achievements of Byzantine and medieval Islamic scholarship could hardly be more striking, despite the fact that both civilizations were dominated by religion. The only area where Islamic beliefs hindered new thinking was in philosophy, and here medieval scholars often got into trouble for putting forward unorthodox ideas. Nevertheless, thinkers like Ibn Sina (980-1037) and Ibn Rushd (1126-1198) had played a major role clarifying and commenting on the ancient Greek philosopher Aristotle, whose ideas dominated all non-religious thought in both medieval Muslim and Christian cultures. It was these men who, with various contemporaries, were actually responsible for transmitting Aristotelian concepts back to western Europe and, as a result, became authorities themselves, their names being westernized to Avicenna (Ibn Sina) and Averroes (Ibn Rushd).

Less acknowledged is the progress made by Muslim engineers, craftsmen and farmers in various fields of practical or applied technology, irrigation being the most obvious. Here surveyors developed various devices to check the level of canals and ensure a steady flow of water, including a simple form of astrolabe used as a theodolite. Technological advances also underpinned other industries, including the distillation techniques used in making scents from the essential oils of flowers or incendiary weapons from refined mineral oil. Soap was made for both cosmetic and medical purposes, while glass-making was far more advanced than it had been in Roman times and included various enamelling techniques. Chinese paper-making technology reached the Middle East very early in the Islamic era, traditionally after some Chinese clerks had been captured at the Battle of Talas in Central Asia in 751, and was soon accompanied by block-printing. On the other hand, the cursive character of Arabic, Persian and Othmanli (Ottoman) scripts did not lend themselves to movable type printing, which was invented much later in Germany. Sophisticated chemical knowledge did, however, permit the development of new textile dyes, ceramic glazes and decorative alloys used in metalwork.

Where pure science was concerned the Muslims have been called 'pupils of the Greeks', but this ignores the fact that medieval Arabs, Persians and Turks also learned from their pre-Islamic Persian predecessors, as well as from the Indians, Chinese and others. Furthermore, as a result of their own research, Islamic scholars went on to add a huge amount of new information and several daring new concepts. Having inherited the pure science of several civilizations, the Muslims' own concern with precise time and place to establish the correct time and direction of daily prayers led to notable advances in lunar calendars, astronomical tables and geography. Despite lacking accurate chronometers, Muslim geographers had tackled the problem of measuring longitude by comparing the timing of lunar eclipses in different parts of the world. Their results were amazingly accurate, considering such crude methods. Meanwhile, in pure mathematics Muslim scholars translated Indian treatises and adopted India's numerical zero. As a result, the numbering system used today in the western world is called Arabic to distinguish it from the cumbersome old Roman numerals, which had no zero. The invention of algebra, from *al-Jabr* meaning 'restoration', analytical geometry, trigonometry and even spherical trigonometry were all new, invented during the tenth to twelfth centuries, and inherited by later Islamic realms including that of the Ottomans.

Deep interest in light and optics had similarly led to an understanding of refraction, which enabled the depth of the earth's atmosphere to be calculated with great accuracy. A sun-centred rather than earth-centred solar system was suggested in thirteenth-fourteenth century Iran, but, although books were written on this subject, the concept was not widely accepted. It may nevertheless have passed via the Ottoman Turks and Greeks to the great Polish scholar Copernicus by the early-sixteenth century. There were fewer advances in zoology as the study of animals had little practical application, but it was very different with botany. Here Muslims could draw upon ancient Greek and current Indian knowledge which, when added to their own traditions of painstaking observation, produced startling new results which had a direct impact on both medicine and agriculture.

Comparable advances were made in the understanding of contagious diseases and in many regions the charitable *waqf* system financed the development of hot springs as free sanatoriums. In more general terms, however, the interests of Turkish rulers and scholars tended to focus on practical matters rather than scholarship. They were thus enthusiastic in the continuation of earlier Islamic medical science and application. Medicine was, in fact, the field in which medieval Islamic civilization had its most notable scientific advances. These were based upon empirical observation. For example, an interests in optics increased knowledge of how the eyes worked, while mental disorders were seen as 'mental sickness' rather than being ascribed to evil spirits, as still tended to be the case in medieval Europe. There were hospitals in all the main cities. These ranged from the Hospital of Qalawun built in Cairo in 1284, which was able to care for 8,000 patients with a professional staff which included physicians, pharmacists and nurses, to the huge Medical Complex of Sultan Bayezit II outside Edirne. This was started in 1484 and is credited to the architect Hayrettin Ağa. The main building is still a mosque, but this is flanked by numerous residential chambers. The complex also includes a large kitchen and refectory, a bakery and store rooms. The hospital proper is on the western side and has a main courtyard flanked by living quarters for the mentally ill isolated behind a colonnade, and various service or administrative rooms. A medical college or *madrasah* is also attached to the hospital, with what are understood to be living quarters for eighteen doctors or students. Perhaps for security reasons, the medical complex of Bayezit II has its back to the river, whereas it was more normal to integrate such features into the appearance of mosques.

Chapter 15

The Failed Christian Counterattack

The Ottoman civil wars which followed the defeat and death of Sultan Bayezit I had allowed Serbia, Bosnia and Wallachia to throw off Ottoman suzerainty. However, this restored independence would not last for long. During the first of his two reigns Sultan Murat II subdued these three states once again, while also extending direct Ottoman rule westward into Epirus. Murat's younger son Mehmet had already shown himself to be a skilled and enthusiastic soldier, which made him very popular with the Ottoman frontier *beys* and a significant number of the *Kapi Kulu* household troops. They now began urging the elderly Sultan Murat to nominate Mehmet as his heir, though he was not the eldest son. For the present, however, the Sultan had other more immediate problems to face. The dramatic revival in Ottoman fortunes clearly came as a surprise in the Catholic courts of Western and Central Europe and by 1443 the perceived danger had grown so great that another Crusade marched against the Turks. This time it was led by King Wladislaw, who currently ruled both Hungary and Poland.

In addition to trouble on their eastern or Anatolian frontiers, the Ottomans had also suffered a number of painful setbacks in Wallachia. Here they faced a new foe in the person of Janos Hunyadi, one of the greatest heroes in Hungarian and indeed Rumanian history. His origins are unclear for though Janos Hunyadi was born in largely Rumanian-speaking Transylvania, where his huge castle still stands at Hunedoara, he was a member of the Hungarian aristocracy and thus is claimed as a national hero by both countries. Having been appointed as *voyvoda* or governor of Transylvania by the new Hungarian king, Janos Hunyadi promptly defeated several Ottoman raids. Because of the reputation he thus earned on the mountainous Transylvanian frontier, Hunyadi was made the effective military leader, though not titular commander, of the forthcoming crusade.

The first phases of Wladislaw's Crusade were a great success, penetrating deep into Ottoman-dominated Serbia where the strategically important city of Niş was seized. The Crusaders then advanced eastwards, over the mountains into Ottoman-ruled Bulgaria, where Sofia also fell. During this period Sultan Murat was away, campaigning in Anatolia, and with their limited resources the local Ottoman forces of Rumelia could do little except harass the invaders. Now Mehmet hurried back to Europe with a relatively small army of elite *Kapi Kulu* household regiments. He regrouped the now scattered Rumelian forces and tried to stop Janos Hunyadi's larger army in a mountain pass known as the Trayan Gate.

Although the Ottomans were defeated, they soon had the weather on their side as the brutal Balkan winter had now arrived. Hunyadi was obliged to abandon the invasion and, after slaughtering his thousands of Muslim prisoners, he returned to Hungary. Despite this apparent and fortuitous success, the Ottoman Sultanate's position remained highly vulnerable, so the Sultan negotiated a truce in July 1444. The following month the aged Murat accepted the urgings of many of his military leaders and abdicated in favour of his son Mehmet. In fact Murat retired to Bursa where he apparently planned to spend the rest of his days in prayer and study.

His successor, the youthful Mehmet II, enjoyed widespread support and it seemed likely that he could prepare the Ottoman defences for any future Crusader assault. Unfortunately Mehmet's accession also led to increasing friction between the *Kapi Kulu* and the older established Turkish aristocracy. The latter were headed by the Çandarlı family whose most senior member, Çandarlı Halil, was also the ruler's *vizir* or senior government minister. To make matters worse, a series of rebellions now flared up in the Ottomans' Balkan provinces, while resistance stiffened in Albania where the Ottoman conquest was still far from complete. To cap it all, the Pope in Rome now declared that oaths sworn by Christian princes to maintain a truce with the Muslim 'infidels' were not binding. A new Crusade was proclaimed and soldiers flocked from all over Europe to join its ranks. Once again led by King Wladislaw it marched out of Szegedin in Hungary on 1 September 1444 and was joined at Orsova by Janos Hunyadi with his own highly experienced troops. Nevertheless the sources make it abundantly clear that Hunyadi had been most unwilling to break the promise of peace he had made to Sultan Murat, yet he felt honour bound to follow his king.

George Brankovic, the Serbian ruler, refused to join in this renewed attack and instead warned the Sultan of the approaching storm. The local commanders of the Ottoman state's Rumelian provinces now decided that the still-inexperienced Mehmet was too young to cope with such a crisis and so Çandarlı Halil asked Murat to return and take command of Ottoman resistance. The old man abandoned his pious retirement and even persuaded the Genoese to ship his substantial Anatolian forces across the straits to Europe. Clearly the Ottomans did not yet possess a fleet capable of doing this quickly enough. Meanwhile the Crusaders reached Varna on the Black Sea coast of Bulgaria. There, on 10 November 1444, the Ottoman army at first appeared to be losing the day, but Sultan Murat rallied his men while the elite Janissaries stood firm against the Hungarian cavalry. By the time the fighting ended the fortunes of battle had been entirely reversed, the invaders had been routed, and King Wladislaw lay dead.

Once again a victory against the biggest and best-equipped army that Western Christendom could send against them brought huge prestige to the Ottomans. It was also the signal for a renewal of Ottoman advances into the Balkans. To some extent these campaigns were declared to be a punishment for the Christians' breaking of their truce agreements. In most regions resistance to Ottoman forces was crushed or brushed aside, but in Albania the Turks again came up against an extraordinary guerrilla leader, George Castriota who is better known by his Ottoman name of Skanderbeğ (Iskander Bey). He and his followers used their exceptionally rugged and mountainous homeland to defy the Sultan from 1443 to 1468, and even then the Ottomans found it expedient to allow the warlike Albanian tribes to retain a considerable degree of autonomy. Eventually, however, the majority of the Albanian people would convert to Islam and became some of the Ottoman Sultanate's fiercest defenders.

Another Crusade was launched four years later and was again led by Janos Hunyadi. Again the Serbian ruler, George Brankovic, refused to turn against his Ottoman neighbours but Skanderbeğ of Albania sent soldiers, as did the ruler of Wallachia. This time Sultan Murat met the invaders in Kosova, routing them at what history knows as the Second Battle of Kosova (18-20 October 1448) on much the same battlefield as the Serbs had been defeated by Bayezit I almost a century before.

One of the first places to feel the renewed wrath of the Ottomans was Wallachia. Here one of the strangest figures in European history had appeared on the scene. Vlad Tepes or 'Vlad the Impaler', who is generally believed to have been the historical reality behind the legends of Dracula, was born around 1430 at Sighişoara. Here his father, Vlad II Dracul, held a relatively unimportant border command post under the Hungarian crown.

This Vlad Dracul was also being groomed as the Hungarian King's candidate as *voyvoda* or autonomous governor of Wallachia, and indeed he achieved that position in 1432. Vlad II Dracul had to retain or more accurately to regain this title by force four year later, at the head of a dissident faction of Wallachian *boyars* or noblemen. He now switched allegiance and became a supporter of the Ottoman cause, taking part in two raids into Hungarian-ruled Transylvania. Changing sides once again, Vlad Dracul joined the Hungarian Crusade against Sultan Murat in 1443 but argued against the new Crusade which came to grief at Varna the following year. For a while he even held the famous Janos Hunyadi captive and so, in 1446, Hunyadi had Vlad Dracul dethroned. However, the Hungarian-supported *voyvoda* who replaced him reputedly betrayed the Hungarians at the Second Battle of Kosova.

The younger Vlad, the future *Tepes* or 'Impaler', had been brought up in his father's palace at Targovişte with several brothers, but at the age of around thirteen his family's varying fortunes forced him to lead a nomadic and sometimes terrifying life. This must surely have had some influence upon his later cruel and bizarre conduct. In 1444 Vlad Tepes and his brother 'Radu the Handsome' were sent to the Ottoman court as hostages for their father's good behaviour. Given their unpredictable father's action, the two boys suffered a precarious existence in the Turkish fortress of Egrigöz in western Anatolia.

In 1447 Vlad II Dracul and his eldest son Mircea were killed by dissident Wallachian *boyars* and Vladislav II, a man more pliable to Hungarian wishes, was made *voyvoda*. The Sultan now freed Vlad Tepes, and gave him an Ottoman officer's rank and a small number of Ottoman troops before sending across the Danube into Wallachia. There he briefly captured Targovişte in 1448 but was soon driven into exile again. For the next eight years Vlad Tepes lived by his wits, moving between Ottoman territory, Moldavia and Transylvania, sometimes as a tolerated pawn in the power game, sometimes as a fugitive. Finally winning the support of Janos Hunyadi, Vlad Tepes fought his way to the bloodstained throne of Wallachia in September 1456. He then swore formal oaths to both the King of Hungary and the Ottoman Sultan, and began the first of his two eventful reigns.

The fact that Vlad Tepes became the relentless and quite successful leader of Wallachian resistance to Ottoman domination has, however, been obscured by the horrendous savagery with which he slaughtered huge numbers of enemies as well as those he believed to be unreliable. The most famous epitaph to Vlad Tepes is the name by which he is remembered – 'The Impaler' – and the fact that he became identified with the mythical and terrifying figure of the vampire Dracula.

The dramatic, often violent, and occasionally bizarre events which marked both the Ottoman conquests and the resistance which it prompted did not directly impact all the inhabitants of these regions. In general the urban populations were most exposed, because their towns and cities tended to be the targets of military campaigns. In the countryside the fertile lowlands and the main communications routes were obviously more vulnerable than the less densely populated highlands. In fact in many regions rural life, agriculture and local trade remained virtually unchanged. In many respects this had already remained unchanged since Roman times, despite huge loss of Byzantine territory to Muslim conquest during the earlier medieval period.

Above all the loss of Egypt, traditionally the 'bread basket' of the Romano-Byzantine Empire, had for a while caused severe food shortages which had a particular impact upon the army and within the cities. As a result the Byzantine imperial authorities had tried to increase food production by improving the generally appalling conditions endured by their remaining peasantry. Nevertheless it continued to remain illegal for a peasant family to change its place of residence and special documents were required for travel near the frontiers. The gulf between landowners and rural labourers remained vast. Furthermore, taxation largely fell upon the peasantry, most of those who tilled the fields being paid labourers, serfs or slaves throughout Byzantine history.

Perhaps not surprisingly, by the eleventh century there were few small freehold farmers left within the Empire, and their status continued to decline. At the same time the aristocratic elite was moving out of the Byzantine cities into the countryside where they bought up the best land. Then in 1204 the entire Byzantine world had been shattered by the Fourth Crusade's seizure of Constantinople and much of the surrounding heartlands of Byzantine civilization. Thereafter, the surviving fragmented Byzantine states went very much their own ways. The 'Empire of Trebizond', for example, was based in territory that was very different from that of other Byzantine states. Here the Pontus mountains and southern coast of the Black Sea were lush and in places almost subtropical. In the fertile coastal plain land-holding continued to be on a very small scale whereas in the mountains and the small amount of the Anatolian plateau still controlled by the Byzantine 'Empire of Trebizond', large-scale ranching gradually replaced arable farming.

Here, in stark contrast to most other remnants of Byzantine territory further west, a free peasantry flourished to the end. A peasant *gonikeia* or small family farm could, for example, be inherited, mortgaged, sold or farmed but it could not be abandoned without government permission. Even the bulk of Trebizond's still-warlike aristocracy remained relatively small landowners or *archons*, who were more like rich peasants than minor noblemen. The only great barons seem to have been from the semi-independent ranching areas of the southern frontier.

Of course village life and the villages themselves differed considerably in such varied climatic conditions as those of even the reduced and fragmented fourteenth- and fifteenth- century Byzantine territories. In many parts of the Byzantine Empire they had been associated with an aristocratic family's villa, just as had been the case in Roman times. Apart from the local priest, other essential members of the community were the blacksmith, potters, brick makers and those operating watermills for irrigation and power. Many of the larger villages also had shops. Fruit groves outside the settlements were owned by individual peasant families, as were the fields beyond, but the more distant pasture land was usually held in common by the village as a whole.

Agricultural implements consisted of simple hand tools and wooden ploughs pulled by oxen or mules. In stark contrast to the situation within the medieval Islamic world, Byzantine crops were largely unchanging, and even irrigation itself probably declined as a result of invasions and the general disruption of rural life. In fact, Byzantine agricultural technology remained backward when compared to the advances seen in the neighbouring Muslim countries or the developments seen in western Europe. Virtually all the substantial areas of intensive agriculture were along or close to the coasts.

Silk manufacture had, however, been introduced from Asia back in the mid-sixth century, supposedly by two monks returning from China with silkworm eggs hidden inside a bamboo stick, but rice was not grown until the very end of the Byzantine era. Surprisingly, windmills were not apparently adopted despite being widespread in both Europe and the Islamic world, while watermills and ploughs remained almost unchanged. Nevertheless, several parts of the Byzantine world remained major exporters of wine, olive oil, cereals, dried fruit, nuts, timber, cattle and sheep. Trebizond, for example, was particularly fertile and well-watered, though the slopes of some valleys were so steep that men supposedly had to tie themselves to trees for safety while working terraced fields.

Most agricultural work was heavily labour-intensive, August and September being the busiest months. Cereals were reaped with simple hand-sickles, threshed and then ground in local watermills. A remarkable manuscript on the 'Labours of the Month' was, in fact, made for a

Byzantine aristocrat in the Empire of Trebizond named Prokopios Chantzames in 1346. In it the otherwise unknown artist John Argyros showed late Byzantine rural life in great detail.

The animals found in the Byzantine countryside similarly remained traditional. Mules were the most common beasts of burden, oxen being used for threshing, pulling carts or ploughs and providing the energy to pump water. In upland areas cattle raising was generally associated with a transhumant or semi-nomadic way of life, as it was across most part of Turkish-ruled Anatolia. Here flocks wintered in the more sheltered valleys then grazed the mountain pasture in summer. Down on the coasts fishing was an even more important activity, often being done at night with the aid of lamps attached to the boats to attract fish. The peoples of certain places like Crete earned additional income by breeding hunting dogs while elsewhere peasants caught singing birds which found a ready market in towns and cities. Annual fairs or markets were another vital aspect of Byzantine rural life where peasants could borrow from money-lenders if they got into difficulties.

Chapter 16

Vassalage & Renaissance

The final half century or so of the Byzantine Empire of Constantinople was a period of raised and dashed hopes, of imperial humiliation, desperate attempts to get help from Western Europe and a final, almost epic and certainly heroic, collapse. The defeat of a huge Crusader army at Nikopol in 1396 had been a severe blow for Emperor Manuel II in Constantinople. As he later wrote to his teacher Cydones; 'To prudent men, life is not worth living after that calamity, that deluge of the whole world [the Biblical Flood], but one worse than that in so much as it carried off men better than those of old.' The Ottoman siege, or more accurately blockade, of Constantinople which had started before the disastrous Crusade was now pressed harder. The victorious Sultan Bayezit I also demanded that Emperor Manuel II hand the city over to John VII, who was more sympathetic or perhaps more subservient to the Ottoman position. Many of the desperate inhabitants of the 'Great City' agreed. Meanwhile the Sultan and his aides were so confident that they once stood on a hill overlooking Constantinople, discussing who should get which palace after the Byzantine capital fell. However, the massive fortified walls still defied their assaults and Bayezit scaled down the siege to the status of a blockade once more.

A reconciliation between the rival Emperors Manuel and John further calmed the situation, but Manuel's lengthy visit to Western Europe from 1399 to 1403 resulted in no real help being sent. By the time Manuel delivered the funeral oration for his late brother, the Despot Theodore of the Morea in 1407, the very names of the defeated western Crusaders stuck in the throat of such a cultured and now embittered Byzantine gentleman. Indeed Manuel now referred to them as; 'The great army which was struck down at Nicopolis – I mean that collected from the Pannonians, the Celts and the Western Galatians, at all of those names I shudder at, as an entirely barbaric thing.'

In fact the remnants of the Byzantine Empire had already withdrawn into its cultural shell. On the other hand the Ottoman catastrophe at Ankara in 1402 almost certainly enabled Byzantine Constantinople to survive for another half century. While some Christian states in the Balkans tried to take advantage of the resulting Ottoman civil wars (see Chapter 14), and were later punished as a result, the Byzantines were more cautious or more clever. The Emperor, having been virtually reduced to the city and immediate environs of Constantinople, managed to regain a significant amount of territory without provoking too much Ottoman wrath. Emperor Manuel II initially supported Bayezit's son Sülayman in return for that Ottoman ruler handing over the south-western coast of the Black Sea, perhaps including the important port of Varna, as well as the Chalkidiki Peninsula on the northern coast of the Aegean Sea, Thessaloniki and perhaps a small area south-west of that city. Inland, the fortified town of Vize (Greek Bizya) was also handed back to the Byzantines.

Much if not all of this was lost after Sülayman was defeated. Nevertheless, Manuel now supported Mehmet against Musa, ferrying him across the Bosphoros in the handful of remaining Imperial galleys and allowing him to use Constantinople as a base. Once Mehmet had defeated Musa, he rewarded Manuel by handing back much of the territory previous ceded by Sülayman, this time certainly including the Black Sea port of Varna. On the other hand, the writing remained on the wall for Byzantium and in 1437 the Emperor John VIII again travelled to Italy with a final desperate plea for help. As vassals of the Ottomans the Byzantines were not even permitted to strengthen the walls of Constantinople. On the contrary they had to send troops, of whom they already had very few, to help their Ottoman suzerain whenever he summoned them. Their presence in the Sultan's army was of no real military value but had huge political significance, enhancing the Ottoman ruler's prestige and symbolizing the Byzantine Emperor's now humble status.

The only Byzantine territory which had real, if still limited, military potential was the *Despotate* of the Morea in southern Greece. Here the military elite now included Greeks, Albanians and Slavs, as well as descendants of Venetian and other Italian or French knights from the virtually defunct Latin Crusader Principalities. Two Greek scholars named Plethon and Bessarion, who would later play a key role in the Italian Renaissance, meanwhile took a keen interest in military affairs, though very clearly writing as 'armchair generals'. Plethon, for example, advocated a properly trained full-time citizen army supported by the labour of demilitarised peasants; an idea based upon his not entirely-correct interpretation of the armies of ancient Greek Sparta. His student, Bessarion, went further by demanding that prisoners no longer be used as slave labour, but be offered full citizen rights along with the associated military obligations. He also suggested that a new fortified capital be built on the Isthmus of Corinth to defend the Peloponnese from attack from the north – in other words from Ottoman territory. Whether these academic ideas had much practical impact is unknown, but a defence known as the *Hexamilion Wall* was certainly erected across the Corinth Isthmus more than once. Unfortunately, despite its one hundred and fifty three towers plus castles at each end, this *Hexamilion Wall* was not a very strong structure. Initially built in only twenty-five days, it failed totally whenever the Ottoman Turks decided to make a serious assault.

If the Byzantine world was in terminal decline in the political or military sense, it was flourishing culturally. Furthermore, this remarkable final flowering was despite an appalling economic situation. Byzantine art had always been overwhelmingly religious in both subject and inspiration. Most secular art was reserved for what might now termed the 'minor arts', including textiles, jewellery, ceramics, some metalwork and small luxury items for the ruling elite. Though deeply Christian, Byzantine art was nevertheless also rooted in the previous civilizations of the Eastern Mediterranean and Persia while the Graeco-Roman elements, though very obvious, tended to be rather self conscious. In many cases they seemed to have been inserted as a sort of cultural declaration that the Byzantine Empire was descended from ancient Rome.

Nevertheless Byzantine religious art remained the fountainhead for most western European religious art throughout the medieval period and indeed until the Renaissance. Meanwhile the Byzantine minor arts absorbed ideas from an even greater variety of sources as the Middle Ages progressed. Externally, Byzantine art's biggest influence was of course on fellow Orthodox and eastern Christian cultures such as the Orthodox Balkans and the Christian Caucasus, though here Armenian and Georgian arts themselves served as sources of ideas for Byzantine craftsmen. The biggest and most important cultural colony of Byzantium was, however, Russia, which had been at least officially converted to Orthodox Christianity back in 988. Its arts, crafts and architecture remained directly inspired by those of the Byzantine world, though they were modified to suit local climatic or cultural conditions. In fact Byzantine or post-Byzantine art continued to have a major influence upon Russian art until at least the eighteenth century, and in certain respects continues to do so to this day.

Large-scale sculpture never flourished in the Orthodox Christian countries and stone carving was almost entirely limited to decorative patterns executed with supreme craftsmanship. Secular and religious scenes were nonetheless carved on the exterior of churches in Georgia, Armenia and to a lesser extent in some parts of the Balkans. Nevertheless, most surviving Byzantine figurative art consists of traditional manuscript illustrations and even more traditional mosaics or wall-paintings. This vigorous art had an even greater impact upon neighbouring Christian cultures, with the entire interiors of medieval Orthodox Christian churches sometimes being covered with religious scenes. In what is now Romania, and particularly in the northern province of Moldavia, this spread to the exterior church walls at the end of the Middle Ages.

From the twelfth to the fifteenth centuries, just when the Byzantine Empire entered upon its final decline, Byzantium enjoyed its own artistic renaissance. This was seen in minor arts as well as larger works, though Byzantine ceramics never achieved the standards seen in the Islamic Middle East and nowhere near the craftsmanship of Far Eastern potters. Yet Byzantine ivory carving could compete anywhere while other eastern Christian craftsmen earned reputations in various minor arts such as cloisonné enamelware.

Much of medieval western European music also stemmed directly from the Byzantine world, where musicians used a variety of ancient Graeco-Roman as well as recently-adopted Middle Eastern instruments. There was a particularly strong Islamic influence where stringed instruments were concerned. Much of the music still used in Orthodox religious services has apparently survived virtually unchanged since medieval times, but whereas it used an eight-tone system, secular music tended to use a more complex sixteen-tone system, perhaps inspired by the extraordinarily complex music of the Byzantines' Muslim neighbours. In return, Byzantine influence, or perhaps more accurately a somewhat distant Byzantine heritage, could be found in some aspects of Ottoman Turkish music. However, this is more tenuous than might be expected, for the simple reason that the Turks not only brought with them an astonishingly sophisticated musical heritage from Central Asia, but were under a much stronger Arabo-Persian Islamic musical tradition.

Literature was the most self-consciously 'classical' and all too often archaic aspect of Byzantine culture, though not much secular Byzantine literature actually survives. Heroic epics were clearly written for recitation, probably by the poets who played a major role in secular festivals. One of the most famous examples was the *Epic of Digenes Akritas* which seems to have been written down in its oldest surviving form near the Syrian frontier some time during the eleventh century. Rulers also employed professional panegyrists to praise them, while other writers wrote savage satires about those in charge of the Empire. Meanwhile literature for the ordinary people tended to be humorous and considerably influenced by Middle Eastern tales such as those in the *Thousand and One Nights*.

As in western Europe, language, literacy and literature were used as powerful weapons in the struggle between competing cultures. Two Slav scripts, for example, were developed early in the medieval period, the *glagolitic* and the *Cyrillic*. These became tools in the struggle between the Orthodox and Catholic churches to dominate Balkan Christianity, a struggle which the Byzantine Orthodox Christian Church largely won.

Byzantine civilization was so conscious of its own classical Greek and Roman past that it held the ancient scholarly authorities in even greater awe than did western European scholars. Perhaps as a result, Byzantine scientists, and even doctors, added relatively little to what they had inherited from their predecessors. Much more originality, however, was shown in religious philosophy than it was in secular scholarship.

Meanwhile, the practical aspects of applied science and technology were not rated very highly in the Byzantine Empire, and this had the paradoxical result of freeing practical scholarship from the shackles of the past. Byzantine engineers and technicians were in many ways very advanced and highly practical in the way they went about solving technological problems. The magnificent architecture and above all the great domes of the Byzantine world, from the vast sixth-century church of Santa Sofia in Istanbul to the jewel-like fourteenth-century convent of Santa Sofia in Mistra, are perhaps the most dramatic witnesses to this practical technology.

The same went for water-collection and storage systems, siege engineering in both attack and defence, and in shipbuilding. The most famous of all Byzantine weapons, Greek Fire, was a particularly dramatic example of how medieval technology was turned to devastating use. It was a petroleum oil-based form of pyrotechnics invented in the seventh century which became, in effect, a medieval flame-thrower to be used on land and at sea. In the latter case Greek Fire was famous for its ability to continue burning on the surface of the water. Other devices, most obviously those used in siege warfare, similarly showed the Byzantine willingness to learn from eastern neighbours and consequently included ideas that can be traced back to China, having reached Constantinople via the Muslim Arabs and Turks.

In complete contrast, Byzantine Greek geographers seem to have learned remarkably little from their eastern neighbours, despite close commercial links. It almost seemed like a conscious rejection of new information and a preference for clinging to an archaic, Mediterranean or even Greek-centred view of the world, even after much more accurate and extensive Arab maps had become available during the twelfth and thirteenth centuries. Some other Arabic books were translated into Greek, but had less impact than they did in western Europe. Even medicine remained firmly based on the ancient Greek and Latin authorities with minimal input from the more advanced Muslims.

Not surprisingly, Byzantine doctors and surgeons were steadily outstripped not only by their eastern rivals but also by the Italians and other western Europeans. This was not to say that the science of medicine was not taken seriously in the Byzantine Empire – far from it. The government provided a certain amount of medical services and hospitals in the main cities, but these were minimal and not as numerous as might have been expected in such a rich, sophisticated and urbanized civilization.

The most positive aspects of health care in the Byzantine world were, in fact, directly inherited from the Roman past and included the provision of adequate, secure and clean drinking water. The only new aspect of this concern with drinking water relied upon Byzantine engineering skills rather than medical science and resulted from the simple fact that the Byzantine Empire was so frequently invaded. Thus the old Roman system of aqueducts which brought water from beyond the fortified walls into the main cities proved too vulnerable to interruption by invading forces, so they were largely replaced by huge underground cisterns from the start, especially from the eleventh century onwards.

The one area where Byzantine physicians do seem to have taken a distinctly modern view was in the field of mental health. For reasons which are not fully understood, the Byzantines were very aware of the problems of mental stress. They not only tried to provide help, but also believed that a house or hospital with an uninterrupted view of the sea was an excellent way of calming those suffering from psychological disorders.

As already stated, the death throes of the Byzantine Empire saw a sudden final flowering of Byzantine art, architecture and scholarship. Several figures stand out but the ferocity with which they disagreed with one another is astonishing. In the fourteenth century, the main debate was between those who wanted to fight the advancing Turks and save the Empire, and those who advocated retreating into a world of mystical contemplation. By and large, the latter won the day.

Even in the last final crises of the fifteenth century the main issues remained religious, though they now had a sharper political edge. Above all there was the question of whether the Orthodox Christian Church should accept union with the Latin Catholic Church on the latter's terms, and under the overall authority of the Pope in Rome. Here three further names stand out. The first was John Bessarion (1395-1472), the titular Patriarch of Constantinople and head of the Orthodox Church in Nicea (now Iznik), who was the leading advocate of union. The second was Gennadios Scholarion, who is said to have preferred domination by Muslim Turks to domination by Catholic westerners. He would eventually become Patriarch of Constantinople from 1453 to 1459, but only after it had been conquered by the Ottoman Turks.

The third, and perhaps most interesting, was George Plethon, who died around 1450. His solution to the problem of the dying Byzantine Empire was as radical as Bessarion's, but he looked much further back into Greek history for inspiration. As a philosopher rather than a churchman, Plethon envisaged an agricultural Utopia based upon ancient Sparta, with a citizen army of warriors maintained by demilitarized serfs. But, despite being so backward looking, Plethon was genuinely aware of the need to use new technologies. Eventually he fled to Italy, where he lectured on Plato and had a huge impact on the development of Renaissance Humanism. Eventually returning to Greece, he died about ten years before the last real European bastion of Byzantium, the fortified city of Mistra in southern Greece, fell to the advancing Ottoman Turks. Mistra, it is interesting to note, was built on the slopes of a great hill which actually overlooked the ruins of Plethon's beloved, and somewhat idealized, Sparta.

Chapter 17

The Ottomanization of Anatolia

*F*ollowing the crushing defeat of Sultan Bayezit I by Timur-i Lenk outside Ankara in 1402, Timur permitted or actively encouraged the re-emergence of the independent Turkish *beyliks* which had so recently been conquered by the Ottoman. However, these never regained their old strength and survived for only as long as the Ottomans were diverted by a series of civil wars or were more concerned about events within their European provinces. Once stability returned to the Ottoman Sultanate, the new Ottoman ruler quickly set about using these same European provinces as a springboard from which to regain lost territory in the east. In some ways this can be seen as an European conquest of much of Anatolia, mirroring the previous Anatolian Turkish conquest of the Balkans during the fourteenth century. Even so it took Bayezit I's successors many years to reach those eastern frontiers which he had established before 1402.

At first it had seemed possible that the Ottomans would be driven from Asia altogether. The most immediate threat was probably posed by Isfandiyar Mubariz al-Din who had regained control of the *beylik* of Candar and after whom the Candar Oğullari ruling family subsequently took its name. He had already extended his power from his family's original powerbase at Sinop to control Kastamonu, Safranbolu and Samsun, as well as the Black Sea coasts between. He now formed an alliance with the revived Karaman Oğullari *Beys* of south-central Anatolia. Further east Ottoman rule was threatened by the growing power of the Qara Qoyunlu or 'Black Sheep' Turcomans.

Sultan Mehmet I rose to all these challenges, defeating Isfandiyar and forcibly transferring most of his Turcoman fighting men to Ottoman-ruled Bulgaria, where they were settled near the city of Plovdiv. The town that developed as the centre of this new warrior community came to be known as Tatar Pazarcik, 'The Market of the Tatars' (now Pazardzhik). As this transfer proved to be such a success, similar population transfers developed into a normal aspect of Ottoman policy. The result was to remove troublesome groups from Anatolia and turn them into generally reliable, permanent garrisons within the Ottoman-ruled Balkans. The Candar or Isfandiyar Oğullari eventually lost their last of their independent territory to Sultan Mehmet II in 1462 but remained a locally dominant family for many generations.

Anatolia was nevertheless still a source of trouble for Mehmet I's son and heir, Sultan Murat II. His first problem was the ambitious adventurer Cüneyt Bey at Aydın, but once he had been removed with Genoese help, the Ottomans could move south to reoccupy the *beyliks* Menteşe and Teke. This brought the entire Aegean coast of Anatolia back under the Sultan's control, a fact which would soon enable the Ottomans to build up a significant navy of their own. Meanwhile, in return for Genoese maritime assistance, Sultan Murat allowed Italian merchant enclaves to be re-established along the Black Sea coast.

Murat also tried to weaken the powerful *beylik* of Karaman by sowing dissention within the ruling family of the Karaman Oğullari. This was partially successful and the new ruler of Karaman, Ibrahim Bey, became an ally of the Ottomans rather than of the rival Mamluk Sultanate of Syria and Egypt. The latter had meanwhile been extending their influence, particularly in the strategic and fertile coastal region of Cilicia. The next *beylik* to be taken over by the Ottomans was Germiyan whose last ruler, Ya'qub II, bequeathed his lands to the Ottoman Sultan on his death in 1428. This now left the whole of western and central Anatolia either under Ottoman rule or that of its vassals; the only exceptions being the few restored Genoese trading enclaves on the Black Sea coast. Eastern Anatolia still largely remained beyond Ottoman reach, with the independent Byzantine 'Empire of Trebizond' in the north-east and largely Mamluk-dominated minor rulers in the south-east.

Despite their promises of friendship and support, the Karaman Oğullari proved to be the least reliable of the Ottomans' supposed allies against their Christian European foes. As a result, this dynasty was eventually overthrown by the Ottoman Sultan in 1475. The neighbouring Ramazan Oğullari of Cilicia became Ottoman vassals in 1516, having previously been more closely linked to the Mamluk Sultans of Egypt and Syria whom the Ottomans conquered only a year later. In 1521 the Dulkadir Oğullari who ruled Maraş and Malatya at last followed the Ramayan into the Ottoman sphere of influence.

From its very beginning, Islamic civilization had been city-based and the expansion of population and agriculture which characterized its early centuries was mirrored by a huge extension of trade. Most of these Islamic cities also grew organically, which accounted for their narrow winding streets and separate quarters inhabited by different religious groups. Though perhaps strange and curious to many modern eyes, this form of urban organization proved to be a highly efficient way of getting goods in and out of the commercial centres while preserving that privacy which was central to Islamic family life. However, such cities could not function without the suburbs that soon developed beyond their walls. These included prosperous residential areas for the wealthy, as well as semi-slums for casual workers. Rubbish dumps were also found outside the walls, as were clearly defined cemetery areas which nevertheless often came to be inhabited by vagrants and criminals. Beyond one of the main gates of such archetypical Islamic cities there was often a large open 'place of prayer' which was used for religious festivals, and possibly for public executions. Another form of clearly defined open space outside a city's fortified walls was the *maydan*, one or more of these military training grounds being characteristic of medieval Islamic cities. They were nevertheless less typical of Ottoman cities in Anatolia and the Balkans, although one area on the north side of the Golden Horn outside Istanbul did come to be known as the *Oq Maydan*, or 'archery training ground'.

Of course the appearance of such cities differed considerable, according to the local climate and local urban traditions. This having been said, Islamic cities were nevertheless invariably dominated by the merchant middle class. People also tended to have a loyalty to their own quarter or urban zone, each of which in turn tended to be inhabited by people of a specific religious affiliation or ethnic origin. Perhaps as a result there was little sense of shared citizenship. Instead the extended family formed the foundation of social organization, business dealing and relations with urban or government authorities. A wealthy householder's tenants could also form part of this economic and social unit.

The role of the state tended to be focussed on in the Arab regions had long been known as the *Dar al-Imara*. This was in practice the local governor's office, usually located in a city's citadel. The governor's primary role was, meanwhile, that of defence, law and order, which often resulted in a peculiar mixture of both autocracy and autonomy within a particular city. Each quarter, and even each large tenement block, had its own elected leader to deal with such authorities, while each quarter was traditionally expected to organize its own young men into a militia to defend both the quarter's interests and, when necessary, the city as a whole.

Meanwhile, the head of the family remained its undisputed master within the home, though such a family would go to the local *qadi* or Islamic judge if it had serious internal disputes. As already stated, the *qadi* and the *muhtasib* were the two senior representatives of municipal authority. The latter's responsibilities covered many things in addition to his primary role as supervisor of markets. These included the quality of drinking and bathing water, the width of public streets, outbreaks of disease and the prompt burial of the dead. On the other hand, the urban authorities had virtually no jurisdiction beyond their walls, which was why cemeteries often became dens of thieves.

Another characteristic aspect of Islamic and very clearly Ottoman urban life was the *waqf*, known in Turkish as the *vakif*. This was essentially a religious charity which dealt directly with the *qadi* and the religious authorities. Such a *waqf* often owned, through gifts and endowments, many of the public baths and even factories within a town and used their revenues to support assorted charitable establishments. These in turn ranged from schools to irrigation systems for orchards outside the city. It was a system which would be extended deep into eastern Europe in the wake of the Ottoman conquests.

Most of the main cities in Turkish-ruled Anatolia and the Balkans had existed for hundreds if not thousands of years, and their Romano-Byzantine plans, fortifications and other facilities did not disappear under Turkish rule. On the contrary, these were usually restored and considerably improved, first by the Seljuks in Anatolia and then by the Ottomans both in Anatolia and in the Balkans. In contrast, the new towns which the Seljuks had established in conquered Byzantine territory had many Central Asian characteristics, though also reflecting existing Romano-Byzantine urban traditions. For example, these new foundations tended to be more spread out than the older towns, with scattered market-gardens, orchards, markets, running water and numerous public fountains. The Turks also greatly increased the numbers of *hamams* or public bath-houses which in turn differed from Romano-Byzantine public baths in lacking a large immersion or 'swimming' pool. Instead they were typified by their constant supplies of running hot and cold water which flowed into several smaller basins. The Seljuks and their Ottoman successors similarly changed the public faces of one-time Byzantine cities by building numerous mosques, *madrasah* Islamic schools or 'teaching mosques', along with hospitals for both physical and mental disorders.

Another distinctive new form of public buildings were the *imaret* soup kitchens and accommodation provided virtually free of charge to the poor. Many of these charitable foundations were financed and administered by the *waqf* system which itself depended upon a rapidly increasing number of revenue-providing properties given in perpetuity for just such purposes. Although religious foundations of all faiths were exempt from taxation in the Islamic world, users of *waqf* land paid taxes to the administrators of the *waqf*, who then used these revenues to support the main *waqf* charities such as the *imaret* soup-kitchens. Similarly the urban population paid taxes to the urban authorities just as military fief-holders paid their taxes to superior officers and freehold landowners paid their taxes to the state treasury. Unmarried men often had to pay an additional levy until they found a wife.

As in other traditional Islamic cities, special areas outside the city walls or perimeter were reserved for animals who had been brought to market for slaughter as food. Similarly, most smelly or otherwise unwholesome industries were obliged to locate just inside, or preferably outside, the city limits. The more valuable or prestigious the goods involved in a specific trade, the closer to the centre of the city or town that trade would be located. As a result, goldsmiths and book sellers tended to cluster around the main mosque in the heart of an Ottoman city. There were no officially recognised guilds in Turkish cities but, as in other parts of the Islamic world, each *esnaf* or craft association was supervised by a man recognised by the authorities. By the Ottoman period the *esnaf* was used by the government as a means of gathering taxes from the urban artisan class. Each trade also tended to develop a sense of shared identity, often attending the same mosque and in some cases forming militia units to defend the city walls. Again, as characteristic of all Islamic cities, slaves were rarely employed in industry or agriculture since slavery was primarily seen as a source of trained domestic servants or élite professional soldiers. Indeed the title *Kul* or slave would become a source of pride, adopted even by free men, during the Ottoman period.

Technology and the industries of Islamic civilization were in many ways very advanced. By the time of the rise of the Ottoman Sultanate, distillation techniques already supported a flourishing perfume industry, while new chemical ceramic glazes had resulted from the constant attempt of Muslim potters to compete with high value imported Chinese ceramics. A scientific approach to metallurgy had also made it easier for Muslim smiths to adopt new steel technologies from China and India. Relatively rapid, long-distance communications had similarly helped the spread of such technologies and by now lay at the very heart of the later medieval Islamic world's flourishing commercial links with China, south-east Asia, India, east Africa, sub-Saharan west Africa and Europe.

In turn, Islam's main exports were manufactured luxuries, including wood carving, metal and glass, textiles, lustre ceramics and tiles. The disruption caused by the Mongol invasions of the thirteenth century had led to a serious industrial decline, but the peace which the Mongol 'World Empire' brutally imposed on most of Asia in turn led to a rapid revival in trade with the rest of the world, if not a complete revival of industry. This, then, was the economic situation inherited by Ottoman cities and their craftsmen, amongst whom the makers of carpets, fine ceramics, perfumes and sword-blades were probably the most highly regarded by their European customers.

The Islamic systems of contracts upon which such trade relied had remained virtually unchanged throughout the medieval period. Merchants bought and sold on commission, often with capital borrowed from a rich lender or jointly invested by several merchants, who could be Muslim, Christian or Jewish. However, business partnerships had tended to be made for one commercial venture only, though bonds or kinship enabled trade links to be made and maintained across huge distances. Each time trade items passed through one of the cities which formed nodal points in this extraordinary trading network, the local government imposed a tax, which could result in very high prices when goods eventually reached their final destination. Yet the Muslim world never became completely reliant upon foreign markets, either for exports or imports, and remained largely self-sufficient throughout the whole of the medieval period. It could, in fact, be argued that it was the failure of the Ottoman Sultanate's self-sufficiency in the face of the staggering economic expansion of early modern Europe which really started to undermine its power and independence from the seventeenth century onwards.

Transport within the Ottoman Sultanate, like that of the longer-established Islamic states of the Middle East, was simple but effective. Each town had areas outside its gates where pack animals assembled. The main markets within the city often had large secure warehouses, while *khans* (*hans* in Turkish) or *caravanserais* provided accommodation for merchants in cities along the major trade routes. Surviving thirteenth and early-fourteenth century *hans* on the high plateau of central Anatolia tend to be around thirty kilometres apart, which represented nine hours walking time for loaded pack animals.

In contrast, the science of maritime navigation was already very advanced. Navigational instruments including the *kamal*, which was a rudimentary sextant to calculate the altitude of stars, as well as the Chinese magnetic compass, were in widespread use. When combined with the detailed geographical knowledge which characterized the medieval Islamic world, it is hardly surprising that Muslim sailors could sail across oceans rather than skirt round their edges as medieval European mariners tended to do. Muslim Arab sailors had also reintroduced large three-masted merchant ships to the Mediterranean a couple of centuries before the rise of the Ottomans. They also developed a specialized horse-transporting galley called a *tarida*, while it is worth noting that the *caravels* which took Christopher Columbus to America were developed from an earlier Islamic vessel, the *karib*. Nevertheless, such technological sophistication could not alter the fact that, by the twelfth century, Mediterranean trade was dominated by western European, largely Italian sailors. It would be some centuries before the Ottoman Empire had the wherewithal and will to challenge this domination. Even then the Ottomans would only manage to regain control of the Black Sea, the Aegean Sea and to some extent the eastern Mediterranean.

Chapter 18

Mehmet Closes in on Constantinople

The fall of Constantinople to the Ottoman Turks in 1453 is sometimes seen as marking the end of a Roman Empire which had been established before the birth of Christ. It is also sometimes seen as the inevitable fall of an isolated city, a relic of the past surrounded by a vast, overwhelmingly-powerful and expansionist superstate which took Constantinople almost as an afterthought. In reality the siege and conquest of Constantinople was neither of these things. The admittedly-fragmented remnants of the Byzantine Empire, which was of course the old Roman Empire by a later name, lasted several more years. Nor was the siege en entirely one-sided affair. In reality the Ottoman conquest of Constantinople in 1453 was a massive undertaking, while its success was important for its symbolic and psychological impact upon Christian Europe, and because it gave the vigorous new Ottoman state a multi-faith, multi-ethnic and multi-cultural capital city which remains unique in both European and Islamic history. In fact the true importance of 1453 was not in marking the end of something ancient but in marking the start of something new.

The Ottoman 'empire', as the Ottoman state already was, had been reestablished as a unified state by 1415, following the disasters of Timur-i Lenk's invasion two decades earlier. Nevertheless the Ottoman elite was still divided between those who clung to a heroic, almost romantic ideal of religiously-inspired and almost freebooting *gazi* frontier warfare and those in favour of military and administrative centralization. Generally speaking the old Turkish tribal armies and the Ottoman feudal elite still opposed such centralization while the provincial administration, the urban merchant class, the Muslim peasantry and above all the *Kapi Kulu* favoured a concentration of power in and around the Sultan.

This struggle for and against centralization was also complicated by other competing strands; for example those from an *ulema* (orthodox Islamic religious background) who represented a refined and tolerant classical Islamic culture and those more recent, sometimes superficial and often highly unorthodox converts who believed that Ottoman destiny lay in war against its Christian neighbours. Sultan Mehmet II, the Conqueror of Constantinople, was advised by men from both traditions; the *Grand Vizier* Çandarlı Halil being from the former whereas the *Second Vizier* Zaganos Paşa was from the latter. However, Çandarlı Halil was also close to the old Turkish feudal and *gazi* section of Ottoman society whereas Zaganos was from the *Kapi Kulu* and an emphatic centralizer. The Byzantines did try to take advantage of such potential divisions within the Ottoman ruling elite, but the failure of these efforts simply made Sultan Mehmet II more determined to crush Byzantine Constantinople once and for all.

Although there was widespread settlement by Turkish Muslims in depopulated regions such as eastern Thrace and central Bulgaria, one remarkable feature of Ottoman rule in the Balkans is the way in which huge territories were first conquered and then governed for centuries by relatively small numbers of troops and administrators. By the mid-fifteenth century a new Ottoman elite had nevertheless emerged, largely replacing the first wave of feudal and virtually-autonomous conquerors. Much of the land was now divided into *timar* fiefs, allocated by the Sultan to his *sipahi* cavalry, both Muslim and Christian, but always remaining the property of the state. The *timariots* or *timar* holders were not particularly rich and their fiefs could also be taken away, but they were numerous, entirely dependant upon the Sultan's favour, and served as a useful counterbalance to the powerful landowning Turkish aristocracy of Anatolia. This, plus the extraordinary economic and population expansion of what are now eastern Bulgaria, north-eastern Greece and Turkish Thrace, meant that, by the time of the final Ottoman assault upon Constantinople, this had become the new heartland of the Ottoman state.

The conquest of Constantinople had been a dream of Islamic armies ever since the first unsuccessful assaults by the Arab Umayyad Caliphs in the eighth century. Since then many *hadiths*, or pious sayings concerning the inevitable fall of the city to Islam had been attributed to the Prophet Muhammad, most of them spurious. Nevertheless the dream continued to develop, eventually even suggesting that the ruler who took Constantinople would be the *Mahdi* or 'Rightly Guided One' under whose leadership the Islamic triumph would be complete. Alongside this Islamic motivation, the Turks themselves had come to focus their dream of the *Kizil Elma* 'Red Apple', to which destiny led the Turks, upon Constantinople. In earlier pagan times it had been the capital of the rival Khazars, and in later years the *Kizil Elma* would shift to Budapest, Vienna or Rome. But for now many Turks believed it was their destiny to capture the ancient capital of the 'Roman' or Byzantine Empire. How seriously the Ottoman Sultans took such beliefs is unknown but Mehmet II *Fatih* or 'the Conqueror' and his immediate predecessors had adopted the title of *Sultan-i Rum*, *Padishah-i Rum* or *Khan-i Rum*, all meaning 'ruler of the Romans', and thus claimed to be heirs not only to the Turkish rulers of Anatolia but of Byzantium and Rome.

The Byzantine Emperor still held territory beyond the walls of Constantinople itself but these few towns and provinces were no threat to the Ottomans on their own. In addition to a few northern Aegean islands and the *Despotate* of the Morea or Peloponnese in southern Greece, the Emperor in Constantinople had direct rule over the Thracian coast well into what is now Bulgaria, plus a shorter coastal stretch along the Sea of Marmara. Inland, however, there was virtually nothing left and even the little town of Vize seems to have fallen, not for the first time but now finally, to the Ottomans around 1422. The interior around Pinarhisar was now known as the 'Land of Gazi Mihail' and was dominated by Mihail's descendants, the powerful Mihaloğlu family.

While the remaining Byzantine coasts, like Constantinople itself, could provide dangerous naval bases for the Ottomans' powerful maritime rivals in Italy, the only major Latin or Catholic European power which faced the Ottomans on land was Hungary. In fact, the struggle between Hungary and the Ottoman state for control of the strategically- and commercially-vital Lower Danube river from Belgrade to the Black Sea had been going on since the late-fourteenth century. It drew in Serbia and Wallachia, both of which were claimed as vassal states by the Ottomans and the Hungarians, and in many ways it was this struggle for the Danube which eventually sealed the fate of Constantinople.

More immediate in the memory of Sultan Mehmet II, were the events of 1444. During that year the Ottoman empire had been virtually cut in two when the remnants of the Byzantine Empire had served as a naval base for a Western European Crusade. At the same time a major land invasion had been launched from Hungary. Even the Byzantine Despot of the Morea, Constantine Palaiologos – the future and last Emperor of Byzantium, Constantine XI – had struck northwards, attacking the Sultan's Latin vassals in Athens and encouraging the Vlachs and Albanians of central Greece to throw off Ottoman suzerainty. An Islamic religious uprising in the Ottoman capital of Edirne had added insult to injury.

For Mehmet II, who had become Sultan at the age of twelve in July

1444 when his father abdicated, the events of that year were also a personal humiliation. The situation had become so serious that Çandarlı Halil, the *Grand Vizier*, had convinced Mehmet's father Murad to return, defeating the Hungarian Crusaders at the epic battle of Varna and forcing the Byzantines back into the Morea. In 1446 Murad formally reassumed the title of Sultan while young Mehmet and his warlike *lalas* or 'advisors', including Zaganos Paşa, were sent to govern the small Anatolian province of Manisa.

Mehmet II may have smarted from his temporary deposition but he also noted that Christian galleys, operating in the Dardanelles, the Sea of Marmara and the Bosphoros, had almost succeeded in confining Murad and his army to Anatolia, the wrong side of the water, during that Crusade of Varna. In fact Murad's forces were obliged to cross the Bosphoros under the protection of shore guns which managed to sink one of the enemy's galleys. It was a lesson well learned, for on this same spot Mehmet II later built his great fortress of Rumeli Hisar to guarantee the free passage of Ottoman troops between Asia and Europe. Sultan Murad still wanted a smooth succession for his son, particularly as another pretender to the Ottoman throne named Orhan was being sheltered, virtually under house arrest, by the Byzantine Emperor in Constantinople. So Mehmet was taken on campaign against the Hungarians in 1448 and the Albanians in 1450, perhaps to teach him the arts of leadership and how to govern a little better.

In 1448 Emperor John VIII of Byzantium died without heir and the imperial crown passed to his brother, the Despot of the Morea Constantine Palaiologos, now Constantine XI in Constantinople. But the great city was now a pale shadow of its former self, its population never having revived following the Black Death a hundred years earlier. At the same time the inhabitants of the Byzantine Empire's remaining possessions had for decades been abandoning vulnerable coastal or low-lying villages and towns for the relative safety of upland villages, many of which had rudimentary fortifications. The only exceptions may, paradoxically, have been the little coastal towns of Thrace, near Constantinople but also closest to the Ottoman capital of Edirne. Otherwise the Emperor claimed suzerainty over the northern Aegean islands ruled by the Genoese Gattilusi family, over Skyros which was ruled by the Venetians, and over the other Northern Sporades islands which were actually held by pirates. Meanwhile the Byzantine Emperor was himself a vassal of the Ottoman Sultan, as were his subordinates, the *Despots* of the Morea. Far to the east the Byzantine 'Empire of Trebizond' was an entirely separate state ruled by a rival dynasty and to the north the strange little principality of Mangoup in the

Crimea was little more than a turbulent offshoot of the wealthy Genoese colonies along the Crimean coast.

In purely military terms the Byzantine Empire was now a very minor player in the events of south-eastern Europe. Constantine Palaiologos' dream of restoring Byzantine control over Greece by expanding the *Despotate* of the Morea had been crushed by an Ottoman campaign in 1446. The Byzantine navy was a thing of the past and even the fourteenth-century naval alliance with Genoa had evaporated. Nevertheless the Byzantine Empire did still have armed forces, several important fortifications beyond Constantinople, a fair number of ships including galleys and merchant vessels, and it currently held the strategic island of Imroz off the mouth of the Dardanelles. The famous Hexamilion Wall across the entire Ithmus of Corinth was supposed to protect the Byzantine Despot of the Morea. It had been repaired at great expense but it could not resist artillery and offered no obstacle to a determined Ottoman assault. The walls of Constantinople, however, would prove a very different matter.

The Byzantine Empire was not the most powerful Christian presence in the southern Balkans in the mid-fifteenth century. The richest were Venice and Genoa, which together controlled most of the islands and several coastal enclaves. The goods carried by their ships ranged from Chinese silks and German sword-blades to timber, bulk grain and slaves. At the centre of this network was the Crimean peninsula, whose coasts were largely controlled by the Genoese, along with the neighbouring outpost of Tana. A sharp deterioration in relations between the various linguistic and religious groups within the Genoese Crimean colonies had, however, led to a revolt in 1433 during which the local Greeks tried to ally themselves with the sub-Byzantine principality of Theodore of Mangoup.

The Venetians and Moldavians had also tried to form an alliance against Genoese domination of the Black Sea. Venice and Genoa had already fought over the small but strategic north Aegean island of Tenedos (now Bozcaada) lying outside the very entrance to the Dardanelles. Now it was theoretically demilitarized, though still used by the Venetians as a naval base, and offered shelter to ships awaiting a favourable wind to take them through the Straits. It may actually have been uninhabited, as the Venetians had removed the previous population to Crete. Though Genoa tended to allow far greater autonomy to its colonial outposts, the Genoese remained the most powerful external presence in the northern and eastern Aegean.

The old Latin Crusader Principality of Athens was now ruled by a noble family of mixed Italian and Catalan origin which maintained links with the Spanish Aragonese rulers of southern Italy. Since 1451 the ruler of Athens had been an infant, Francesco I, under guardianship of his mother and her lover, the Venetian Bartolomeo Contarini. All that remained of the once extensive and powerful Byzantine Despotate of Epirus were three coastal castles and the Ionian islands, ruled by the Italian Leonardo III Tocco. The armed forces available to the assorted Western European outposts consisted almost entirely of mercenaries, plus the occasional local militia. The Catalans also had a strong tradition of alliance with the Turks while Catalan pirates remained a menace to one and all. In fact, some years after the fall of Constantinople the captain of the Ottoman flagship based at Gallipoli was reported to be a Spaniard. Whether he was also a convert to Islam is unknown. To the north some Albanian clans had accepted the leadership of an Ottoman renegade, George Castriota, better known as Skanderbeğ, and were maintaining a bitter resistance to Ottoman conquest while at the same time clashing with Venetian outposts on the Albanian coast.

These assorted Christian outposts did not seem to pose much of a challenge to the Ottomans. To the east, however, Ottoman domination of what is now Turkey was far from complete. Here the Karaman Oğullari were occasionally obliged to accept Ottoman overlordship, though remaining latently hostile and ever willing to take advantage of Ottoman weakness. Beyond them the Dulkadir Oğullari were generally friendly to the Ottomans in the fifteenth century. The Mamluk Sultanate of Egypt and Syria also controlled Cilicia but as yet took little interest in Ottoman affairs. The Aq Qoyunlu and Qara Qoyunlu, 'White-' and 'Black-Sheep-Turcomans respectively, remained significant powers in eastern Anatolia. The Qara Qoyunlu in particular were often seen by Venetians and other westerners as potential allies against the Ottomans. Meanwhile in northern Anatolia the Candar Oğullari remained loyal vassals of the Ottoman Sultan and the ruling *bey*, Ismail, would play an interesting role in the fall of Constantinople.

North of the Black Sea the old Mongol Khanate of the Golden Horde would fall apart upon the death of its current ruler, Khan Kuchuk Muhammad (1423-59). In fact one significant part of this vast state had already broken away around 1430 when Hajji Girei created what would become the Khanate of Krim (Crimea). This also included the relatively fertile wheat-growing prairies north of the Crimea itself and around the Sea of Azov. Not long after the fall of Constantinople the Khanate of Krim and the Ottoman Empire would jointly expel the Genoese from the Crimea after which the Khanate would become a militarily potent vassal of the Ottomans.

Beyond the Khanate of Krim the race to inherit the remnants of what had been Golden Horde territory was being won by the extraordinary Catholic joint kingdom of Poland-Lithuania rather than by Orthodox Christian Russia. In fact Russia was increasingly absorbed in its own considerable problems, with expansionist Poland-Lithuania to the west and assorted crumbling Khanates to the east. The affairs of the Byzantine Empire and the Orthodox 'Mother Church' in Constantinople seemed far away, and after the Ottoman victories of 1444 and 1448 the Metropolitan of Moscow declared the Church of Russia to be *autocephalous*. This obscure bit of Orthodox Church politics not only meant that the Russian Church was now autonomous, but it meant that Russia itself virtually turned its back upon Byzantium.

Of the other Christian powers which took a serious interest in Byzantine affairs, few were able or willing to offer much assistance. The Aragonese had only recently won control of southern Italy where they were more concerned to consolidate their position. Their authority in Sicily was of longer standing but was so ineffective that various Sicilian coastal towns behaved like independent pirate states, praying upon Christian and Islamic shipping alike. The Papacy in Rome had recently shown an increased interest in Crusades to save Constantinople and the Eastern Churches from Ottoman conquest, but seemed powerless to do more than encourage others to take up the sword. Hungary might seem to have been the only Latin Catholic kingdom capable of challenging the Ottomans. In reality its efforts were not very effective and from 1427 to 1442 Hungary had been on the defensive. This was followed by a more aggressive but even more unsuccessful phase from 1443 to 1448, since when the Hungarians had again been losing ground to the Ottomans. In fact the Ottomans were now in a position to raid the Hungarian heartlands from their permanent garrison bases in the Balkans.

Mehmet II's determination to conquer Constantinople became clear almost as soon as he returned to the throne on the death of his father in 1451. He inherited an empire which was in good condition with few external problems. Internally, however, the young Sultan Mehmet wanted big changes. He did not yet feel strong enough to remove the highly experienced and cautious *Grand Vizier* Çandarlı Halil but he did depose Ishaq Paşa as *Third Vizir*. Instead Ishaq was sent him off to be the *Beylerbeyi* or governor and senior military commander of Anatolia, a position he still held during the siege of Constantinople. Sultan Mehmet instead made his own *lalas* or advisors, Zaganos Paşa and Şihab al-Din Paşa, the *Second* and *Third Viziers*. The youthful Sultan also sent his step-mother, the princess Maria Brankovic, back home to Serbia and replaced her advisers with his own men. Mehmet now showed that streak of ruthlessness which would come to characterize his reign by having his younger brother Küçük Ahmet assassinated. This removed a potential threat to stability but still left the Ottoman pretender, Prince Orhan, safe within the walls of Byzantine Constantinople.

These actions did not yet impress his neighbours, the Byzantine Emperor and the Bey of Karaman, who both regarded him as in inexperienced youth whom they could manipulate. Perhaps they were more influenced by the enthusiasm with which Sultan Mehmet II set about greatly extending his father's palace on Tunca Island outside Edirne. This was indeed a magnificent place but within its beautiful chambers Mehmet and his warlike closest advisers had decided that a great victory was needed to secure the young Sultan's position, not only in relation to his neighbours but with his own powerful *Grand Vizier*, Çandarlı Halil and the old Ottoman aristocracy.

The conquest of Constantinople would also remove the threat of a seaborne Crusade using the capital of the rump Byzantine Empire as a base from which to cut the Ottoman Empire in two. Furthermore, its capture would forestall the danger of the Byzantines handing over Constantinople to Western Europeans who might be better able to defend it. Furthermore, possession of the great city would enable the European and Asian halves of the sprawling Ottoman state to be integrated in a way which had not yet been possible, and would permit the Ottomans to become a great naval as well as a land power, just as the Byzantine Empire had been in earlier centuries. Mehmet II summed up the situation more simply; 'The gaza [Holy War] is our basic duty as it was in the case of our fathers. Constantinople, situated in the middle of our domains, protects our enemies and incites them against us. The conquest of this city is, therefore, essential to the future and the safety of the Ottoman state.'

To attack Constantinople with potentially hostile neighbours on the other Ottoman frontiers would nevertheless be risky, so Karaman and Hungary had to be dealt with first. Very shortly after Mehmet II came to the throne for the second time Ibrahim Bey of Karaman, believing that the young Sultan was inexperienced and ineffective, invaded the disputed Hamid-ili region and went on to encourage various other parts of Anatolia to shake off Ottoman domination. It took a relatively brief campaign for Mehmet to teach Ibrahim how wrong he was.

The Byzantine Emperor Constantine XI also thought Mehmet ineffective and he twice tried to extract concessions by threatening to let loose Prince Orhan to stir up an Ottoman civil war. The only result was to encourage Mehmet II to make peace with Karaman by marrying Ibrahim Bey's daughter and returning home even more determined to crush Constantinople. Meanwhile the elderly *Grand Vizir* Çandarlı Halil used his considerable diplomatic skills to appease the Ottomans' other neighbours. On the second occasion that Byzantine envoys to Bursa threatened to let Prince Orhan loose, Çandarlı Halil's impatience boiled over; 'You stupid Greeks,' he said, 'I have known your cunning ways long enough. The late Sultan [Murad] was a tolerant and conscientious friend of yours. The present Sultan Mehmet is not of the same mind. If Constantinople eludes his bold and impetuous grasp it will only be because God continues to overlook your devious and wicked schemes.'

Mehmet merely regarded these feeble threats as justification for his forthcoming campaign against what remained of the once mighty Byzantine Empire. On his way back to Edirne from Bursa the Sultan's passage across the Dardanelles was blocked by hostile Christian ships, and so he crossed the Bosphoros instead, via the existing Ottoman castle of Anadolu Hisar. This is said to have been the moment when Zaganos Paşa proposed building another and bigger fortress on the opposite shore, the Rumeli Hisar, an idea which Sultan Mehmet adopted with enthusiasm.

Once back in his capital of Edirne, the Sultan took control of the sometimes troublesome Janissary infantry regiments away from Çandarli Halil, replaced the *Grand Vizir's* man as their *Ağa* or commander and also placed his own ultra-loyal *Kapi Kulu* 'slave recruited' officers in command of other infantry units. The Janissaries were meanwhile reorganized as a personal guard corps under the direct control of the Sultan and became, perhaps for the first time, a truly elite infantry formation.

Mehmet's expulsion of the Emperor Constantine's tax collectors from various Ottoman villages in the Strymon valley in Macedonia, where the Byzantine ruler had previously been allowed the local revenues, was little more than a symbolic act. Now that Mehmet II was determined to crush Constantinople, the *Grand Vizir* Çandarlı Halil feared for his own position and even his life because many in the court referred to him as a friend of the infidels. Late one night he was summoned to the Sultan's private rooms and came with a bowl of gold coins, fearing the worst. In fact Mehmet still could not afford to oust the powerful old politician and merely wanted Çandarli Halil to promise his support during the forthcoming campaign. Mehmet II also had doubts about the popularity of his aggressive new policy amongst the ordinary people and troops, and so would walk around Edirne at night with his closest confidants, dressed as common soldiers and listening to talk in the camps and taverns.

In Constantinople Emperor Constantine XI knew what was looming and sent urgent messages to the west, bringing news and asking for assistance. Venice was perhaps in the best position to help and on 14 February 1452 the Senate finally answered the Emperor. However, the Venetian reply included nothing but excuses plus a promise to send armour and gunpowder. Many Venetian senators seemed, in fact, to regard Constantinople as a lost cause and were arguing in favour of better relations with the Ottomans.

Çandarli Halil, aware of these mixed feeling in Western Europe, successfully blunted Byzantium's appeals for aid by renewing trade and other agreements with Venice and Hungary. In fact the Ottoman government was making it clear to all the European powers that it would behave reasonably with any state that did not oppose the Ottoman conquest of Constantinople. The *Grand Vizier* also got Sultan Mehmet II to renew his father's agreements with the vassal states of Serbia and Wallachia.

The building of Rumeli Hisar marked the start of active operations. In 1451 orders had been sent out to collect materials and recruit masons, lime slakers, carpenters and other workers. There was now panic in Constantinople where people openly stated that; 'These are the days of the Anti-Christ. This is the end of the city.' The Emperor Constantine sent an embassy to complain that the Sultan had not asked permission to build a castle within Byzantine territory. In his reply Mehmet II said that the area involved was uninhabited, that Christian ships had previously attempted to stop him from travelling between the two halves of his realm, and that anyway the Emperor owned nothing outside the walls of his city.

To build Rumeli Hisar, however, Mehmet II needed a fleet powerful enough to stop outside interference, particularly as lime was slaked in the mountains of western Anatolia and timber brought from northern Anatolia, both on the other side of the Bosphoros. A story told by the Serbian soldier, Konstantin Mihailovic, that the Ottomans had no ships before this date, and that thirty-five had to be built secretly in a forest 'four Italian miles from the coast', is a myth. Nevertheless the sudden appearance of an Ottoman fleet of six war-galleys, eighteen smaller galliots and sixteen supply ships which sailed from Gallipoli, through the Sea of Marmara and anchored in the Bosphoros, took the Christians by surprise. Sultan Mehmet II himself seems to have accompanied his fleet, probably studying the sea-walls of Constantinople as he sailed by, perhaps on 26 March as Alexander Ypsilanti, the eighteenth-century *phanariot* (Ottoman Greek) Prince of Wallachia, claimed.

The work itself began in April 1452 where the Bosphoros was at its narrowest and swiftest, about eighty-eight metres across. The fortress was designed by a certain Müslihuddin, probably a convert to Islam, and an anonymous monk who was certainly a recent convert. Each mason had two assistants and was responsible for half a metre's width of wall. Members of the military and governing elite set an example by carrying stones while ready-made columns were taken from various abandoned churches. The overall work was supervised by Çandarli Halil, supported by the three subordinate *vizirs*. Each *vizir* was allocated a tower to complete, Çandarlı Halil's being the most important at the centre of the east wall, while the Sultan took responsibility for the walls between these towers. It was a remarkable achievement for five hundred skilled workmen to complete the great triangular fortress between 15 April and 31 August 1452.

Nevertheless, the work was not without incident and there were brawls between Ottoman soldiers and local Byzantine civilians. The worst clash came when troops of Mehmet's brother-in-law, Qara Bey the governor of Edremid, were grazing their horses near Epibatos (Bivados) west of Constantinople. Local villagers objected to their crops being eaten, particularly as Epibatos was itself a significant Byzantine fortress which needed all available grain supplies with a war looming. The Emperor Constantine also wanted all available grain to be brought inside the city with a siege threatened. Men on both sides were killed and some Ottomans who had strayed too close to Constantinople were arrested by the Byzantine authorities. They proved to be eunuchs who worked in the Sultan's *harim* and they begged to be released on the grounds that their heads would be forfeit if they failed to return to their duties in time.

Quarrels continued and although the Emperor Constantine tried to placate Mehmet by sending the Turkish workers food and drink, the Ottoman Sultan executed two Byzantine emissaries. It was an official declaration of war, though it was now hardly needed. Everyone knew what Rumeli Hisar meant. To the Turks it was *Bogaz kesen*, to the Greeks *Laimokopia*, both of which meant 'Cutter of the Straits', or 'of the Throat'. Once completed, the new fortress was garrisoned by four hundred men under Firuz Bey. His duties were to stop all ships and make them pay a toll. Those which refused would be fired upon and if possible sunk by the cannon which were soon mounted along the shore. The biggest of these was said to fire a ball weighting 600 pounds (surviving cannonballs at Rumeli Hisar weigh 450 pounds).

Sultan Mehmet now returned to Edirne by land, once again pausing for a few days to study the massive walls of Constantinople. The Ottoman fleet under Baltaoğlu Sülayman Bey, soon to be the *Kapudan Paşa* or commander the navy, left a week later and returned to its main base at Gallipoli. Throughout the autumn of 1452 troops of the Palace regiments and from the Rumelian or European provinces assembled around Edirne while throughout the Ottoman state armourers were hard at work. The Sultan himself spent much of his time studying the latest military ideas from east and west, including siege machines, developments in siege engineering, fortification and above all the use of gunpowder artillery. One of his advisors appears to have been an Italian self-taught scholar, traveller and collector of ancient Greek and Roman antiquities, Ciriaco de Pizzicolli, better known as Ciciano of Ancona.

Many other assorted experts were attracted to Mehmet II's court and army, ranging from famous Jewish doctors to a Hungarian gun-founder named Urban. This Urban had awaited the Sultan in Edirne, having abandoned Byzantine employment because the Emperor Constantine could not or would not supply him with the necessary funds and materials. When asked if he could make cannon capably of breaking the walls of Constantinople, Urban replied that he could. Mehmet also wanted cannon to block the Bosphoros and here Urban, as a gunmaker rather than artilleryman, admitted that he was not qualified to work out the ranges. Mehmet II offered the Hungarian whatever he needed and told him to make the guns. Ranges could be sorted out later.

It took about two months to make the cannon for Rumeli Hisar but on 10 November they opened fire on two Venetian ships which were returning from the Black Sea. The crews had a fright but reached Constantinople safely. So the Ottoman gunners adjusted their ranges and fifteen days later a third Venetian ship was hit and sunk. Giolamo Minotto, the Venetian *Baillie* (Consul) in Constantinople, failed to save the crew from execution but he did win the release of two small galleys commanded by Gabriele Trevisan, *Vice Captain of the Gulf*, and three cargo ships which they were escorting from the northern Black Sea.

When Sultan Mehmet heard the news he ordered Urban to make a cannon twice the size of the first and capable of shooting a ball weighing over one thousand pounds. It took seven hundred men and fifty pairs of oxen to move the completed weapon which was set up outside the Sultan's new palace for a test firing. The people of Edirne were warned to expect a huge bang and the next day Urban's monster gun duly hurled a massive stone cannonball over a mile – and six feet into the earth.

Under the circumstances it was not surprising that Emperor Constantine sent his men to gather as much grain, other food supplies, wine and even winnowing fans as possible from those areas still under Byzantine control and bring them inside Constantinople. Many people meanwhile evacuated into the city. During the winter of 1452-3 the Emperor sent his available transport ships to the Aegean islands, those under Byzantine control and perhaps others as well, to purchase food and military equipment. One particularly large ship sailed to Genoese-ruled Chios where it bought wheat, various types of grains and beans, olive oil, dried figs and carob-beans. Unfortunately it was itself trapped by contrary winds and would not be able to sail homeward until after the Ottoman siege of Constantinople had begun.

Throughout the winter men and women were hard at work in the city, improving the defences. Emperor Constantine even ordered silver in the churches and monasteries to be melted down for coin to pay his troops. A widespread story that a large sum of money given to some Greek monks to pay for repairs to the walls was buried, and found later by the Turks, is another myth. On the other hand there was considerable dissention within the Greek Orthodox Church concerning the question of union with the Latin Catholics. Many highly-respected priests, monks and nuns maintained that it was folly to flirt with the Schismatic Latins when only God and the Virgin could now save their city.

As yet only warm words arrived from Venice, the Pope, the German Emperor, Hungary, Aragon and France. Nor was there any help from other Byzantine provinces, neither from the separate Byzantine 'Empire of Trebizond' which was more concerned to defend its own frontiers nor even from the *Despotate* of the Morea. Here the all-too-often quarrelling brother *Despots* Demetrius and Thomas faced a raid in force by Ottoman troops under Turahan, the *Uc Beyi* or frontier commander in Macedonia, as well as Ahmad Bey and Umar Bey from Thessaly. They attacked the Morea on 1 October 1452, easily stormed the Isthmus of Corinth, ravaged Arcadia and the plateau of Tripolista as far as the Gulf of Coron and captured Navarino. On the other hand they failed to take Siderokastron and a unit which had been sent towards Leondarion was defeated by Byzantine troops under Matthew Asanes, brother-in-law of the joint *Despot* Demetrius. Ahmad Bey was captured and taken to Mistra, the capital of the Despotate. It was a small and perhaps surprising success for Byzantine arms, but the Ottoman raiders had fulfilled their task. No help for Constantinople would come from the Morea.

For their part the remaining Latin enclaves in Greece and even the Crusading Military Order of the Hospitallers in Rhodes were too weak to do anything. It was the same in the Balkans, where the *Despot* George of Serbia would remain loyal to his Ottoman overlord. The *Voivode* Vladislav

II of Wallachia similarly refused to turn against the Ottomans without direct Hungarian support. According to the Byzantine statesman and chronicler George Sphrantzes, the great Hungarian military leader Janos Hunyadi had demanded Mesembria (Misivri) or Selymbria (Silivri) in return for helping Constantinople, promising to garrison them with his own men. 'When the war began,' Sphrantzes wrote, 'Mesembria was given to Janos. I personally drafted the gold-sealed document. Michael's son, the brother of Theodosios from Cyprus brought it to him.' Sphrantzes also claim that that the Aegean island of Lemnos was given to King Alfonso V of Aragon and southern Italy so that he could use it as a naval base from which to help Constantinople. Nothing came from either of these remarkable proposals. Furthermore a great deal of money was supposedly sent to the Genoese rulers of Chios for soldiers who similarly never arrived.

Meanwhile the rival Princes Peter III and Alexander II of Moldavia were quarrelling with each other and were in any case more concerned about their relationship with Hungary and Poland. Even the heroic Skanderbeğ of Albania was preoccupied with own problems. Orthodox Christian Russia was too far away to help and claimed to be shocked by the Greek Church's flirtation with the Latins. Similarly the other Turkish rulers in Anatolia were either friendly towards the Ottomans or were frightened of them.

The sinking of a Venetian galley in the Bosphoros meant that the Venetian Republic was now technically at war with the Ottoman empire, but this did not mean that Venice could act quickly. In the fifteenth century, it took at least a month for even the most urgent message to get from Constantinople to Venice, via the Venetian colonial outposts of Negroponte and Corfu. The Senate was nevertheless clearly concerned about how to protect its merchant convoys through the Bosphoros, past the guns of the Rumeli Hisar. Gabriele Trevisan, the Venetian *Vice Captain of the Gulf*, was sent back to Constantinople where he was supposed to remain if the city came under Ottoman attack. In such a case he, all his ships and their crews were to help in whatever manner they could.

Further reports from Constantinople caused further alarm in Venice where the Senate now decided to arm two large transports, each to carry four hundred soldiers, accompanied by fifteen galleys to sail for Constantinople on 8 April. Meanwhile the Venetian authorities in Crete sent two warships to Evvoia where they would be placed under the command of Zaccaria Grioni who had recently come from the Byzantine capital and would have the latest news. Although the Senate sent messages to various other rulers urging prompt action, Venice's own preparations remained painfully slow.

The naval command structure was changed and the fleet for Constantinople was eventually put under Giacomo Loredan, the *Captain General of the Sea*. He was already on his way east and was now ordered to wait at Modon for the galleys commanded by Alvise Longo. Further delays followed and in the end Longo was told to take his fleet through the straits to Constantinople but only of they could avoid a direct clash with the Ottoman navy. There he should put himself and his men under the Venetian *Baillie* or governor of Venetian residents until Loredan arrived to replace Trevisan and take overall command. In the event Alvise Longo set sail from Venice on 19 April with only one warship, another fifteen vessels remaining in port because of a shortage of money. Five of them perhaps set out after 7 May but in the event the Venetian fleet which eventually assembled in the Aegean was too late to save Constantinople.

Meanwhile the Venetians already in Constantinople had to decide what to do. Girolomo Minotto, the *Baillie*, persuaded Trevisan to disobey his standing orders and remain in the Byzantine capital under Minotto's authority. Various other Venetian merchants, captains, crews and soldiers were also currently in Constantinople, on their way home from the Crimea. One of them was Giacomo Coco, captain of one of the ships which had successfully run the gauntlet of cannon fire from Rumeli Hisar, while Nicolo Barbaro, whose account remains one of the most important sources of information about the siege, had been travelling as a Venetian ship's surgeon. In December Minotto summoned a meeting of his council, at which the Emperor Constantine was also present. Here most of the leading Venetian citizens voted to remain and it was therefore agreed that no ship should leave without the *bailli's* permission on pain of a massive fine of 3,000 *ducats*. Nevertheless, on 26 February 1453 six ships from Venetian Crete and one from Venice itself defied the *bailli's* orders and fled from the Golden Horn carrying seven hundred people.

In Rome the Pope naturally saw Constantinople's predicament as another opportunity to convince the Greek Orthodox Church to accept Union with the Latin Catholic Church, and to accept Papal authority. So, in November 1452, Cardinal Isidore arrived in the Byzantine capital in a Venetian galley. The Cardinal had set off with some archers and hand-gunners from Naples and on his way stopped off at the island of Chios where he enlisted more Italian troops. There he was also joined by Archbishop Leonard.

As a result Cardinal Isidore reached Constantinople with a unit of around two hundred soldiers. These were widely seen as the advance guard of a much larger force which would save the city and consequently the Cardinal was given a great welcome by Emperor Constantine. On 12 December a joint or Unionate service was held in the ancient church of Santa Sofia and the leaders of the Orthodox Church agreed to a Decree of Union, though both sides agreed that this Decree would be re-examined once the Ottoman threat had passed. Meanwhile much of the ordinary Orthodox clergy, monks, nuns and large numbers of common people were furious, protesting and rioting in the streets. This anti-Union faction found their leader in a well known monk named Gennadios from the Monastery of the Pantokrator in Constantinople.

Isidore's handful of troops were not the only fighting men to make their way to the beleaguered Byzantine capital. In November 1452 Venice's great maritime rival, Genoa, decided to send help whilst also asking her allies, France and Florence, to contribute. As a result, in January 1453, Genoese galleys with seven hundred first rate troops arrived in the Golden Horn under the leadership of Giovanni Giustiniani Longo. They certainly impressed the Byzantine diplomat and chronicler Dukas who described them as; 'two huge ships which were carrying a large supply of excellent military equipment and well-armed youthful Genoese soldiers full of martial passion.' Giustiniani Longo's reputation was such that the Emperor Constantine XI promptly made him commander of all the soldiers and militiamen defending Constantinople by land with the rank of *protostrator*. Longo also received one of the Byzantine Empire's few remaining possessions, the northern Aegean island of Limnos, as a reward for his service.

Chapter 19

Preparing for the Siege

As was the case with all the main early Ottoman campaigns, the Sultan himself was in real and overall command. Mehmet II was one of Murad II's sons by his first or chief wife, a Turkish woman possibly named Huma Khatun. Born at Edirne on 30 March 1432, he was nevertheless only the fourth son and thus unlikely to become Sultan and, at the age of eleven, he was sent with his two *lalas* or advisors to govern the province of Amasya. Around 1450 Mehmet was married to his first wife, Sitt Khatun, daughter of the ruler of the Dulkadir principality in eastern Anatolia, a traditional ally of the Ottoman against the Karamanids.

The young Prince, and subsequent Sultan, Mehmet had a strong interest in both ancient Greek and medieval Byzantine Greek civilization. His heroes were Achilles and Alexander the Great and he could also discuss the Christian religion with some authority, which was not of course unusual amongst educated Muslims. Within his own Turco-Persian Islamic cultural context Sultan Mehmet II would became a leading patron of poets and writers as well as being responsible for the building of several *madrasah* schools. He earned the nicknames of *Fathi* 'The Conqueror' and *Abu'l-Fath* 'Father of Victory' following his conquest of Constantinople, but he was also known as *Abu'l-Khayrat* or 'Father of Good Works'. He provided pensions for no less than thirty Ottoman poets and each year sent large sums to the Indian poet Khoja'-i Jihan and to the Persian poet Jami. Meanwhile Mehmet II was himself a poet, writing under the pseudonym of 'Avni, and although he was not in the first rank, some of his verses show talent:

I asked her, why across your cheeks,
  So disordered roam your tresses?
It is Rumeli, she replied,
  Where high starred heroes gallop

Other verses by the poetic Sultan proclaimed his zeal to fight for the Faith. On the other hand many of Mehmet II's own subjects, Muslims and Christians alike, regarded him as a tyrant and he was widely credited with ordering the execution of no less than 873,000 people. Mehmet was certainly very ruthless and a very different character from his father Murad II and it is possible, though unlikely, that his son Sultan Bayezit II eventually had him poisoned.

Facing Sultan Mehmet was the last Emperor of Byzantine Constantinople, Constantine XI Palaiologos. He had been born into the ruling imperial family in Constantinople on 8 February 1405, the fourth son of Emperor Manuel II and his wife Helena Dragas. As a younger son he, like Mehmet, would not have expected to inherit the throne and was sent to the Morea in southern Greece in 1428, to share the role of *Despot* with his brothers Theodore and Thomas Palaiologos. Here he ruled for twenty years, greatly strengthening local defences, including the Hexamilion Wall across the narrow Isthmus of Corinth. For a brief period his troops even reconquered Patras, Athens and Thebes to the north.

Constantine Palaiologos was clearly a brave, energetic, successful soldier who also showed himself to be a generally cautious military leader. Following the death of his childless elder brother John VIII, Constantine became Emperor on 12 March 1449 and, as Constantine XI, ruled until his death in battle on the fateful day of 29 May 1453. Unfortunately Constantine was much less effective as an Emperor than he had been as a *Despot*. He was flexible in religious matters and was willing to accept Church Union but seemingly lacked diplomatic skills. Furthermore he badly misjudged both the domestic opposition within Byzantine territory and the real situation in the Ottoman camp. Above all Constantine failed to appreciate Sultan Mehmet II's determination and his capabilities.

Nevertheless Constantine XI Palaiologos would become a heroic figure in Greek history. Following the fall of his capital many Greeks even maintained that this last Emperor was not dead but had been turned to marble and would one day be awakened by an angel to drive the Turks from Constantinople. He would then restore the Byzantine Empire; a dream which, in its modernized version as the *Megali Idea* 'Great Idea', would lead a revived Greece to catastrophe in Turkey in the 1920s. Otherwise the only known, and still somewhat dubious, relic of Emperor Constantine XI is a fine sabre in the Armeria Reale of Turin whose blade bears a Greek inscription which states; 'Christ, you, the invincible King, the Word of God, Master of all things – For the ruler and faithful autocrat Constantine.'

Ottoman forces undoubtedly outnumbered the defenders of

Constantinople in 1453, yet the degree of difference has almost always been greatly exaggerated. The overall population of the city, excluding Galata, was probably now between 40,000 and 50,000 people with a regular or full-time garrison of only a few hundred. Some scholars put the actual numbers of men defending the walls of Constantinople in 1453 at between 6,000 and 8,500, including barely trained local militias plus Venetians, Genoese and other foreigners. These figure may, however, be on the low side as the list of defenders actually drawn up by the Byzantine government official Sphrantzes gave a total of 4,973 Greeks, both professional soldiers and militiamen, plus two hundred resident foreigners. This was so low that Emperor Constantine XI told Sphrantzes to keep the result of his survey, conducted shortly before the siege actually began, secret to avoid undermining morale. The Italian and other elite western European troops who arrived with Cardinal Isidore and Giustiniani Longo must then be added to Sphrantes' sum, along with crews and marines from the large number of Italian ships bottled up in the Golden Horn, not to mention those who crossed the Golden Horn secretly from Galata and the 'renegade' Ottoman Prince Orhan with his followers. A grand total of nine thousand men defending the Byzantine capital is probably closer to the truth.

By the fifteenth century the remnant of the Byzantine Empire was too poor to hire many mercenaries. Defence therefore depended upon local troops and militias, foreign volunteers who were sometimes religiously motivated, plus a handful of European mercenaries who, for whatever reason, found themselves at the Emperor's gate. Some Europeans had already fought for Emperor Constantine's predecessor, John VIII, including Catalans and other Spaniards but, like those western mercenaries and volunteers who served in other fifteenth century Balkan armies, most seem to have come from relatively humble backgrounds and few were members of the knightly aristocracy.

Even so there were small units of properly equipped cavalry inside Constantinople during the final siege, and the soldiers who had accompanied Emperor John VIII to Italy in 1437 included two distinct types of horsemen. The first were the armoured *stradiotai*, who would probably have rated as relatively-light cavalry in Western Europe. Secondly there were the less well equipped *gianitzaroi* whose name was probably a corruption of the Catalan term *ginetari*, javelin-armed skirmishers fighting in what was considered the 'Moorish' manner. They were certainly not Byzantine *Janissaries*.

Although the garrisons of the remaining outlying towns in Byzantine hands were now tiny, they were supported by urban militias, while it is also clear that the more powerful Byzantine noblemen had their own substantial military followings. Even at the end, Byzantine soldiers who held land as *pronoia* fiefs were not mere militarized peasants but formed a local social as well as military elite. Many, particularly within the Despotate of the Morea which was the only substantial bloc of territory still in Byzantine hands, were of non-Greek origin. They included Slavs, many Albanians and fewer descendants of previous Latin Crusader or Italian settlers. Nevertheless a minor clash near Patras during a civil war of 1429, and described in detail by Sphrantzes, who actually took part, was fought by Greek soldiers under Greek officers. Plethon's famous scheme to change the army of the *Despotate* of the Morea along ancient Spartan Greek lines had, in fact, a great deal in common with the existing system of small *pronoia* fiefs for a military class supported by tax-paying farmers.

The Byzantine militias within Constantinople appear to have been quite highly structured, perhaps based upon the fact that the city itself now consisted of little more than separate village-sized settlements within the vast ancient walls, with a more substantial urban area at the easternmost end around the great Church of Santa Sofia. Parts of the latter area were, however, the quarters of resident foreign merchants such as the Venetians. Each quarter or 'urban village' probably had its own militias, organized under a *demarchos* and supervised by imperial officials. These militias maintained law and order but also defended a nearby stretch of city wall. The many monasteries in Constantinople also helped defend the neighbouring walls. Monks themselves did watch duty in their monastery's *vigla* observation towers, so references to monks patrolling the ramparts of the Byzantine capital are no surprise. Furthermore, Constantinople already had a substantial Turkish Muslim population but how many of them chose to support the Ottoman pretender, Prince Orhan, in the final siege is unclear.

The military organization of these remaining Byzantine forces is unclear. The little army in Constantinople itself may still have been known as the *politicon* army. Whether it, or the troops elsewhere, were still really divided into *allagia* regiments is simply unknown, though the similarity between Ottoman provincial military organization and that of Byzantine forces several generations earlier suggests continuity. In the *Despotate* of the Morea Byzantine crossbowmen seem to have been something of a local elite and to have formed themselves into 'brotherhoods' rather like those seen in medieval Italy, and there seems no reason why this should not have been the case in the capital.

Written sources make clear that the most heavily equipped Byzantine troops wore plate armour in Western European style. Most of it would, in fact, have been imported from the west. During the final siege of Constantinople the defenders, Italians and Byzantines alike, normally had heavier armour than those Ottomans who were attacking them. Late Byzantine Greek popular literature also confirms close similarities between Byzantine and Western European armour, though these are often described in archaic Greek terms. The Byzantine defenders clearly had firearms during the final siege. Most were almost certainly bought from Italy, Hungary or the Balkans since the only evidence of the Byzantine Empire making its own was the presence of the Hungarian gunmaker Urban working in the Byzantine capital before offering his service to Sultan Mehmet II. In fact the cannon used to defend Constantinople in 1453 largely seem to have been gifts from Genoa. The same was probably true of gunpowder as the Byzantines seem to have been seriously short of saltpetre. Even though these guns were considerably smaller than the Ottoman 'great guns', they still made the walls shake if mounted on top. One of the largest Byzantine cannon also burst during the siege, leading to the gunner being accused of treachery. The defenders of Constantinople also had many smaller handguns. Late Byzantine names for such weapons were *molybdobolon* or 'lead thrower', *skopeta* which came from the Italian word *schiopetto*, and *touphax* which, perhaps significantly, came from Turkish word *tüfek*.

A remarkable description of late-Byzantine cavalry training in the Hippodrome of Constantinople, written by Bertrandon de la Broquière not many years before the fall of the city is supported by less specific information from elsewhere. Bertrandon saw the Despot of the Morea with twenty to thirty 'knights' exercising with their bows near Santa Sophia. 'Each,' he said, 'was carrying his bow and galloping the length of the square [Hippodrome]. They threw their hats ahead of them and then the one who could strike closest, shooting backwards, was considered the best.' This exercise clearly was learned from their Muslim foes, though not necessarily from the Ottoman Turks. He also saw horsemen jousting in the Byzantine manner, which was even stranger to Bertrandon:

> A great post was planted in the middle of a square with a large plank, three feet wide and five feet long [tall] attached to it. Perhaps forty horsemen came galloping one after the other, each with a slender shaft in his hand and doing all sorts of tricks. They were not in armour. When they had galloped around for half an hour, forty to eighty reeds like those we [the French] use for a thatched roof were brought out. The master of ceremonies started and took one of the sticks which flexed very much while he was riding, and charged as

fast as a the horse could go and hit the target, full tilt, so much that he broke his stick without too much of a shock. They then started to shout and play their instruments, which were drums like the Turks.

The tactics of most *stradioti*, whether Balkan or Byzantine, seem to have been comparable to those of the Ottoman *akincis* rather than the armoured *sipahis*, with an emphasis on raiding, speed, evasion and flanking attacks. Perhaps this was a result of the overwhelmingly defensive character of Byzantine warfare by the fifteenth century. Apart from an over-ambitious strike northwards by Constantine Palaiologos when *Despot* of the Morea, the only real offensive operations by these last Byzantine forces was during frequent but small scale civil wars. One such skirmish was again described by the courtier-soldier-historian Sphrantzes. Here in 1429 the army of the *Despotate* was attacking Patras which was held by troops loyal to the town's Latin Archbishop. The Byzantines constructed a field fortification of myrtle branches outside the main gate but were then struck by a sortie of defending cavalry, some of whom may have been horse-archers, though these bowmen could just as well have been infantrymen. The Emperor Constantine wanted to similarly attack the Ottomans as they erected their siege lines outside Constantinople in 1453, but was dissuaded by his advisors.

The famous land walls of Constantinople had been improved various times since they were built centuries earlier, but their essential layout remained the same. The only major changes lay at the northern end where a single twelfth-century wall and towers enclosed the Blachernae Palace. The other main change dated from between 1433 and 1448 when the lower, outermost of the land walls were rebuilt in a final attempt to repel the Ottoman threat. A low wall or breastwork had, in fact, already been erected along the inside of the moat in 1341. A different defensive feature which played a major role in the final siege was a floating chain or boom which ran from the Tower of Eugenius below Acropolis Point to a tower in the sea wall of Galata, on the northern side of the Golden Horn. It was supported by massive wooden floats.

Another aspect of the defence of Constantinople which is not always appreciated was the city's ability to grow a great deal of food within its walls and, under normal circumstances, to obtain fish from the sea. So much of the land within the fortifications was now uninhabited that there was space for animals to graze, not to mention orchards and vegetable gardens. However, the participation of a powerful Ottoman fleet during the siege of 1453 meant that Byzantine fishing boats no longer dared venture out of harbour.

The Byzantine ports and villages along the Black Sea coast of Thrace were abandoned apparently without a fight, as were some places on the Marmara coast when the Ottoman advanced towards the city in 1453. Other places put up a fierce resistance and for reasons which remain unknown the garrisons of the Princes' Islands in the Sea of Marmara, at Therapia, Selymbria and Epibatos clung on for some time. Therapia was on the Bosphorus, north of the Ottoman blockade fortress of Rumeli Hisar while Selymbria and Epibatos were behind the Ottoman siege-lines on the Marmara coast. All could, perhaps, have hoped to serve as points of contact with the outside world while Constantinople was itself invested.

The lack of a proper navy was a fatal handicap for the defenders of Constantinople, the last real Byzantine fleet having been destroyed by the Genoese in the fourteenth century. Nevertheless the Emperor Constantine XI did have some galleys and merchant vessels or transports, most of which seem to have been bought from Italian shipyards. The Byzantines also commandeered all the vessels caught in the Golden Horn at the start of the siege, except for those moored along the quays of the autonomous Genoese suburb of Galata, while similarly taking control of ships which arrived during the course of the siege.

In January 1453 Sultan Mehmet II returned to the capital of Edirne where large numbers of volunteers were enthusiastically mustering for the forthcoming campaign. In addition to the Rumelian provincial forces, the Palace Regiments and the inevitable camp followers, there were merchants who expected to supply Ottoman troops with food and other necessities. Early in 1453 a large Serbian vassal contingent also arrived, reportedly consisting of 1,500 well armoured Christian cavalry plus auxiliaries under the *voivode* of Jaksa. These men did not, however, take a very active part in the actual siege, although the Serbian miners who arrived later from Novo Brdo did so. According to the Italian Giacomo Tedaldi there were, in fact, many Christians in the Ottoman ranks who were allowed to worship as they wished during the course of the siege.

Meanwhile Daği Karaca Bey, the *Beylerbeyi* of Rumelia, had sent many of his men to prepare the roads from Edirne to Constantinople so that they would not break up under the strain of an army and, more importantly, so that their bridges could cope with the massive cannon which were now being constructed, fifty carpenters and two hundred assistants building wooden bridges or strengthening others. There was no reported resistance from Byzantine forces in the open countryside and Karaca Bey's pioneers were free to cut down large areas of vines and orchards outside the walls of Constantinople, ready for the Ottoman army to make camp and to provide a clear field of fire for their artillery.

Then in February Karaca Bey's troops began to take the remaining Byzantine towns of Hagios Stefanos, Heraclea, Pyrgos, Anchialos and Mesembria. In most places there was no resistance, no destruction and no removal of the Orthodox Christian populations. Only those places which resisted were sacked and had their fortifications dismantled. Three places resisted effectively, Silivri and Epibatos on the Marmara plus Therapia on the Bosphoros which were therefore bypassed.

Bursa was the main assembly area for Ottoman units from Anatolia and, according to Dukas, three such regiments crossed the Bosphoros during the winter of 1452-3 to help Karaca Bey's Rumelians watch Constantinople. During March large numbers of *azap* infantry and *sipahi* cavalry were similarly shipped, soon followed by their commander Ishaq Paşa, the *Beylerbeyi* of Anatolia and husband of Mehmet II's father's widow.

It took much of February and March for the Ottoman army to bring its massive guns to the walls of Constantinople. This was again the responsibility of Karaca Bey. Three 'giant' guns were the most difficult, the biggest built by Urban requiring sixty oxen to pull it. The guns were then assembled eight kilometres from the walls, guarded by Karaca Bey's troops. In March the Ottoman fleet under Baltaoğlu gathered outside Gallipoli and sailed for Constantinople where it established its base at the Diplokionion 'Double Columns' bay on the Bosphoros just north of Galata.

Meanwhile the Byzantines were by no means inactive. They still had access to the sea and during the winter of 1452-3 their few remaining galleys had raided Turkish coastal villages as far away as the Erdek peninsula on the far side of the sea of Marmara. Many captives were taken and these were promptly sold as slaves. On 26 February Pietro Davanzo's ship slipped out, followed by six Cretan merchant ships laden with cloth and seven hundred people aboard. They reached Tenedos (Bozcaada) safely but the arrival of the Ottoman fleet off Constantinople in March meant that any future communication with the outside world had to slip out quietly by night or fight its way through an enemy blockade.

The first task of the Ottoman fleet was impose a tight blockade and then to force the floating boom across the entrance to the Golden Horn. Most of these ships were newly built from the Aegean coast of Anatolia, but some were old and had needed recaulking or repair. Estimates of the size of Baltaoğlu's fleet also vary wildly but a remarkably specific and credible report by Jehan de Wavrin, which was probably taken from an official Burgundian document, stated that there were eighteen war-galleys, sixty to seventy smaller *galliots*, and sixteen to twenty small craft. The usually highly accurate Giacomo Tedaldi also specifies that these were sixteen to twenty *palendins* suitable for carrying horses.

Though the Byzantines were now almost entirely confined within the walls of Constantinople, they did what they could to strengthen their defences. However, Archbishop Leonard of Chios noted that; 'The greater part of the Greeks were men of peace, using their shields and spears, their bows and swords, according to the light of nature rather than with any skill. The majority had helmets and body armour of metal or leather, and fought with swords and spears. Those who were skilled in the use of the bow or the crossbow were not enough to man all the ramparts.' It also seems that around a thousand of the best Byzantine troops were kept back as a reserve within the city, ready to help whichever section of wall was most threatened, but the size of Constantinople meant that it took them too long to reach the breach when the fall finally came.

On 2 April 1453 the floating chain or boom was drawn across the entrance to the Golden Horn, supervised by the Genoese engineer Bartolomeo Soligo. The Genoese in Galata had already received a letter from home saying that a ship with five hundred troops on board was on its way to reinforce them. Nevertheless the people in Galata had a hard choice to make. Should they maintain their neutrality and perhaps see Constantinople fall or should they help their arch-rivals but fellow-Christians, the Venetians, defend the city? The authorities decided on neutrality, but some Genoese men and ships slipped across the Golden Horn to fight alongside the Byzantines.

Within Constantinople the Venetians had no such choice. Most lived under Byzantine authority and had their livelihoods to defend, while those sea captains who chose to remain also fought hard under the committed and inspiring leadership of the Venetian *Baillie*, Giolamo Minotto. For his part the Emperor Constantine XI had huge faith in the military expertise and reputation of Venice, even asking Minotto's men to parade along the walls with their banners to show the assembled Ottoman troops who they would soon be fighting. The keys of four vital gates in the land-walls were entrusted to the Venetians Catarino Contarini, Fabruzzi Corner, Nicolo Mocenigo and Dolfin Dolfin, while the defence of the Emperor's own Blachernae Palace was entrusted to the Venetian *Baillie*. Giustiniani Longo, meanwhile, commanded as many as 2,000 Greeks and Italians on his vital central section of the land walls, facing Sultan Mehmet II's own position.

Other measures carried out before the Ottomans moved forward to their siege lines included the clearing of a ditch around the otherwise exposed Blachernae walls. Anticipating an artillery bombardment, the Byzantines had large bales of wool and leather sheets either at the ready or already hung outside the walls. Needless to say, these medieval methods were of little help against the Ottomans' modern cannon. Each bastion or tower of the walls from the Golden Gate to the Horaia Gate facing Galata was manned by an archer, supported either by a crossbowman or a handgunner, while Loukas Notaras in the Petrion quarter also had a number of mobile cannon as a reserve. This quarter was furthermore surrounded by an additional wall or stockade on its inner side, facing the open agricultural part of what is today the centre of Istanbul. Several other such isolated quarters may have been similarly defended on the inside, almost certainly including Studion and Psamathia to the south.

Sultan Mehmet II and his elite Palace Regiments left Edirne on 23 March 1453, by which time the bulk of Ottoman forces were assembling about four kilometres from the land-walls of Constantinople. A later source maintains that the main Ottoman encampment was on the other side of the Golden Horn, in an area later called the Oq Maydan. If true, then this was probably the site of the pioneers', labourers' and non-combatants' camp – relatively safe from sorties by the defenders of the city.

The artillery was already in position closer to the city, presumably defended by other units. Its fourteen and eventually fifteen emplacements were relatively evenly-spread along the land-walls. Three batteries faced Blachernae, including one of Urban's giant guns. Two batteries faced the Charisius Gate, four the St. Romanus Gate, and three the Pege Gate, with the two remaining batteries perhaps facing the Golden Gate. Artillery positions 'behind Galata' may not have been established until later. Additional batteries of smaller cannon were established alongside those of the big guns, and perhaps also elsewhere since there are said to have been sixty-nine Ottoman cannon all-told in fifteen batteries.

On Easter Day, 2 April, and the same day that the Byzantine boom was drawn across the Golden Horn, Sultan Mehmet II and his entourage established their tents on Maltepe Hill facing the St. Romanus Gate, where the Sultan was also accompanied by his spiritual mentor, Aq Shams al-Din. On the sixth the bulk of the Ottoman army moved forward from its assembly positions, probably marching along the main road from Edirne, with the Rumelian contingent forming the van, the Sultan's Palace Regiments the centre and the Anatolians the rear. They paused for prayers about a kilometre and a half from Constantinople, then moved up to their siege lines. Thus the Rumelians were now on the left, the Sultan in the centre and the Anatolians the right. Half of the army was kept in reserve at the rear, perhaps including much of the Sultan's own Palace Regiments and the auxiliaries or volunteers. The *Second Vizir* Zaganos Paşa and Daği Karaca Bey of Rumelia took a few thousand men to occupy the hills on the other side of the Golden Horn, those under Zaganos Paşa including many Albanian recent converts to Islam. Meanwhile a small unit under Kasim Paşa was sent forward to keep watch on Galata.

Archbishop Leonard stated that as the Sultan's army moved forward, its troops carried 'pieces of lattice-work made out of branches and slips of trees to protect his soldiers'. He also maintained that they could have been attacked at this point by a sortie from the walls before they could complete or occupy their siege fortifications. The Ottoman siege lines now consisted of a continuous field fortification over four kilometres long from the Marmara coast to the Golden Horn, with a trench fronted by an earth rampart and a lower wooden palisade pierced by posterns or entrances and wooden turrets.   According to the Byzantine chronicler Laonicus Chalcocondylas the Ottoman infantry; 'dug trenches outside the fosse [the main moat of Constantinople], and made openings in the earth which was thrown up, through which they could fire their cannon at the Greeks and shoot arrows at them without exposing themselves and without suffering any other trouble at their hands, for it was not possible to hit them there.' The two sides were now so close that the Turks mocked the long beards of their Greek opponents, threatening to make dog-leads out of them.

As the Ottomans assembled for their great assault, little was being done in Europe to help Constantinople. In late March or early April the Pope sent three large Genoese ships full of arms and provisions but they soon found themselves stormbound at Chios. The Venetians reacted even more slowly and it was not until 11 May that Loredan set out for the Byzantine capital. A few days later news that the siege was under way caused near panic in the Senate, which promptly decided to order three more warships from Evvoia, Corfu and Crete to join Loredan's fleet at Bozcaada.

In Hungary the young King Ladislas came of age in 1453. The experienced regent János Hunyadi was reduced to the status of Captain-General while Ladislas took the field against a powerful rebel, Peter Aksamit of Liderovic. During the siege of Constantinople Hunyadi reportedly proposed a seaborne campaign to outflank the Ottomans but this idea came to nothing. Clearly the most powerful state on the Ottomans' European frontier was neither willing nor able to rescue the remnants of Byzantium.

Chapter 20

The Conquest of Constantinople

O n the morning of 6 April, as the Ottomans moved forward to their siege lines, the Emperor Constantine XI left his palace and joined Giustiniani Longo at the St. Romanus Gate. It was the start of the active siege of Constantinople which would last fifty-four days. It would also be a slow, patient, yet bloody struggle during which trusted messengers could still cross from one side to the other, primarily between the Ottoman Grand Vizier Çandarlı Halil and the Emperor Constantine. The Ottoman artillery bombardment also began on the 6 and was continued on the 7, bringing down part of the wall near the Gate of Charisius. Urban's giant gun also did considerable damage to the walls of the Blachernae sector where it could be set up at close range because there was no real fosse or moat. On the second day of firing, however, the big gun started to overheat. This was temporarily solved by sponging the interior of the barrel with oil after every shot, but on 11 April the gun either cracked or started to leak gases. It cannot have actually burst as it was repaired and brought back into action some time later. A more widespread problem for the Ottoman artillerymen was that their guns often slipped in the mud of April rain showers.

The first Ottoman infantry assault seems to have been launched on 7 April against the centre of the land-walls defended by Giustiniani's men. It was clearly a probing attack by ill-equipped irregulars and volunteers who nevertheless advanced with great courage and enthusiasm, supported by archers and handgunners who attempted to keep the defenders' heads down. They were met by the defenders at the outermost wall, on the very edge of the fosse and were driven back with relative ease after which the damaged sections of wall were repaired by night. Meanwhile Byzantine artillerymen were using their relatively few and small cannon in anti-battery work against Ottoman artillery positions. The guns commanded by the Bochiardi brothers were notably effective, until the largest Byzantine cannon burst. However, it seems as if the defenders were soon running short of powder and shot. Thereafter the Byzantine guns were largely limited to the anti-personnel role, each gun shooting from five to ten walnut-sized bullets as an early form of grape-shot.

Constantinople's crossbowmen were similarly proving themselves a force to be reckoned with. During the first days of the siege the defenders made several sorties, taking a number of Ottoman prisoners, but Giustiniani decided that they were losing more than they gained and so withdrew his outnumbered men from the edge of the moat to the first main wall. There was now a short pause during which Sultan Mehmet ordered several artillery batteries to be repositioned. On 11 or 12 April the Ottomans reopened their artillery bombardment, after which it remained almost continuous, despite problems with the elevation and aiming of the Ottoman guns. According to Leonard of Chios;

> Then they placed a terrible cannon, an even larger which burst..., near that part of the single wall called Caligaria... It fired a stone which measured eleven of my palms in circumference. The bursting of this big cannon continued to annoy the Sultan, and to sooth his vexation he ordered another, much larger even than the first, to be made. It was never completed by its maker, thanks to the efforts, as it was said, of our friend the Vizier Halil.

There is almost certainly some confusion here, and the Archbishop was probably referring to the great gun *Basiliske* which had been moved to the main battery facing the Gate of St. Romanus after being repaired. Here the *Basiliske* brought down an almost two-metre-wide section of wall with its second shot. These huge cannonballs were sufficiently valuable for Ottoman troops to risk using nets to drag them from the fosse in front of the walls to be used again. Apparently a Hungarian ambassador from János Hunyadi arrived in the Ottoman camp as an observer around this time and, according to Dukas, actually advised the Ottoman gunners on how best to lay their guns. Previously they had fired constantly at one point on the wall, but this Hungarian supposedly taught them to fire three shots to form a weakened triangle, after which a shot from one of the great guns would bring down the cracked structure. On the other side the defenders soon got used to the psychological impact of Ottoman artillery fire, though there was little they could do to stop their walls crumbling.

Mehmet now also sent troops with lighter mobile artillery to take two outlying Byzantine forts. These operations went smoothly and the defenders were executed for their persistent refusal to surrender. Meanwhile the Ottoman fleet's first tentative attack upon the floating boom across the mouth of the Golden Horn failed. Baltaoğlu decided to await the arrival of additional ships from the Black Sea before trying again on the twelfth. Again the Ottoman fleet was driven off despite launching a ferocious attack, largely because the Christian ships, though fewer, were much taller.

On the night of 17-18 April the Ottomans launched a surprise night attack on the Mesoteichon sector of the land-walls. The Emperor himself was on a tour of inspection elsewhere but after a four-hour battle the defenders under Giustiniani Longo drove the Ottomans back. It was probably on the following day, perhaps to maintain the Ottoman army's morale, that the fleet was sent to seize the Princes Islands, which it did with ease.

Two days later the Ottoman fleet suffered its most serious reverse when the three large Genoese-Papal armed transports carrying weapons, troops and food, which had previously been delayed by adverse weather at Chios, suddenly appeared off Constantinople having been joined by another large Byzantine ship carrying wheat from Sicily. Furthermore they had passed through the now unguarded Dardanelles unchallenged. Clearly the Sultan was furious and ordered Baltaoğlu to capture them or not return alive. The Christians' sails apparently looked like islands rising from the sea of smaller Ottoman ships which closed around them. In fact the height of the Christian sailing ships gave their heavily armed defenders a huge advantage and as the struggle came level with the Golden Horn, the prevailing current propelled the Christian vessels towards safety. During the afternoon, however, the wind dropped and the entire battle drifted towards the shore, probably just north of Galata, where the excited young Sultan Mehmet II urged his horse into the sea as he shouted orders to Baltaoğlu. The latter pretended not to hear since the Sultan, though a fine general, had no experience of naval warfare.

Eventually three Genoese ships came to the Byzantines' assistance and in the desperate fight which followed Baltaoğlu was wounded in the eye while Sultan Mehmet became ever more angry. Then, as the sun set, the wind returned, enabling the four Christian ships to push the Ottoman craft aside and run for the Golden Horn. Dusk was falling and in the gathering gloom Baltaoğlu could not reassemble his ships, so he ordered them back to the Diplokionion harbour while Sultan Mehmet urged his horse further into the waves, summoning his sailors to stand fast.

This highly-visible defeat clearly had a serious impact on Ottoman morale, while that of the defenders was raised, particularly in the light of their previous successes against Ottoman assaults upon the land-walls. The need for heads to roll is reflected in a letter sent to Mehmet II by his mentor, Aq Shams al-Din;

> This failure on the part of the navy caused a lot of disappointment and sorrow [in the Ottoman camp]. There seems to have been an opportunity, the loss of which created new concern. In the first place the religious one; the Christians rejoice and make a fuss, in the second place people in our camp ascribed this to your misjudgement and lack of authority... Under the circumstances you have to make proper enquiries into such dissention and neglect, and punish severely those who were responsible for it lest they commit the same neglect when the time comes to attack the walls and to fill the trenches.

Next day the brave but unlucky Baltaoğlu was brought before the Sultan and publicly threatened with execution. It is unlikely that Mehmet really intended to kill such a brave and skilful commander and the testimony of fellow officers and Janissaries as to Baltaoğlu's courage and determination may have been prearranged. In the event Mehmet stripped Baltaoğlu of his rank and possessions and had him flogged which, since Baltaoğlu was one of the Sultan's *kuls* or 'slaves', he was entitled to do. According to Christian sources the disgraced naval commander spent the rest of his days in obscurity but the Turkish sources say nothing, though a later chronicler using now lost Turkish and Balkan documents mentions Baltaoglu's presence during the final successful Ottoman breakthrough. Meanwhile he had been replaced as commander of the fleet by Hamza Bey.

While all this was going on, the Ottomans apparently missed an opportunity at the land-walls. Here, on 21 April, their artillery brought down a large tower whose ruins partially filled the fosse near the Gate of St. Romanus. But the Sultan was at Galata so an attack could not be mounted before the defenders plugged the breach with beams and rubble. Following this additional setback Mehmet II summoned his advisers and commanders to a war council at Diplokionion. The Grand Vizier Çandarlı Halil reportedly urged that the Sultan reach a compromise with the Emperor in return for certain political rights over Constantinople and an annual tribute of 70,000 gold pieces. Zaganos Paşa, the other *vizirs* and Shaykh Aq Shams al-Din argued for a continued attack, with which the Sultan agreed.

One of the Sultan's first orders was to have most of the cannon taken off the Ottoman warships and mounted ashore to bombard the Italian and Byzantine ships in the Golden Horn. The most important of these were defending the floating boom, but in this position they were shielded from Ottoman fire by the suburb of Galata. It was at this point that Mehmet was personally credited with devising a new form of long range mortar. It is unlikely to have been one of the guns from the fleet and was probably a heavier weapon from one of the land batteries. The barrel was now mounted at a high angle while the gunners were taught how to judge the range and drop their shot into the Golden Horn area. According to Mehmet II's Greek biographer Kritovoulos, told them to; 'get the measure by mathematical calculations' in one of the first clear examples of the new science of ballistics in Ottoman military history.

At the same time work was either started, or more probably speeded up, on the construction of a wooden slipway from the Bosphoros, across the vine-covered hills behind Galata and down to the Golden Horn. Sultan Mehmet and his advisers clearly realized that they must take control of this inlet and the only way to do so was to get their ships inside. Since the fleet had failed to force the boom, the ships must be taken overland. It was not, of course, the first time that such a portage of warships had been constructed. Nevertheless it remains an astonishing feat of imagination, engineering, determination, and brutally hard work on the part of those men who pulled the ships once the slipway had been constructed.

By 22 April this slipway was complete and, perhaps under the cover of an artillery bombardment of the Golden Horn, some of the smaller warships were hauled across the hills. They moved on rollers and reportedly even used their sails to provide extra power, or at least slid into the Golden Horn with their sails already up and skeleton crews aboard. Zaganos Paşa's artillery were already stationed along the shore, ready to repel any attempt by Italian or Byzantine ships to interfere. Full crews were immediately put aboard and eventually seventy two of the Ottoman fleet's smaller craft, some thirty of them being galleys, took control of the Golden Horn.

Presumably believing that the Ottoman fleet in the Bosphoros was now seriously weakened, the defenders decided to attack it with fire-ships by night as it lay anchored at the Diplokionion. Whether this rash attempt was betrayed by a traitor in Galata, as some Christian sources suggest, or was simply spotted by a sharp-eyed Ottoman sentry is unclear. It was certainly defeated with serious loss. However, the defenders of Constantinople still hoped for relief while the increasingly worried Emperor Constantine XI had sent a scout ship to look for the anticipated Venetian relief fleet. By late May Sultan Mehmet II was also concerned at the prospect of a fleet arriving from the west and he now considered that enough of the walls had been battered by his army for a final assault to be launched.

On 3 May the defenders placed guns on or in front of the Golden Horn walls to fire over the water at maximum range, hoping to drive back the Ottoman ships. The Ottomans replied by assembling batteries to bombard the Golden Horn walls and to force the Christian ships still further up against the boom. More dramatic was the impact of Sultan Mehmet's newly devised long-range mortar which opened fire on 5 May, sinking a supposedly-neutral Genoese merchant ship owned by a certain Barnaba and moored close to Galata.

Between 9 and 13 May Venetian ships in the Golden Horn handed over their war material to the Emperor and on 10 May Alvise Diedo was given command of all the ships, while Gabriele Trevisan took his forty men to help defend the walls. Further skirmishing in the Golden Horn eventually forced all Christian ships, except those guarding the boom, into or around the small Prosphorianus harbour next to the boom.

Meanwhile the boom itself remained a problem for the Ottoman fleet, which made tentative demonstrations or attempted surprise attacks on 16-17 and 21 May, though none were pressed home. At the same time Ottoman engineers and sailors constructed a pontoon bridge across the Golden Horn, close to the angle of the Blachernae and Golden Horn walls. It was wide enough for five men to walk abreast and substantial enough to carry wagons or artillery, though reports that heavy cannon were actually mounted on the floating bridge seem impossible. They were probably on batteries defending each end and, in the case of the northern bridgehead, capable of bombarding Blachernae from a new angle. A Byzantine attempt to destroy the pontoon bridge with fire-ships failed and from then on this new link between Ottoman forces on each side of the waterway proved very useful.

The bombardment of the land-walls, the real key to the ultimate capture of the city, continued and on 2 May the mighty *Basiliske* was returned to its original position; probably opening fire again four days later. Also on 6 May more guns were concentrated in batteries facing the St. Romanus Gate sector and made another breach. It was enlarged on the seventh but was still only about three metres wide, and an Ottoman assault the following night failed. This seems to have been the occasion when, according to Balkan and Russian chronicles, a Greek nobleman named Rhangabe killed Sultan Mehmet's standard bearer Amir Bey. But according to Alexander Ypsilanti, using Balkan and perhaps Turkish sources, Ottoman soldiers under Paşa Murad seemed likely to break through until the Greek *boyar* Rhangabe seriously wounded Paşa Murad. Rhangabe was then killed by Mehmet's standard bearer (*alamdar*) Mustafa and a soldier named Umar Bey.

The Ottoman attackers were surrounded and in danger of being wiped out until Mustafa turned the tide. Now a general route of the Byzantine defenders seemed likely until Giustiniani and the *voyvode* Theodore joined in. The Emperor Constantine was in conference with Loukas Notaras and the *Eparch* Nicholas at the time. They galloped to the scene on horseback and drove the Ottomans back through the breach, the Emperor personally playing a leading role in this fighting.

A particularly intensive Ottoman bombardment continued from 8-11 May, a new breach being made near the Caligaria Gate. This was followed by an evening assault on the twelfth, which penetrated the Blachernae Palace before being driven back. Two days later additional guns were brought across the pontoon bridge from behind Galata and the Valley of the Springs to join the batteries facing Blachernae. They were not particularly effective and two days later moved on to join those opposite the St. Romanus Gate which already looked the most promising sector.

The Ottomans also started to undermine the land-walls. Most of the miners appear to have been Serbians from the Novo Brdo area, sent by the Serbian Despot and placed under the command of Zaganos Paşa. They eventually excavated fourteen separate tunnels, beginning some distance back to avoid being seen and initially aiming towards the Charisius Gate. But this was in the Lycus river valley and the ground proved unsuitable, either wet or too sandy, so the miners tried again, aiming for the Blachernae wall near the Caligaria Gate. This time they were discovered and defeated by a Byzantine countermine, excavated under the direction of Johannes Grant, which broke into the Serbian shaft on 16 May. Further Ottoman mining efforts were defeated on 21 and 23 May, several miners being captured. They included an Ottoman officer who was tortured to reveal the location of all the remaining mines, and by 25 May all had been destroyed.

Zaganos Paşa had meanwhile ordered the construction of some large wooden siege towers. These were not moveable but, being partially filled with earth, served as strong points and cover for both men and scaling ladders before an assault. On the night of 18-19 May one such tower was blown up with barrels of gunpowder during a sudden sortie by the defenders. Others were destroyed by various means after which the remainder were dismantled as failures.

On the other side the defenders found it increasingly difficult to plug breaches in the Lycus valley sector once the fosse had been largely filled, even when working at night. Instead they erected their own stockades within the gaps, made of rubble, barrels filled with earth and baulks of timber carried from inside the city by men and women alike. It was also increasingly difficult to launch sorties because the shattered gates made the defenders too visible. On the other hand there were still postern gates which had been walled up before the siege began. One of these was the Kerkoporta. This was reopened on the Emperor's orders and used for notably successful flank attacks, mostly by cavalry led by the Bocchiardi brothers, against Ottoman attempts against the northern part of the land-walls.

Nevertheless morale was declining within Constantinople. Early in May, Emperor Constantine demanded additional funds from the churches and monasteries to buy food for his troops. There seem to have been few real shortages, despite the year's poor harvest, but livestock within the walls was dwindling fast while the fishermen were now unable to fish, even in the Golden Horn. Distribution of bread to men on the walls was inadequate and many would return home to eat or tend their allotments or vines when enemy activity was slack. There was increasingly-open grumbling against the Emperor and growing tension between Italians and Greeks. On one occasion the Venetians, who had been constructing wooden mantlets in their own quarter near the harbour, demanded that the Greeks carry these to the land-walls. Perhaps resenting the Venetians arrogant behaviour, the Greeks demanded payment or food for their families, and this nearly led to a brawl.

Worse still the *Hodegetria*, the holiest icon in Constantinople which was supposedly painted by the Apostle Luke himself, slipped from its platform while being carried in procession around the city. A violent thunderstorm then forced the entire procession to be cancelled. Next day, probably 12 May, an unseasonable fog shrouded Constantinople and a strange effect of light appeared to hover around the Cathedral of Santa Sofia. This was, interestingly, reported by both sides and in the highly-charged atmosphere of the time caused widespread concern. Muslim leaders declared that it was a foretaste of the Light of the True Faith which would soon shine within the ancient building, but Christian leaders came up with no explanation to reassure their followers. Instead some of the most senior advised the Emperor to leave Constantinople and continue the struggle elsewhere.

Constantine XI, however, refused, saying; 'I pray you, my friends, in future do not say to me anything else but "Nay sire, do not leave us". Never, never will I leave you. I am resolved to die here with you..'

On 23 May a small reconnaissance boat returned from beyond the Dardanelles. Ottoman ships tried intercept it but failed; perhaps they had been told not to try too hard for the news it brought cast Emperor Constantine into despair. There was no relief in sight. Omens seems to follow hard on each others' heels and on 24 May there was a lunar eclipse, which this time upset the Ottomans as much as the defenders. Clearly the strain was telling on both sides and Sultan Mehmet reportedly tried to bribe Giustiniani Longo, knowing how vital he was to the defence.

Mehmet II was worried enough to send a final embassy into Constantinople to try and negotiate a surrender. This seems to have followed Byzantine enquiries, via the Genoese in Galata, as to the Sultan's terms. The final Ottoman embassy was headed by Mehmet's brother-in-law, Isfandiyaroğlu Ismail Bey, the vassal ruler of Kastamonu and Sinop, who had friends amongst the Byzantine ruling elite. In return the Byzantines agreed to send a low-level delegation to the Sultan's camp, but in the event Mehmet's terms were the same as before, and just as unacceptable.

On 26 May rumours started to spread in the Ottoman camp that a Christian relief fleet had in fact set sail and would soon break their siege. For their part Sultan Mehmet and his senior commanders now called a council of war to decide whether or not to risk an all-out assault. Zaganos pointed out that Mehmet's hero, Alexander the Great, had conquered half the world when still a young man. His views were supported by many of the younger military leaders, including the Bey in command of the irregular volunteers, but Çandarlı Halil still argued in favour of a compromise and emphasized the continuing danger from the west. According to Archbishop Leonard of Chios even Turahan Bey, the commander of the armies of Thrace who was normally a supporter of Çandarlı Halil, no longer dared support his caution. Zaganos Paşa similarly insisted that this time the Ottomans' western foes would not unite and the Sultan must take the opportunity to capture Constantinople before relief arrived. In fact, the Venetian fleet had already left port and news also arrived that the Hungarians were preparing to march. Emperor Constantine XI probably knew this as well, and that was why he had refused the Sultan's terms.

Mehmet II decided to send Zaganos Paşa to sound out the opinions of the men, perhaps knowing full well what answer his *Second Vizir* would bring back. According to a sixteenth-century rewriting of the Greek chronicle by Sphrantzes, Zaganos reported; 'I have spoken with many soldiers and know how they feel. Joyfully lead them into battle and victory will be ours.' The following day, the twenty seventh of May, Sultan Mehmet toured the entire army while heralds announced that the final attack by both land and sea would be on the twenty ninth.

Senior officers were told that their men would be permitted a general pillage of the city except for its fortifications and buildings. Celebration bonfires were lit and from 26 May onwards there was continuous feasting in the Ottoman camp, most notably opposite the St. Romanus Gate. Criers announced that the first man onto the wall of Constantinople would be rewarded with fiefs and high rank in the administration, while those who fled would be punished. Religious leaders similarly toured the encampments to encourage men to fight well and telling them about the famous warrior and Companion of the Prophet Muhammad, Abu Ayyub, who had died during the great Arab-Islamic attack upon Constantinople in 672.

Following the fall of the city Abu Ayyub's grave was 'rediscovered', though in reality it had probably never been lost by the Muslim merchant community which lived in Constantinople. Today it can still be visited in the Mosque of Eyüp in a suburb of the same name, overlooking the Golden Horn just north of the Blachernae walls. Zaganos Paşa is said to have been responsible for the final preparations while Sultan Mehmet II reportedly announced that; 'I have decided to engage successively and without halt, one body of troops after another until the enemy, harassed and worn out, will be unable to resist further.'

During the evening and night of 27 May the defenders on the walls of Constantinople saw the Ottoman encampments so full of torches that some thought the enemy were burning their tents before retreating. In reality they were stockpiling weaponry, while every ship also had its lights illuminated. At midnight all were extinguished and work ceased. The defenders did not cease, however, and spent the entire night repairing and strengthening breaches in the wall as well as they could. Particular attention was paid to the very battered sector around the Gate of St. Romanus, where bulwarks were erected and new defensive entrenchments excavated. Giustiniani Longo now asked Loukas Notaras for his reserve of artillery to be sent to this part of the wall. Notaras refused, Longo accused him of treachery and they almost came to blows as the Italian reportedly drew his sword. Emperor Constantine intervened, but the bitterness seemingly remained.

The following day was dedicated to prayer and rest in the siege lines while Sultan Mehmet visited every unit, north and south of the Golden Horn, and including the fleet under Hamza Bey. The Sultan also summoned the leaders of Galata to their wall and warned them not to allow their people to help Constantinople. Final orders were now sent to the Ottoman commanders while Admiral Hamza Bey was told to spread his ships around the entire sea walls and erect scaling ladders where possible.

Zaganos Paşa was to send some of his men help the ships in the Golden Horn while the rest should cross the pontoon bridge and assist in the attack upon the Blachernae walls. Karaca Bey and the Rumelians would be to their right as far as the Gate of Charisius. Ishak Paşa and Mahmud Paşa with the Anatolians would attack the walls between the Gate of St. Romanus and the Marmara shore, though focussing mainly around the Third Military Gate. Sultan Mehmet II himself with Çandarlı Halil and Saruja Paşa would direct the main attack against the walls in the Lycus valley. No guns would be fired on the day before this final assault but, in late afternoon as the setting sun shone in the eyes of the defenders, the Ottoman troops came out of their camps and began to fill the fosse while the artillery brought their moveable guns as close as possible. Meanwhile the eighty assorted ships which the Ottomans had brought into the Golden Horn spaced themselves along Constantinople's northern wall between the Xyloporta and the Horaia Gate, while those outside the boom spread themselves more widely along the sea walls as far as the Langa harbour. It then began to rain. Nevertheless the Ottomans continued quietly working into the night, only ceasing around 1.30 in the morning of 29 May.

For their part the defenders had similarly been rearranged. Manuel of Genoa with two hundred archers and crossbowmen guarded the districts around the Golden Gate and probably the Studion quarter. The scholar Theophilos Palaiologos commanded forces around the south of the Pege Gate, while Giovanni Giustiniani Longo with four hundred Italians and the bulk of the Byzantine troops was responsible for the most threatened sector around the Gate of St. Romanus. The Myriandrion area where the walls had been partially demolished went to the brothers Antonio, Paolo and Troilo Bocchiardi.

Girolamo Minotto was placed in overall command of the defenders of the Blachernae Palace area where Theodorus from Karyston, described in Greek sources as 'the best archer on earth', and Johannes Grant *'an able military engineer'* defended the Caligaria Gate. Archbishop Leonard of Chios and a certain Hieronymus with their men guarded the Xyloporta. Cardinal Isidore's men probably defended the walls immediately to the right of the Xyloporta. Loukas Notaras took charge of the Petrion district as far as the Gate of St. Theodosia; five hundred archers and perhaps hand gunners manning these walls facing the Golden Horn. Gabriele Trevisan with fifty soldiers seems to have guarded the central section of the Golden Horn walls while the crews of Cretan ships manned those around the Horaia Gate, probably under Trevisan's command. Antonio Diedo retained command of the vessels arranged in battle order. The Catalan consul Pére Julia defended the Bucoleon district as far as the Contoscalion harbours. The Ottoman Prince Orhan and his followers were almost certainly still stationed near the Langa harbour while Jacobi Contarini's men defended the sea walls of the Langa harbour as far as Psamathia, but probably no further as no Ottoman ships approached the further sector of sea walls.

The remainder of the Byzantine aristocracy and their followers, including the local militias, went to their allotted places. Demetrius Cantakuzenos, his son-in-law Nikephoros Palaeologos and others took up position at the Church of the Holy Apostles ready to provide reinforcements where needed. The Emperor himself and various attendants including Sprantzes made constant tours of inspection to boost the defenders' morale. Monks and clergy similarly conducted constant religious services and processions both within Constantinople and around its walls as the people shouted: 'Kyrie eleison! Avert from us, Lord, thy just threats and deliver us from the hands of our enemy!' The quarrels of only a day before seem to have been forgotten as Orthodox and Latin Christians joined in prayer, including a Latin service in Santa Sophia.

The assault began about three hours before dawn on 29 May, St. Theodosia's Day. There was a final ripple of fire from the Ottoman artillery and then the first attack by Ottoman irregulars and volunteers swept forward led, according to Alexander Ypsilanti, by Mustafa Paşa. Their role was to tire the defenders and although their weaponry was rudimentary and their losses high, they pressed on to the sound of drums and trumpets. The main attack focussed around the battered Gate of St. Romanus. Here Giustiniani Longo had once again taken 3,000 of his best men down to the outer wall, while the other walls behind them were patrolled by observers with a better view of the Ottoman preparations. Despite terrible casualties few of the Ottoman volunteers retreated until, after two hours of fighting, Sultan Mehmet ordered a withdrawal. Around the same time the Ottoman ships attempted, with continuing lack of success, to get close enough to the walls to erect scaling ladders. Inside the city church bells and wooden gongs were sounded, all defenders hurried to their posts, women carried water to the fighting men and helped tend the wounded, while children and the elderly crowded into the churches to pray.

After another intense artillery bombardment it was the turn of the Anatolian divisions. They had formed the southern or left wing of the Ottoman array but now Anatolians in notably fine armour also attacked the St. Romanus Gate area. Perhaps the Christian sources are combining the actions of Anatolian provincial *sipahis* and *azaps* with those of Anatolian regiments in or attached to the Sultan's division at the centre of the Ottoman line. They marched forward, many carrying torches in the pre-dawn gloom, but found their movements hampered by the narrowness of the breaches in Constantinople's walls. More disciplined than the previous irregulars, the Anatolians occasionally pulled back to allow their artillery to fire. During one such bombardment a large cannonball struck squarely into one of the defender's stockades, bringing down a large section. Three hundred Anatolians immediately rushed the gap but were again driven off. Attacks elsewhere were equally unsuccessful, though they did stop the defenders sending reinforcements to the vital St. Romanus Gate and Lycus valley sector. Fighting was particularly intense around the Blachernae walls where Zaganos Paşa faced Minotto and Karaja Bey faced the Bocchiardi brothers.

This second wave of assaults continued until about an hour before dawn when they were called off. Sultan Mehmet had only one other corps to throw into combat; his own Palace Regiments and his valuable *Janissary* infantry. According to Ypsilanti, uncorroborated by any other known source, the three thousand *Janissaries* were led by Baltaoğlu and they attacked the main breach near the St. Romanus Gate as if not caring whether they lived or died. Many were armed with handguns though some also seem to have hurled javelins before they closed with the enemy. All sources agree that these *Janissaries* advanced with terrifying purpose and discipline, slowly and without noise or music, while Sultan Mehmet accompanied them as far as the edge of the moat. From there he encouraged and consoled his men individually by name since they were, after all, his own.

This third phase of fighting lasted about another hour before some *Janissaries* on the left found that the Kerkoporta postern, previously used to such effect by the defenders, had been left open or at least not properly closed after the last sortie against Karaja Bey's men. About fifty soldiers broke in and rushed up the internal stairs to the top where the old Theodosian wall joined the twelfth-century walls of Blachernae. Here they raised their banner.

These courageous men were nevertheless almost immediately cut off and were in danger of being wiped out when the Ottomans had a great piece of luck – a stroke of luck which their discipline and excellent command structure enabled them to utilize to the full. Giovanni Giustiniani Longo was standing in one of the wooden turrets or ramparts which filled the breach when he was struck by a bullet through the back of his arm. This penetrated the fully plated chest and back-plates of his cuirass, probably through the arm-hole and caused an agonizing wound, though perhaps no one yet realized it was mortal. According to the highly reliable Giacomo Tedaldi, the wounded Giustiniani entrusted his sector to two Genoese noblemen and was taken, but more likely walked, to the rear. The Emperor Constantine had been nearby and called out; 'My brother, fight bravely. Do not forsake us in our distress. The salvation of the City depends on you. Return to your post. Where are you going?' Giustiniani simply replied: 'Where God himself will lead these Turks.'

He was taken to his own ship in the Golden Horn, but when Giustiniani's men saw him leave they thought he was running away. Panic spread rapidly, spurred on by the sight of an Ottoman banner still flying on the wall to the north. Those outside the main walls rushed back in an attempt to retreat through the breaches in their own defences, but were hampered by their own numbers. Others fell into gaps in the battered defences or into what remained of the fosse.

Precisely what happened next is, perhaps inevitably, obscured by legend. Sultan Mehmet is himself credited with recognizing the confusion in the defenders' ranks and sending a unit of *Janissaries*, led by another man of giant stature named Hasan of Ulubad, to seize the wall. This Hasan reached the top of the rubble which filled the breach but was then felled by a stone (he is now commemorated by a naive statue in his home village of Ulubad). Seventeen of his thirty comrades were also slain but the remainder stood firm until further Ottoman soldiers could join them. Other sources credit Zaganos Paşa with seizing the initiative and sending in a *Janissary* unit, but perhaps this was a parallel event at the northern end of the walls.

One way or another the Janissaries took control of the taller inner wall near the St. Romanus Gate, and by appearing behind the defenders they added further to their panic. Other Ottoman troops now poured into various breaches and word spread that the Ottomans had also broken in via the harbour, which may or may not yet have been true. It was about four o'clock in the morning and dawn was breaking as yet more Ottoman banners appeared on the Blachernae walls. Here the Bocchiardi brothers cut their way back to their ships in the harbour, but Minotto, his son Giorgio with Giovanni Loredan and most of the Venetians were cut off and captured. According to Dukas the defenders of the Golden Horn wall maintained a successful defence until some of the first Ottoman looters – not yet regular troops – appeared behind them. Many then escaped over the wall to their ships while the Ottoman sailors outside erected ladders and swarmed over the same walls. A different story maintains that the sentries at some of these gates threw their keys outside the walls, believing a prophecy that the people of Constantinople would destroy the invaders once they were trapped within the ancient walls.

Clearly the defence now collapsed. Its foreign troops tried to reach their ships in the Golden Horn. Many succeeded, although a large number of the better equipped men were captured while in the lengthy process of trying to remove their armour before swimming to the ships. The local Greek militiamen fell back to defend their homes from looting. Many defenders in the Lycus valley section of land-walls were trapped and captured.

Local officials in the Studion and Psamathia areas surrendered their quarters to the first proper Ottoman troops who appeared. The Catalans below the Old Palace resisted until all were killed or captured. Ottoman sailors certainly broke through the Plataea Gate and some through the Horaia Gate while others spread along the walls to open other gates. Some time later Admiral Hamza Bey, with the more disciplined crews still under his control, led some ships around Acropolis Point through the now broken boom into the Golden Horn where he captured the remaining Christian ships.

The death of the Emperor Constantine XI is entirely lost in legend, though there are three main versions. The most commonly accepted maintains that Constantine and his immediate companions charged into the fray as the Ottoman soldiers poured through the main breach near the Gate of St. Romanus. One story says that he shouted at his enemies; 'Is there no Christian here? Who will take my head?' before being struck in the face and back. The Emperor then fell and was killed. Another version says that Constantine leapt into battle without a helmet because had recently removed it to grab a moment of sleep. A different legend amongst both Turks and Greeks is found in its most complete version in the history by Tursun Bey. It maintained that a band of naval *azaps* had dressed themselves as Janissaries so that they could enter the city, presumably because the Sultan had already issued his order preventing any but authorized units going beyond the main defensive wall. In this way they were able to plunder and while doing so came across the Byzantine Emperor in a back street, killing him without realizing who was.

A variation on this story, found in Ibn Kemal's chronicle, adds that the skirmish took place near the Golden Gate where the Yediküle fortress would soon be built. Taken together, these latter stories offer a credible account of Constantine XI's last moments as he fled southwards towards a tiny harbour just inside the point where the Sea of Marmara walls joined the massive land walls, perhaps heading for a boat which could have taken him to the *Despotate* of the Morea to continue the struggle. Less believable are a story in the *Memoires* of Pope Pius II that Constantine was trampled to death by cavalry, and a legend that a now-lost tomb near the Vefa Maydan was that of the last Byzantine Emperor. Other stories suggest that this tomb was the last resting place of the heroic *Janissary* Hasan of Ulubad, the first soldier to mount the breach at the Gate of St. Romanus.

There is strong evidence that news of the Ottoman break in was not initially believed in all the separate quarters of Constantinople. It is almost certain that some areas continued to resist, though probably only against the first looters rather than the Sultan's regular troops. These were sent into the city to take control while the bulk of the army was ordered to remain outside. Under Islamic Law the Ottoman army was permitted to sack a city which had offered armed resistance, but the Sultan wanted to take his future capital as undamaged as possible.

Mehmet's troops now advanced methodically, taking control area by area and protecting each quarter from looters. Some sailors or marines clearly entered via the Golden Horn and Marmara coast, looting Constantinople on a massive scale before Ottoman troops forcibly put a stop to it once the minimum period permitted by Islamic Law had been reached. The luckiest looters were camp followers or men from the fleet, many of whom left their weapons on the beach before entering the city to seize whatever they could. Each gang of pillagers appears to have respected the marks of 'ownership' daubed on the buildings by their predecessors.

The notably rich Orthodox churches and monasteries suffered worst, but the survival of the Church of the Holy Apostles from sack, despite being on the main road from the breached land-walls to the centre of the city, is clear evidence of the control Mehmet II had over his troops at this highly charged moment. Perhaps he intended to keep it as the main Orthodox Church while converting Santa Sofia into Constantinople's main mosque. It was, in fact, allocated to the Patriarch shortly afterwards and its subsequent abandonment was also the Orthodox Patriarch's own decision.

A concentration of surviving churches, which were not converted into mosques, in the Petrion and Phanar (Fener) quarters of north-western Constantinople, and in the Psamathia quarter in the south-west suggest that these areas obtained generous surrender terms after the defence of the land-walls collapsed. The later Ottoman traveller and commentator Evliya Celabi similarly wrote that the families of some fishermen in Petrion claimed to be descended from Greeks who opened their gates to Sultan Mehmet II and so obtained tax privileges. Writing around the same time Dimitri Cantemir retold a story he had read in a history by Ali Effendi of Plovdiv, a secretary of state under Sultan Selim I. This claimed that the Orthodox Patriarch told Sultan Selim I that the text of an agreement bearing Sultan Mehmet II's signature and allowing various churches to remain undisturbed, had recently been lost in a fire. To confirm the Patriarch's claim some very old retired *Janissaries* then swore that; 'they were present at the taking of Constantinople and with their own eyes saw the Greek nobles come out of the city and present the Sultan, still in a tent outside the walls, the keys in golden bowls and require and obtain [from the Sultan] the grant of the three mentioned conditions.'

Some of the defenders of Constantinople could not escape, however. Prince Orhan tried to escape disguised as a monk and got through an archer's embrasure in the sea walls before being captured and pushed with other prisoners into the hold of a ship. There he was recognized by a man who had helped defend the same tower and who now earned his own release by identifying Orhan. The Prince's head was immediately cut off and taken to Sultan Mehmet by the ship's captain who was suitably rewarded. Some sources say that this same captain found Loukas Notaras amongst his prisoners but took him alive to Mehmet.

Clearly the ordinary people of Constantinople were treated better by their Ottoman conquerors than their ancestors had been by the Fourth Crusade back in 1204. Only about 4,000 Greeks were killed in the taking of the city, which was very few in the circumstances. On the other hand, many members of the Byzantine elite had fled into the great Church of Santa Sophia, apparently believing an ancient prophecy that the infidels would turn tail at the last minute and be pursued back beyond Persia. Instead, Ottoman looters broke down the cathedral doors and dragged these people off into slavery or for ransom. Men were tied in pairs with ropes, the women with their own belts. Religious statues were smashed, because Muslims regarded these as idols. Jewels were prised from the icons, altar clothes divided as spoil, while a *Janissary* cap was reportedly put on the main Crucifix and paraded around.

Mehmet II sent men to find the Emperor's body, which was recognized by its purple shoes. The head was then removed and placed on a column in the Augusteum to prove that Constantine XI really was dead. The Sultan himself remained outside the land-walls until about noon on 29 May when he and his entourage finally rode through the city to the Santa Sophia Cathedral. There he stopped further damage and sent a preacher up into the pulpit to proclaim the Islamic declaration of faith, thus making the venerable building into a mosque. After the place was cleaned the Sultan joined other worshippers in afternoon prayers. According to Tursun Bey, Mehmet next went to an upper gallery inside the great dome of Santa Sophia to look at the view which still amazes visitors, then went outside the dome. From here he surveyed the decrepit state of Constantinople and quoted a verse by the famous Persian poet Firdawsi; 'The spider serves as gate-keeper in Khusrau's hall, the owl plays his martial music in the palace of Afrasiyab', though others say Mehmet spoke this verse when he saw the ruins of the Blachernae Palace. On 1 June Mehmet II ordered all looting to stop and sent his army back to camp outside the walls, re-entry being prohibited on pain of severe penalties. Only now did the garrisons of the outlying castles of Silivri and Epibatos surrender peacefully. The siege and conquest of the Byzantine capital of Constantinople was concluded.

Chapter 21

Greece Falls to the Turks

he Ottoman conquest of Constantinople, now Istanbul, in 1453
had a profound impact within the Ottoman Sultanate. Henceforth
the religious, political and above all military struggle with
neighbouring Christian states focussed more upon the Ottoman ruler's own
actions rather than on those of the autonomous frontier heroes of earlier days.

The impact of the fall of Constantinople on the Byzantine world was of
course catastrophic and sent shock waves across Orthodox Christendom as
a whole. Many people blamed it on the disloyalty of the Byzantine military
elite. Although conversion to Islam was never as widespread within Greek-
speaking communities as it would be amongst the Slavs and above all the
Albanians, conversion did become common in what had been the Byzantine
aristocracy. Conversion was even more commonplace amongst the Greek
Orthodox clergy, perhaps because the faith of many had been severely
shaken by what was widely seen as 'Divine Punishment'.

In the immediate aftermath of the Ottoman conquest of Constantinople
much of the old Byzantine upper classes fled, some to the tiny quasi-
Byzantine principality of Theodore Mangoup in the mountains of southern
Crimea, others to the Byzantine 'Empire of Trebizond' or to the Byzantine
Despotate of the Morea in southern Greece. This Despotate had formed part
of the Empire of Constantinople but was now torn apart by internal
dissentions and rebellions between and against the co-*Despots* Demetrius
and Thomas. There was also bitter rivalry between Greeks and Albanians
within the *Despotate*, especially within its army.

In October 1454 Sultan Mehmet II sent Turahan Bey to help the
Despots, who were already his vassals, regain control over southern
Greece. However, as soon as Turahan returned from the Morea, civil war
flared up again and in 1460 the Sultan finally lost patience. Its capital,
Mistra, fell to Ottoman forces on 29 May 1460, exactly seven years after
the fall of Constantinople, and the Despotate was incorporated directly

within the Ottoman Sultanate. This coincidence of date cannot have been accidental.

The remaining Latin possessions also fell and it is fascinating to note that Sultan Mehmet allowed special privileges to the newly conquered city of Athens because of his own deep interest in the Classical civilisation of ancient Greece. Some Genoese outposts lasted longer, the port of Enez (Ainos) at the mouth of the river Marica on the Aegean coast of Thrace remaining under the rule of the Genoese Gattilusi family, though under Ottoman suzerainty. Palamedes Gattilusi was also entrusted with the island of Imroz, which had been Byzantine territory under the direct rule of the last Byzantine Emperor of Constantinople. The similarly ex-Byzantine island of Limnos was allocated to Dorino I Gattilusi, the lord of Lesbos (Mytilini). Both ruled as vassals of the Ottoman Sultan and paid him an annual tribute, but in 1460 Enez was transferred to Demetrius, the deposed co-Despot of the Morea. Elsewhere the Gattilusi family retained Lesbos under Ottoman suzerainty until 1462 while a Genoese *Mahona* or 'merchant commune' held the island of Chios as late as 1566. The Ottomans then transferred it to the Jewish Duke Joseph Nasi of Naxos.

Meanwhile the Ottoman conquest of Constantinople and Greece came as a terrible shock to a Western cultural elite which was increasingly influenced by the Renaissance and its admiration – almost worship – of ancient Greek civilisation. Nowhere was this more apparent than in Italy, the birthplace of the Renaissance. Here the Humanists, who spread the idea that the Classical Civilisations of Greece and Rome should be the source of European ideals in art and culture, were appalled at the idea that Greece should now lie under Turkish domination. As the renowned scholar Aeneas Sylvius Piccolomini, the future Pope Pius II, wrote; 'Here is a second death for Homer and for Plato too … Now Muhammad reigns amongst us. Now the Turk hangs over our very heads.'

Even though some writers pointed out that the Ottomans were good and honest people, horrendous propaganda soon led to the widespread image of 'The Terrible Turk'. Ottoman victories over Europeans were also seen as somehow unnatural, along with the Turks' supposed blind obedience to their officers. Nevertheless most Europeans still felt secure behind the powerful Catholic Kingdom of Hungary, and the fate of the Orthodox Christians was regarded as God's punishment for their weakness and sins.

All that was now left were the Venetian enclaves, which were well fortified, well provisioned and could be supplied from the sea by the Venetian fleet. As yet the Venetians were still the strongest naval power in the region, which made these enclaves too strong for the Ottomans to take until they could defeat the Venetians at sea. The Venetian colonial territories around Greece and the Balkans were also well garrisoned, not least by regionally recruited troops of whom the most renowned were *Stradioti* light cavalry. Their name came from the Greek *stradiotai*, which simply meant soldiers. Many of the first *Stradioti* who signed up for Venetian service during the fifteenth century were, in fact, ex-Byzantine troops of Greek origin, Venice first recruiting them in 1464 to fight the Ottoman Turks in southern Greece. Other units then entered permanent Venetian service in 1470. Thereafter they were enlisted in increasing numbers because they proved so effective in Balkan colonial warfare, both as light cavalry and as marines.

Although the first Venetian *Stradioti* had been recruited from Byzantine Greeks, a larger number soon came from Albanian, Slav and Vlach or Rumanian-speaking communities of the western Balkans. Fearless, effective and above all content with relatively low pay, they often enlisted as kinship groups. For this reason they had strong loyalty to their own leaders and, indeed, to those Venetian *proveditori* who earned their trust. The men themselves were usually recruited through the military aristocracy of the western and southern Balkans; such local noblemen also commanding individual units of *Stradioti*.

This Balkan military elite already had much in common with the Italian aristocracy, both being largely town-based but living off the rents of rural estates. However, a relative liberation of the Balkan peasantry following the Ottoman conquest destroyed the economic and socio-political foundations of this Christian aristocracy. Some entered Ottoman service with reduced status while others either fled into the mountains of the western Balkan peninsula, or to the remaining autonomous principalities of what is now Rumania, or to Venetian and Genoese colonial outposts around the Aegean and Adriatic seas.

It is, however, worth noting that the western Balkans already differed considerably from the east, having been under Italian and Hungarian cultural and military influence for centuries. As a result the military elites of these western regions were not as different from their Italian neighbours as might be imagined, particularly those of the coast. Inland, however, many communities seem to have still been organized along extensive clan- rather than smaller family-lines. In particularly the Latin-Rumanian speaking Vlachs (Mavrovlachs or Morlachs) of Bosnia and Herzegovina were a virtually tribal society. They provided large numbers of *Stradioti* light cavalry mercenaries for Venetian and other Western states. Nevertheless, the apparently heraldic shield emblems recorded on their remarkable carved tombstones are believed to have been forms of tribal rather than individual or family identification.

Surprisingly, given the wealth of their 'mother city' and their vital role as a chain of commercial outposts, the fortifications of the Venetian colonial empire were generally of inferior construction during the thirteenth and fourteenth centuries. Only in the fifteenth century would Venice provide its most important outposts with truly impressive, modern and indeed scientific defences. Even at Methoni, which the Venetians retook after a brief Genoese occupation, their new urban defences consisted of small square open-backed towers linked by low walls around a peninsula which was sealed at its northern end by a castle. Inside this walled area stood the town, its port and a cathedral.

Meanwhile the Genoese remained the dominant Western European commercial and naval power in the Black Sea. Here existing coastal fortifications reflected various cultures, the most important being the Byzantine. Elsewhere the military architecture of the rising Romanian states of Moldavia and Wallachia used the old Byzantine concept of a walled enclosure or the traditional earth and timber fortifications of Hungary and the Balkans. During the late-thirteenth and fourteenth centuries, however, Western European influences had reached the north-western coasts of the Black Sea via the Genoese colonial outposts, Hungary and the short-lived Crusader 'Latin Empire of Constantinople'.

The most important Genoese colony was in fact Pera (now Galata), a suburb of Constantinople (Istanbul). Here on the northern side of the Golden Horn, the original Genoese colony was destroyed by its Venetian rivals in 1296. Seven years later the Byzantine authorities gave the Genoese a substantially larger area where they re-established a colony defended by a moat or ditch. In 1313 the *podesta* or local Genoese governor, Montano de Marini, built the first land wall around Pera. A sea-wall was in place before 1324, after which the Genoese added towers to their land-walls, the biggest of which, the Galata Tower, still dominates the skyline.

Elsewhere the Genoese seized substantial pieces of ground which they defended with long walls, though the areas enclosed were not necessarily then filled with buildings. The biggest of these Genoese outposts were established on or near the Crimean Peninsula. Here Kaffa was strongly defended by land and sea-walls which, by 1352, were 718 metres long and incorporated numerous towers. Even this was considered inadequate and Genoa proposed strengthening the fortifications, while increased reserves of food and weapons were stored inside the walled *commune*. The fortifications themselves were, however, still Byzantine-style plain walls with tall rectangular towers. Far to the south, on the Aegean island of Chios, a five-sided *castrum* was erected for the first Genoese rulers in 1346; three sides facing the Greek town, one facing the port and the fifth facing the coast.

The quality of Italian colonial fortifications, particularly those of the Venetians, improved markedly during the gunpowder revolution of the fifteenth century. Newly-strengthened defences emerged as being amongst the most advanced anywhere. In fact the Venetians, who purchased Nauphlia in 1388, refortified it so thoroughly that little trace of previous Crusader construction can be seen. Similarly the new walls that the Venetians built around the promontory of Methoni were designed to resist cannon, while a moat was excavated across the landward side and a *fausse braie* or lower, external fortification, was added in front of the land walls. The fortifications which the Venetians constructed in Cyprus after they took over the island in 1489 similarly demolished many earlier defences and included some notably advanced military architecture with massive, solid earth bastions in the Italian style, as seen at Magusa, Kyrenia and Limassol.

Many Crusader castles in Greece had lost their strategic significance after being reconquered by the Byzantines, but others remained important or even increased in military significance. The most famous was Mistra, which became the capital of the Byzantine *Despotate* in the Peloponnese. Mistra also remained locally important under Ottoman Turkish rule, the castle being slightly altered once again, while several Islamic buildings were added to the town, including a mosque, *hamam* public bath and public fountains for clear drinking water. The Byzantine Despots of Mistra had already modified several other inland Crusader castles, while the coastal fortresses would be even more substantially altered by the Venetians. For example, the existing castle of Vardounia incorporates elements from many different periods, both before and after the introduction of gunpowder.

Constantine Palaiologos, the Despot of Mistra and subsequently the last Byzantine Emperor of Constantinople, took up residence at Clairmont (Chlemutzi) in 1427 and it is possible that most of the existing supposedly 'Crusader castle' was actually built by him. Having been regained by the Byzantines from the Latins in 1429, Patras was certainly rebuilt during this period in a final effort to stem the Ottoman advance. In the event the castle of Patras did manage to hold out when the Turks first took the town, obliging them to retreat. Only in 1458 did both the town and the castle of Patras surrender to Sultan Mehmet the Conqueror.

The fate of those of Western European origin and Catholic religion who had held Crusader castles in Greece was varied. As the Latins lost territory to Byzantine reconquest, the senior aristocracy was either killed or returned to France or Italy. Lower ranking members of Crusader society found it more difficult to leave, many migrating to the Venetian colonies or being absorbed into the last Byzantine military elite. In southern Greece many families were clearly assimilated in this way, and became loyal military supporters of what remained of the Byzantine Empire. Whether they retained any connection with ex-Crusader fortifications is unknown, as is the fate of their descendants under Turkish rule. Many were probably incorporated into the Ottoman military system, along with so many of the Byzantine military class.

The Ottoman impact upon castles of Crusader origin was similarly varied. During the early decades the Turks strengthened some fortifications but most were now irrelevant and were abandoned. Where the early Ottomans did make alterations, these were almost invariably in a continuation of Byzantine military architectural styles, though stronger towers in the Arab-Islamic tradition were modified to incorporate or resist cannon.

Genoese outposts in the Aegean survived slightly longer than those around the Black Sea. Despite the fact that the Ottoman Sultans were more sympathetic towards Orthodox Christians, especially Greeks, than to Latin or Western Catholics, they allowed the Genoese Gattilusi to retain control of Limnos under Ottoman suzerainty and this was probably when the Gattilusi added gun emplacements to their main fortress. However, after several years of chaos and oppression, the local Greeks appealed to the Sultan who handed the island to a member of the ex-Byzantine imperial of family in 1457. Finally, in 1467, Ottoman direct rule was imposed, though the Venetians continued to dispute possession of the island until 1478. Thereafter there was little need for fortifications as the Aegean Sea was now effectively an Ottoman lake.

The Ottomans had taken and garrisoned the reportedly Genoese-held island fortress of Giurgiu in the Danube river in 1394 and fifty years later the recently Genoese enclave of Kilia on the Black Sea coast was occupied by Hungary's local allies. Nevertheless, by twenty or so years after the Ottoman conquest of Constantinople, all the Genoese outposts around the Black Sea had fallen and in the end the main Genoese outpost of Kaffa in the Crimea sought protection from Poland, but this also failed. Most of the local inhabitants refused to fight for Genoa and instead made terms with the Ottomans, who took control in 1479. The fall of Kaffa led to brief attempt at a Genoese-Moldavian alliance against the Ottoman Empire and in the same year Stefan III of Moldavia sent a force of 800 masons and over 17,000 labourers to strengthen the defences of Kilia. Only this fortress and that of Moncastro (Bilhorod-Dnistrovsky) now remained, and their Moldavian garrisons surrendered to a major Ottoman land and sea campaign in 1484. The Black Sea, like the Aegean, would thereafter be an Ottoman lake for several centuries.

Chapter 22

Venetians & Ottomans

The Venetian Republic and its overseas territories or 'colonial empire' would eventually became locked in a life-or-death struggle with the vast Ottoman Empire. In the early years the cautious Venetian authorities tried to avoid conflict and to focus solely on what their scattered 'empire' was really for – namely making money through trade. However, clashes seemed inevitable and became increasingly bitter. The prolonged Venetian-Ottoman wars look at first sight like a David and Goliath confrontation, but in military terms the Venetians were not as small as they might have appeared. From the very dawn of Venetian history all classes were called upon to fight. Venice also grew into a huge city by medieval standards, with a population of some 200,000 by the early-fifteenth century. Furthermore, the Venetian Republic became immensely wealthy while remaining politically united, diplomatically experienced and with a huge navy.

The people of medieval Venice were also noted for brawling and a love of display. While for centuries older men continued to wear traditional long dark cloaks, in the fifteenth century younger men adopted tight-fitting multi-coloured hose. The designs on these leggings often indicated the *Compagnie della Calza* or 'Trouser Clubs' to which the wearer belonged. Sumptuary laws were constantly enacted to curb the extravagant dress of Venetian men and women, but these often led merely to a change in fashion, as when legal but dull outer garments were slit to reveal legal but more sumptuous underclothes.

Venetian love of display paradoxically made this maritime city a European leader when it came to jousts, tournaments and conspicuous consumption by the military elite. Venice was, in fact, seen as a paradox through its ability, as a money-minded republic, to so often defeat warlike feudal princes. Venice similarly enjoyed uncharacteristic stability despite its turbulent politics and occasional military disasters while, by the end of the fifteenth century, the Venetian army remained the only independent Italian military force in Italy. Even the inexorable advance of the Ottoman Turks was at first turned to advantage, Venice snapping up naval bases and colonies at a cheap price or in return for protection. In this way the Venetian Empire reached a pinnacle of power and prosperity in the mid-fifteenth century. The cosmopolitan character of the city meanwhile grew ever more pronounced through an obvious Dalmatian influence on many aspects of life, and the large Greek, Armenian, Muslim and African mercantile communities within Venice itself.

Despite Venice's maintenance of generally good relations with the Ottomans until the late-fifteenth century, Turkish expansion inevitably undermined Italian commercial domination of the eastern Mediterranean, and as soon as the Ottomans turned their attention to the sea a clash became inevitable. In fact Venice's loss of the large Greek island of Evvoia in 1470 marked a turning point which was recognised even at the time. One year later the Venetians were sending armaments to Iran in a classic effort to win allies on their enemy's eastern flank. Nevertheless, these years saw Venice lose domination of the seas, at least beyond the Adriatic, and the start of an epic naval struggle such as had not been seen for centuries.

Venice became a truly imperial power in the wake of the Fourth Crusade which had, in 1204, seized the Byzantine capital of Constantinople and, with Venetian support, temporarily established a 'Latin Empire' in the Byzantine heartland. Venetian power depended, of course, upon its fleets which, whether peaceful or warlike, were commanded by an admiral advised by two government-appointed civilians. Beneath the admiral were *proveditori* administrators and *sopracomiti* galley captains. This chain of command was tightened as the centuries passed, but galley captains always had a tendency to act as free agents, despite the creation of a *Captain General of the Sea* in overall naval command. A system of naval patrols was also set up in the thirteenth century to control the most sensitive seas and, where possible, to cut off enemy supplies.

The limitations of medieval shipping nevertheless meant that Venice could never entirely control any part of the Mediterranean, though Venetian trade could be protected and piracy suppressed. A convoy system was nothing new, but by the thirteenth century escorts of from fifteen to thirty galleys protected many slow and vulnerable merchant 'round ships'. These convoys, their routes and their destinations, were strictly regulated by the government, but if their escorting galleys were lured away or defeated, then

Venetian losses could be crippling. Such convoys were, however, only seen in dangerous seas or during wartime as, for example, when Venice was locked in one of its numerous conflicts with Italian arch rival, the Republic of Genoa.

Furthermore, the very limited operational range of medieval galleys at first confined convoy escorts to a chain of naval bases which constituted the Venetian overseas empire, or to friendly ports. Only the building of much larger merchant-galleys, which were able to defend themselves, enabled this convoy system to be extended beyond the Mediterranean, out into the Atlantic and even to the coasts of England and Flanders. The absence of a Venetian galley fleet could also influence events on land, as when the Byzantines took advantage of such a situation to recapture Istanbul from the 'Latin Empire' in 1261. Furthermore, galleys had to defend their own bases, captains and crews manning the walls whenever they were attacked by land.

Over 3,000 Venetian merchant ships were trading by the mid-fifteenth century, and many of these could be readily converted into warships or at least into military transports. In the Arsenal of Venice itself was a reserve of originally twenty-five, later fifty and eventually a hundred war-galleys. The defensive equipment carried by each ship was closely regulated by the government. In 1255 a small vessel carried five assorted crossbows; a large ship at least eight, plus helmets, shields, javelins, spears and grappling hooks.

Medieval ships also had notably large crews, particularly when 'armed' for a voyage into dangerous waters. Under such circumstances even a merchant ship would then carry at least sixty men, an ordinary galley from 240 to 280. Skilled sailors were recruited in Venice, Dalmatia and Greece while oarsmen came from Venice or its empire, particularly from Dalmatia. Venetian oarsmen were selected by lot from the city's parishes, being financially supported by those who remained behind. From the fourteenth century debtors were also recorded working off their obligations at the oars but there were as yet no galley-slaves. Rowing skills were encouraged through races and regattas in Venice, especially on the feast day of St Paul. Other competitions included a sort of rough water polo, and water-tilting where jousters stood on the stern of each boat as they rowed towards each other, the loser being knocked into the canal. At sea sailors and oarsmen were armed with swords or spears, but changes in weapons technology gradually led to a decline in the military status of the ordinary sailor. Yet all aboard were still expected to fight when necessary, even the merchant passengers, and every man had his weapon, the most important being stored beneath the captain's cabin.

Professional soldiers or marines had always sailed aboard ship, but their role became more important as weaponry became more powerful and expensive. Yet Venetians still used javelins as late as the fifteenth century, while other weapons included cooking pots filled with soap to make the enemy's decks slippery, fire-grenades and blinding sulphur. Swimmers could even attack the foe's hull, threatening to sink him, though in reality very few ships were actually sunk in medieval warfare, the defeated normally being captured.

Crossbows were now the main long-distance weapon, while boarding still decided the final outcome. In 1303 the Venetian government instructed that each galley carry thirty crossbow-men who would also row on the inner benches. Shooting practice was compulsory in Venice, citizens training at the butts in groups of twelve. They also competed in three annual competitions where the government offered rich prizes; valuable scarlet cloth for the winner, a shorter length of cloth plus a new crossbow and quiver for runners up. One group of crossbowmen known as the 'noble archers' were recruited from the aristocracy. They served aboard both war galleys and armed merchantmen from the late-fourteenth century onwards, having the privilege of living in the captain's cabin. Such service could also be the first step in a military or political career. Few professional mercenaries yet seem to have served at sea, and no maritime *condottieri* are recorded until the mid-sixteenth century.

Another important foundation of Venetian naval might was the Republic's ability to mass-produce ships in the Arsenal. These now had the frame-first system which differed from Graeco-Roman shipping in that the frame was constructed before planking was applied, the ancients having made a planked hull to which they then attached ribs. War-galleys were themselves also changing. Though the differences between early medieval Byzantine *dromons* with their two banks of oars and the single-banked Italian war-galley are not yet fully clear, a new system of grouping the oars does seem to have been invented in the eleventh or twelfth centuries. This system, known as *alla sensile* or 'in simple fashion', would itself be superseded early in the sixteenth century. 'Great galleys' designed specifically for long-distance trade in dangerous waters, also appeared in the mid-fourteenth century.

Heavily defended, though bulky and unwieldy, merchant 'round ships' also proved their worth against the Ottomans when the latter suddenly turned to naval warfare late in the fifteenth century. By then Mediterranean ships employed the more efficient stern rudder instead of the steering oars that had been used since antiquity. Though this invention is generally believed to have entered the Mediterranean from northern Europe, recent evidence shows that it was known to Muslim mariners at least as early as the eleventh century. Other technical advances included the compass, which was clearly of Islamic and ultimately Chinese origin.

Ramming was no longer an important naval tactic, the true ram having been replaced by the higher and more flimsy *calcar* boarding 'beak' early in the Middle Ages. But even a *calcar* could smash the enemy's oars and injure his oarsmen. A galley's defences were concentrated in the bow, where a stone-throwing catapult might also be mounted in the wooden *rembata* or castle, and to a lesser extent in the stern, while *impavesati* wooden parapets ran along each side of the ship to protect the oarsmen. Greek Fire and other pyrotechnics were greatly feared, some ships being swathed in protective vinegar-soaked hides or sheets of felt in time of battle.

Yet battles on the open sea remained rare. Apart from defending convoys and suppressing piracy, the primary function of the Venetian galleys seems to have been in 'combined operations', supporting a landing force either to attack an enemy base or defend their own. The Venetians were noted experts when it came to attacking harbours and sea walls. Even the catapult aboard ship was, in fact, called a *litaboli* 'shore hitter'. Wooden towers could also be erected on deck to overtop the land defences while small boats could be slung between the mast-heads to carry crossbowmen and spars could be swung from ropes as battering rams.

When battle between opposing fleets did occur it often began with the same ceremonious courtesy as a land battle. A special flag, with a sword pointing skywards, could be raised to signal a willingness to fight, and enemy standards would be trailed in the water behind victorious ships when they returned to port. A commander's primary tactical consideration was to keep his fleet together. Then he had to make best use both of his low but fast and manoeuvrable galleys and his slow but tall and almost invulnerable 'round ships'. Above all he had to break the enemy formation before overwhelming it piecemeal by boarding. This could be achieved by feigning flight, then turning on the foe, or by catching the enemy's galleys with their sails up and oars stowed. Navigation was almost always within sight of land, so that a concealed part of the fleet could launch an ambush from behind islands, capes or bays. Consequently small scouting vessels had a vital role to play in naval warfare.

The appearance of the first cannon aboard ship did little to change these traditional tactics until the late-sixteenth century. However, such bombards were recorded in the forecastles of a few Venetian galleys in the 1370s and became standard armament during the fifteenth century. Numerous small guns were by then mounted on galleys and round ships to cut down the enemy crew, while a single larger cannon could be placed in a galley's bow to pierce the enemy's hull or topple his mast. This modern weaponry at first proved very successful against Ottoman galleys, whose crews still mostly used composite bows.

The Venetian army was quite as effective as its fleet, despite jibes that the marsh-dwelling Venetians didn't know how to ride properly. Most early-thirteenth century Venetian troops had, indeed, been recruited from the lagoon area plus a few Dalmatian and Istrian feudal contingents. In emergencies, like that of 1294, the Venetian parishes registered all males between 17 and 60 years of age and listed all the weapons they possessed, those called to fight being organised into groups of a dozen. Such domestic troops, conscripts and volunteers, were still preferred to mercenaries in fourteenth-century Venice. Most fought on foot while richer men or aristocrats served as a cavalry, as they did in all Italian cities. A register of 1338 estimated that 30,000 Venetians could bear arms; nor were they a mere rabble, as in some other medieval urban militias. Many were skilled crossbowmen, while others fought with slings and fire-grenades. Venice also had its own local professional soldiers, a small corps of infantry guarding vital castles like Mestre and Treviso, but no full-time Venetian cavalry were as yet recorded in the fourteenth century.

In the second half of the fifteenth century the Venetians suddenly faced full-blown Ottoman Turkish raids deep into the province of Friuli in the far north-eastern corner of Italy. This was something totally new and, despite Venetian experience of war against Turks in their overseas empire, the defences of Friuli at first failed dismally. The Venetians had to withdraw into their fortresses, leaving the countryside to the faster, lightly-equipped Ottoman cavalry. The one major battle also resulted in a serious Venetian defeat although, by assembling a much larger army, the Venetians did beat off later Ottoman raids. Such experiences convinced Venice to employ its own Balkan *Stradioti* 'colonial' light cavalry on Italian soil, to improve domestic military training and to overhaul the system of selective conscription. Even so, another series of Ottoman raids in 1499 proved to be virtually unstoppable.

Command of the Venetian army differed from that of the fleet. An ancient tradition stated that Venetian noblemen could command detachments of no more than twenty-five men, yet an overall *Master of*

Soldiers had been known since the earliest days. The position of *Captain General* appeared as an emergency measure in the fourteenth century but overall management of military affairs still lay with a civilian committee of twenty *Savii* or 'Wise Men'. Remarkable as it might seem, such constant civilian and political interference in military and naval affairs did not affect efficiency; in fact it saved Venice from the military take-overs which plagued other Italian city-states.

Long experience of seafaring and naval warfare gave Venice a supply of men well able to accept the responsibilities of leadership, particularly of infantry forces. Armies were normally commanded by Venetian noblemen, though professionals from the *Terra Firma* Italian mainland provinces and later some mercenary *condottieri* were sometimes given command. Venetian military thinking was, however, singularly cautious; lust for glory running a poor second to achieving victory with the minimum expenditure of blood and treasure.

Another feature of Venetian military life was the *proveditore* or civilian commissioner who accompanied an army and kept a watchful eye on everything, particularly on mercenaries. A series of new *proveditori* roles was set up in the late-fifteenth century, including a combat rank commanding ferocious Balkan or Greek *Stradioti* forces in Italy. By 1509 these supposedly civilian commissioners would also command Italian light cavalry and the artillery.

The elite of Venetian infantry had long been drawn from the ranks of the *Arsenalotti*, the highly skilled and well-paid craftsmen of the Arsenal. They provided guards for the Doge's Palace and other government buildings, acting as a police force and even a fire-brigade, as well as furnishing detachments of well-equipped infantry. The Arsenal itself was a weapons factory and arms store as well as being the most famous ship-building yard in Europe. In 1314 no less than 1,131 crossbows were stored within its walls, while its new rope-making factory, dating from 1303, made thousands of crossbow-strings. The *Compagnie della Calza* 'Trouser Clubs', which had been created in the fifteenth century largely for the entertainment of the young men, provided further trained volunteers when called upon, while the unemployed could also find themselves enlisted.

Venetian forces stationed overseas in the empire *Da Mare* were of more consistent quality and often occupied isolated or hazardous outposts. Apart from the huge booty won with the conquest of Istanbul (Constantinople) in 1204, Venice had carefully selected a number of strategic territories as her share of the shattered Byzantine Empire. She was not interested in large mainland territories which would be difficult to defend and expensive to govern. Rather the Venetians wanted domination of the lucrative trade routes, so they took part of Istanbul itself, a chain of islands and most of the best harbours around Greece. Finally they bought the great island of Crete for 30 pounds weight of gold.

Venice had thus, at one stroke, won an empire. Organising it was another matter. The older Venetian territories in the Adriatic had retained their traditional systems of government, though under Venetian counts or local families of proven loyalty. The new empire in *Romania*, as it was known, would be placed under governors sent directly from Venice, though Crete was slightly different because of its size. Here a Venetian duke was responsible for the island's defences and presided over a new feudal class of colonists, plus those few Greek aristocrats who retained their land. Permanent military forces soon appeared elsewhere in this empire, mostly enlisted from the local military elites, though even in the thirteenth century Italians were being recruited for service overseas. In 1369 Venice's Cretan feudatories rose in revolt. The rising was crushed after bitter fighting, and thereafter the defences of Crete were stiffened by numerous mercenaries, Italian infantry taking a major role though Italian cavalry were more rarely recorded and local *Stradioti* continued to provide the bulk of horsemen.

Each part of the Venetian empire differed in the details of its military organisation. Istria had finally been conquered late in the thirteenth century after a series of amphibious operations by galley fleets. The fortifications of those places, like Trieste and Koper, which had defied Venetian control were dismantled, Koper being placed under the joint rule of a *podesta* civil governor and a *proveditore* military administrator. Zadar, the main Venetian naval base in Dalmatia, frequently revolted against Venetian rule and had, in fact, been recovered during the first battle of the Fourth Crusade. Dubrovnik resisted Venetian control more effectively but was nevertheless ruled by Venice from 1205 to 1358.

Elsewhere the Venetians left day-to-day affairs in local hands while firmly controlling the ports, those islands with a tradition of piracy, and access to the vital forests from which most Venetian ships were built. Otherwise Venice had no interest in the bleak limestone mountains of the Adriatic hinterland. Some cities were, in fact, obliged to supply ships to the Venetian fleet - Zadar no less than thirty fully-manned galleys - while all had to supply sailors, plus militias for their own defence. Though the countryside remained firmly Slav, the Italian character of the major Dalmatian cities was strengthened. Fully-trained crossbow militias became a feature of these cities although Dalmatian peasant warriors still apparently used composite bows of Byzantine or almost Turkish forms.

The Near-Eastern character of Venetian colonial troops in Crete and Greece was even more obvious. The large island of Evvoia, known to the Venetians as Negroponte, was the key to Venetian power in the Aegean. It bristled with fortifications, including a tower built in the midst of the narrow Euripos channel where the complexity of the neighbouring coastlines meant that up to fourteen tides flowed in a single day. Only one of the most senior Venetian administrators was permitted become *Baillie* or governor of Evvoia, and the colony's own flag was flown on a bronze flag-staff outside the Cathedral of San Marco in Venice itself on ceremonial occasions.

Other less important Aegean islands were mere stops along the trade routes or bases from which to control piracy. The Cyclades archipelago, theoretically a fief of the Latin Empire of Constantinople, was actually held by various Venetian families who placed loyalty to Venice above feudal obligations to that short-lived 'empire'. The tiny island of Kithera, off the southern tip of Greece, provided vital communications between Venice and Crete. It eventually had a sizeable garrison and no less than three castles. Corfu, at the mouth of the Adriatic, had fallen to Venice during the carving-up of the Byzantine Empire but was soon lost to the Kingdom of Naples and had to be purchased back in 1386. Other temporary Venetian possessions in Greece included Monemvasia, Methoni, Argos, Corinth, Navpaktos, Nauphlia and even Athens.

As the Ottomans advanced across Greece during the fourteenth century these outposts filled with Byzantine refugees. Many came from the old military elite and took service with Venice as *Stradioti* light cavalry. Among them were famous names like Graitzas Palaiologos from the last Byzantine ruling family who rose to command all Venetian light cavalry. An effort to drive the Ottomans out of the Peloponnese in 1463-4 with an army of *Stradioti*, Italian hand-gunners and *condottieri* heavy cavalry mercenaries failed and would be the last major Venetian land offensive in the east. Thereafter defensive operations were left to naval and garrison infantry and to *Stradioti* who not only fought the Ottomans on their own terms but were much cheaper to maintain than Western-style men-at-arms. Recruited in Greece, Albania and Dalmatia their loyalty was rarely in doubt, their ferocity proverbial, and their habit of collecting the heads of slain foes never seriously discouraged. Nevertheless, signs of declining Balkan and Greek support for Venice had become apparent by the fifteenth century.

It was seen in Crete even earlier. This was a prized possession and Venice had to fight for it against both local Greeks and Genoese free-booters. To ensure its subjection the island was divided into six sections named after the six districts of Venice. Beneath these came 132 knights' fees and 405 infantry *sergeantries* mostly held by Venetian military settlers. Fortifications sprang up all over the island, particularly along the northern coast. However, Crete did not prove to be the land of opportunity originally hoped. Even by 1332 many of the Venetian settler knights were too poor to afford proper military equipment. Many of their feudal serfs were of Arab origin, descended from Muslim conquerors who had ruled Crete centuries earlier. Though unfree, they could be summoned for military service while Greek Cretans were also conscripted when needed. The Cretan talent for savage guerrilla warfare first became apparent during the mid-thirteenth-century rebellion but was, however, equally savagely crushed. Another uprising in the mid-fourteenth century confirmed the Venetians in their view of Cretans as untrustworthy savages, and the latter in their hatred for Venetian colonial rule.

From the Fourth Crusade's conquest of Istanbul in 1204 to the Byzantine regaining of their capital in 1261, Venetian merchants had dominated the Black Sea. This dangerous area spanned the rich caravan routes from Iran and China, and was also an important source of wood from which crossbows were made. In 1261 Venice lost its paramount position to the Genoese who were close allies of a revived Byzantium. Even so, despite their traditional rivalry, these two Italian maritime republics frequently co-operated in the hazardous environment of the Black Sea. This was particularly apparent in the Crimea, where a number of originally Byzantine ports served as termini for the trans-Asian 'Silk Routes', as well as routes north into fur-rich Russia and Siberia. There were, of course, clashes but Venetians and Genoese both feared the might of the neighbouring-Mongol Golden Horde and its successor Khanates more than they did each other. The Italians finally lost the Crimea to the Ottomans in 1479, the Black Sea becoming an Ottoman lake within five years after which the only 'Western' merchant vessels to sail its waters were those of Venice's old Dalmatian rival, Ragusa (Dubrovnik) – now a vessel of the Ottoman Empire.

The first decades of Ottoman history had been landlocked and their supposed capture of the island of Imralı in the Sea of Marmara in 1308 seems impossible, as this was before Ottoman forces had taken possessions of any coastline. It may, on the other hand, have echoed some daring but otherwise unrecorded raid. The small but steadily-expanding Ottoman state actually reached the southern coast of the Sea of Marmara around 1333, with the seizure of Gemlik (Kios), but there is virtually no evidence that they used any of the ports and fishing villages of this shore to range further afield. The Sea of Marmara is, of course, a virtually enclosed stretch of water which then lay next to the Byzantine Imperial capital of Constantinople. It was also a major maritime trade route dominated by the powerful Italian fleets of Genoa and Venice.

However, the conquest of the neighbouring Turkish *beylik* of Karasi gave the Ottomans a much extended coastline, some useful and defensible harbours, and the small raiding fleet already established by the *Beys* of Karasi. This would prove to be a turning point in Ottoman history, not only because it was from ex-Karasi territory that Ottoman forces first invaded and held some European soil, but because the Ottoman Emirate now began to develop as a naval power.

Initially its maritime ambitions were extremely modest. European influence upon the development of the Ottoman fleet was also important, and was apparent from the very start. Yet it would not be the only influence. Ottoman ship-builders, mariners, navigators and tacticians could draw upon the long naval traditions of the Islamic Middle East and the Byzantine Empire. Even so, where the Eastern Mediterranean, Aegean and Black Seas were concerned the Islamic and Byzantine maritime heritages had for centuries been almost identical to those of medieval Italy and the western Mediterranean. It would only be with the arrival of northern European and Atlantic naval traditions and technologies from the late-fourteenth century onwards that all Mediterranean fleets underwent significant changes.

The small Karasi navy inherited by the Ottomans had been built by Greeks and was largely manned by ex-Byzantine sailors and *gazi* warriors. The sailors remained largely Christian, and would do so for many years. Nor were all of the so-called *gazis* Muslims, recently converted or otherwise. Many are likely to have been adventurers, men whom their foes described as pirates. Yet the Ottomans' lack of a more formidable fleet would leave their expanding Balkan conquests vulnerable throughout the fourteenth century. Not until the first half of the fifteenth century did Ottoman ships confront the Venetians whose coastal possessions dotted the eastern Mediterranean.

During those early years most Ottoman naval campaigns were hit-and-run affairs. The earliest version of the *Düsturname Destan* was written by a Turkish poet named Enveri in 1465. The text is a verse history of several earlier dynasties, and one of the most interesting sections deals with the epic adventures of Umur Bey, ruler of the *Beylik* of Aydın (1334-48). However, the maritime warfare it describes is that of the mid-fifteenth century. In these verses Umur has a large *qadirga* war-galley constructed, which he then named the *Gazi*. Otherwise his fleet largely consists of smaller *qayiqs*, a name still used for traditional coastal craft in Turkey and Greece. These medieval *qayiqs* were, however, fighting ships carrying thirty to forty men and having boarding 'beaks'. Although their weapons included some firearms, the mid-fifteenth-century Ottoman fleet, like those of their Turkish *beylik* predecessors, largely relied on bows, crossbows and close-combat weapons for boarding, while trumpets and horns were used for communication and maintaining morale in combat.

During one naval expedition in the *Düsturname*, Umur's little fleet found five enemy *köke* or cogs at the island of Bozcaada (Tenedos). The cog was a northern European type of ship which reached the Mediterranean during the second half of the fourteenth century, where it was soon adopted by Spaniards, French, Italians and others. First Umur studied the enemy;

> Their topsails towered like fortresses,
> > The cogs carried enemies without number.
> Their topsails, solid like fortresses, were full of rocks [the European
> > ships were armed with fighting tops],
> > Large and small crossbows were numberless.

Umur then attacked, and Enveri's description of the ensuing struggle must surely be based upon what the poet heard from Ottoman sailors of his own day:

> They shot at the oarsmen and cried 'Oh Muhammad!' ...
> > Some carried spears in their hands, others had swords,
> Striking without pause the enemies' armour of blue iron.
> > Other brandished cutlasses, crash! crash!....
> The Turks defended themselves from the rocks behind wooden planks,
> > The cogs were broken apart....
> The cogs were chopped into pieces with pickaxes.

On another occasion Umur's ships and their armament were described in greater detail, again reflecting the reality of the mid-fifteenth Ottoman fleet rather than that of mid-fourteenth century Aydın:

> He had built twenty-eight ships,
> > All were greased and coated with pitch.

He had there seven qadirga, seven igribar [smaller galliots]
 And fourteen qayiqs, the construction was rapid.
They armed the ships with crossbows, arrows and tüfeks [early forms of
 hand-gun, arquebus or musket].
 They deployed the sails, they pulled up the boarding ramps....
On each ship they planted banners,
 The drums made a sombre and piercing sound,
The horns, the zurnas [bass clarinets] and the flutes played.

The mention of *tüfeks* in the hands of Turkish naval personnel is particularly interesting at this early date, as they were still a very new form of weapon, even aboard Western European warships. A generation before Enveri wrote his epic *Düsturname*, Sultan Murat II had built a substantial fleet which, in 1430, helped Ottoman land forces capture Venetian-held Thessaloniki. By 1456 the Ottoman fleet had around sixty ships manned by *azap* 'marines', Christian oarsmen and crossbowmen. That year it took control of Genoese-ruled Enez, as well as other islands in the northern Aegean Sea. By 1470 the Ottoman war-fleet had increased to ninety-two galleys, which enabled the Sultan's ships to dominate the Black Sea and the compete with the Italians in the Aegean.

Over the next decades the expansion of the Ottoman navy was quite astonishing, and Western observers were soon claiming that the entire fleet, including fighting galleys and transports, numbered around five hundred vessels. During the 1499-1502 war against the Venetians, an Italian agent reported that Ottoman shipyards certainly launched two great ships of 1,800 *tonilato* (roughly equivalent to modern tonnes), which were the largest vessels yet seen.

The Ottoman Sultanate's administrative and financial system was fully up to the task of maintaining this massive but still young navy. The money came from the maritime *sançaks* or provinces of al-Cezayir, consisting of the Aegean islands and Gallipoli, Galata, Izmit and, at a later date, also Algiers in North Africa. Galley sailors and marines, called *levents*, were recruited from Turkish coastal communities, Greeks, Albanians and, again at a later date, Dalmatians and North Africans. The *kürekçiler* oarsmen included criminals and prisoners-of-war as well as some volunteers. Sailors specialising in all-sail ships rather than galleys were at first called *aylakçiler*, though with the adoption of new styles of Western European 'galleon' warships they came to be known as *kalyonçiler* 'galleon men'.

Several Janissary *ortas* or battalions either specialised in naval service as marines, or had historically close associations with the fleet. Thus the 88th *Orta* had an anchor for its insignia, often tattooed on the men's hands or arms, as did the 8th and 31st *Bölük* regiments. The 25th and 37th *Bölük* had a fish, while the 56th *Bölük* had a galleon. This was probably the unit shown in several Ottoman and European illustrations having a large model war-galley thrust into the plume holder of their distinctive white *börk* cap when on ceremonial parade.

During the first centuries of its existence the primary role of the Ottoman fleet was to transport land forces and, after the adoption of gunpowder artillery, to support them where possible by coastal bombardment. As the Ottoman Sultanate expanded still further, the fleet tried to control or at least to police its exceptionally-long, rugged and indented coastlines. Control of the numerous offshore islands may actually have been easier, though these often still remained havens for Christian pirates.

Chapter 23

The Ottomans Fortify their Empire

The Ottoman seizure of Constantinople (Istanbul) and the subsequent mopping-up of the remaining relics of the Byzantine Empire did more than merely change the political, strategic and economic situation around the Black Sea. The fast-expanding population of Istanbul following the Ottoman conquest in 1453 soon led to food shortages, and so the Ottomans began to look to the fertile grain-producing plains north of the Black Sea as a possible source of wheat for bread.

The fall of Constantinople had also cut Italian trade through the Dardanelles and Bosphoros to the Crimea. This large peninsula was virtually a great island on the northern side of the Black Sea and had for millennia been the main hub of maritime and trade communications for this region. It remained so, though the changed political and military situation almost immediately led to a steady emigration away from the Genoese merchant colonies all around the Black Sea. Many Armenians who had lived in these colonies for centuries under Byzantine and then Italian rule, now moved to the Ukraine or Poland. The same was true of Italian colonists and more temporary residents, Italian craftsmen from the Crimea being recorded as far away as Moscow within little more than twenty years.

Meanwhile Ottoman campaigns elsewhere confirmed Ottoman domination throughout most of the Balkans, though they also suffered significant reverses. Wallachia moved firmly into their sphere, accepting the Sultan's suzerainty which would remain in place for another four centuries. Even Moldavia was theoretically tributary to the Sultan after 1456. In reality it took several decades for Ottoman suzerainty to be accepted as permanent. Stefan III Cel Mare, 'Steven the Great', came to the throne of Moldavia a year later, threw off Ottoman domination and spent much of his reign competing with the Sultan for dominion over neighbouring – and similarly Romanian-speaking – Wallachia.

Stefan Cel Mare was a near contemporary of Vlad Tepes of Wallachia. He was, however, a man of very different character, being a deeply religious patron of the arts as well as an effective military leader and tireless diplomat. The fall of Byzantine Constantinople, followed by Byzantine Trebizond (Trabzon), was disastrous for Moldavian trade. Now virtually surrounded by predatory foes, the Principality had to fight Ottomans, Mongols, Poles, Lithuanians and Hungarians, eventually being obliged to pay tribute to the Ottoman Sultanate in 1456. Stefan III's refusal of further payment when he became *hospodar* or ruler of Moldavia resulted in a series of fierce campaigns and eventually even he had to kneel. Meanwhile Stefan Cel Mare had married his daughter to the son of Grand Prince Ivan of Muscovy, cementing an alliance against the vast and rambling Polish-Lithuanian realm on Moldavia's northern frontier. What his daughter thought about this marriage is unrecorded, though a combined Moldavian-Muscovite army did rout a Polish-Lithuanian force in the Kozmin forest in 1497.

The consolidation of Ottoman power in the Black Sea also had a profound impact in the Middle East, by cutting the largely Genoese maritime link between the Mamluk Sultanate of Egypt and Syria, and the Mongol Khanate of the Golden Horde north of the Caspian and Black Sea. This strategic partnership had existed for centuries, not only bringing wealth to the three partners but also serving as the channel through which slave-recruits for the Mamluk army reached the Mamluk Sultanate. Without it the entire Mamluk system gradually withered. For Genoa the impact was largely financial and, although expensive, was not fatal. The third partner, the Golden Horde, had been in decline throughout the fifteenth century. Its defeat and partial absorption by the rival Khanate of Krim (Crimea) in 1502 can be only partially attributed to events in the Black Sea.

The extraordinary expansion of the Ottoman empire had only occasionally required major fortifications. Ottoman strategy had been offensive rather than defensive, yet the fifteenth century did start to witness a change in Ottoman attitudes to military building. The final siege of Constantinople and its aftermath, for example, resulted in the construction of several varied and impressive fortresses. Even so the imposing Ottoman castles of the mid-fifteenth century were rarely followed up, the following two centuries being a period of almost complete Ottoman domination in the Balkans, central Europe, the Middle East and North Africa. Imposing and expensive fortifications were, by and large, simply not needed.

The Ottoman state had first emerged in a mountainous region with few fortified towns but numerous smaller strongpoints, mostly held by Byzantine *akritai* frontier warriors. As support from the central Byzantine government failed, so these outposts fell to the Turks, often when the local lord simply switched from being a Byzantine *akritai* to being an Ottoman *uc begleri* 'frontier governor'. Under such circumstances the Ottoman *emir*, who was still more of a tribal leader than a territory ruler, had little reason to encourage castle building. As the Ottoman state grew from a frontier nuisance to a mortal threat, the declining Byzantine Empire and Christian powers in the Balkans put considerable effort into upgrading their defences. Virtually all of these eventually fell to the Ottomans who thus inherited an array of powerful fortifications.

On the other hand, Ottoman attitudes to fortification were already changing. This was apparent to the great Moroccan traveller Ibn Battuta who visited Bursa in the 1330s and wrote that the Emir Orhan, 1324-60, possessed nearly a hundred castles, constantly inspecting them to ensure they were in good condition. When the Ottomans reached the coast, however, they faced a different military problem because Christian fleets still controlled the seas and there is strong evidence that the Turks now maintained as well as used captured Byzantine coastal fortifications. During the second half of the fourteenth century the Ottomans demolished many existing fortifications in the Balkan provinces of their fast expanding Empire, but they also strengthened some, especially along their exposed Danube flank at Silistria, Nikopol and Vidin.

Further south the ex-Byzantine fortress and harbour of Gallipoli became the first Ottoman naval base. It was so strategically important that Bayezit I had a fortified inner harbour constructed. Whereas the fortifications of Gallipoli were primarily to defend Ottoman communications across the straits, Bayezit I built Anadolu Hisar in preparation for an assault upon the Byzantine capital of Constantinople in 1395 AD. It stood at the narrowest part of the Bosphoros but, given the limitations of existing artillery, was not intended to close the Strait. Instead Anadolu Hisarı was an observation point and secure position from which small numbers of Ottoman troops could cross the Bosphoros and maintain communications with Ottoman forces already operating on the European side. As part of his more ambitious effort to close the Bosphoros to enemy shipping Mehmet II 'The Conqueror' strengthened Anadolu Hisarı with an additional three towers.

Although the Ottomans used existing fortifications it was from Islamic traditions of military architecture that they drew most inspiration, most notably adopting the *burj* or large tower as the main element in a castle or citadel. To this the Ottomans added emplacements for defensive cannon and much thicker walls as a protection against enemy guns, perhaps having learned much from Genoese coastal fortifications like the Galata Tower overlooking the Golden Horn in Istanbul.

Such 'great towers' formed the basis of Mehmet the Conqueror's fortress of Rumeli Hisar, on the European shore of the Bosphoros. Contrary to a myth that Mehmet based the plan of this impressive fortification upon his own initial in Perso-Arabic script, its shape was actually determined by the lie of the land and was designed by an architect named Müslihiddin. The remarkable speed of construction – a mere four months and sixteen days – depended upon considerable use of prefabricated elements and the Ottomans' renowned organizational skills.

Sultan Mehmet II 'The Conqueror' was just as concerned to 'lock' the Dardanelles and the result was a pair of fortresses built in 1452 AD at the narrowest point of the straits. Kale-i Sultaniye on the Asian side, and Kilidülbahir on the European shore, were completely different from each other, and from Rumeli Hisarı. Nevertheless, both contained thirty cannon which would enable them to cover the Dardanelles at this point.

Once Ottoman rule had been consolidated across the Balkans, relatively few new fortifications were added, except on some exposed parts of the Ottoman state's long coastline. Elsewhere Ottoman garrisons occasionally repaired old Byzantine, Bulgarian, Serbian, Crusader, Genoese and Venetian fortifications in a sometimes crude manner.

A good example of the Ottoman focus on coastal fortification in Greece is the fortress of Aya Mavra on the island of Levkas. Here the collapse of the Crusader rule in 1479 coincided with a major spread in the use of cannon as both offensive and defensive siege weapons. This led to modifications of many fortresses, and on Levkas the Ottomans changed the Crusader castle into a modern citadel, surrounding the castle with lower, sloping walls about three metres thick. A strong semi-circular rampart, constructed north of the two existing square towers, was provided with gun emplacements which dominated the sea approaches to the town, while the main gate was also relocated in the southwest of the site where it was defended by a two-storied circular artillery tower.

The strategic situation was different where the Ottomans faced the Kingdom of Hungary. Here the Derdap Gorge on the river Danube formed a barrier between the Lower Danube Plain dominated by the Ottomans and the Great Hungarian Plain which formed the heartland of the Hungarian state. The northern entrance to this gorge was already defended by the fortress of Golubac which had been updated during the first half of the fifteenth century when the Ottomans were already poised at the southern entrance to the Gorge. During this phase of its development, Golubac was provided with a partially fortified river harbour, though these defences were still in a pre-gunpowder style. Next the rectangular towers of its main wall were given an additional layer of masonry designed to deflect gunfire; this probably being done when the last Serbian rulers were already vassals of the Ottoman Sultan. Only when an Ottoman garrison had been installed was a squat artillery-tower built to defend the river harbour around 1480.

The strategic situation in Albania was different yet again. Here the turbulent character of the country meant that most fifteenth century Ottoman building work was military, though often constructed on earlier fortifications. The citadel rebuilt by Mehmet the Conqueror at Elbasan became a particularly important military centre.

As the Ottoman state increased in size and sophistication, greater emphasis was placed on urban, palatial and what might be called mercantile fortifications. By the time the Burgundian ambassador Bertrandon de la Broquière visited Bursa in 1433 the city consisted of several settlements divided by deep ravines, though only one was fortified. Another town which had a 'palatial' function was Didimotokon in Thrace, its Byzantine citadel being strong enough to serve as a secure place for the Sultans' treasury without significant changes. In contrast the much larger Thracian city of Edirne (Adrianople) became the Ottomans' first capital on European soil. Nevertheless, rather than repair its archaic Romano-Byzantine fortifications, the Sultans built a new palace complex nearby. Though essentially unfortified, the complex contained at least one defensive building, the Cihannüma Kasri built for Murat II early in the fifteenth century. Enough survives for archaeologists to know that this Cihannüma Kasri was a large rectangular building with a tall central tower having a polygonal top.

The first real fortification that Mehmet the Conqueror added to his new capital of Istanbul was the Yediküle, attached to the inside of Constantinople's ancient Golden Gate. It stands on the site of the abandoned Church of the Holy Apostles but was not the first additional fortification in this spot. Around 1390 the Byzantine Emperor John VII had ordered a major strengthening of the towers of the Golden Gate, and between this gate and the coast, to serve as his 'final refuge'. However, these were reportedly torn down on the insistence of the Byzantine Emperor's Ottoman suzerain. Sultan Mehmet II did much more by adding three new towers to the existing towers of the Golden Gate and their neighbouring wall towers, linking them with a high curtain wall to form the

Yediküle or 'Castle of Seven Towers'. Nevertheless, this was not a defence against external attack, but would have served as a refuge in case the still overwhelmingly Greek and Christian population either rose in revolt or joined forces with a new crusade.

In contrast with the initially dangerous situation in Istanbul, the high degree of security within the Ottoman state almost certainly accounted for the fact that new *hans* or caravanserais along its trade roads were generally less fortified than those of the previous Seljuk and *beylik* periods. Other *hans* were located in towns where they became centres of craft manufacture and in almost all cases their defences, insofar as they existed at all, were against thieves and rioters rather than the brigands or highwaymen.

A substantial number of Turks settled in the Balkans in the wake of the Ottoman conquests and by the early-sixteenth century Muslims formed a quarter of the entire population, especially in Thrace and central Bulgaria. Settlement was, however, concentrated in major fortified cities and along important communication routes. The centralised character of the Ottoman Empire also meant that fortresses remained under strict government control. As Konstantin Mihailovic, a Balkan Slav soldier who served in the mid-fifteenth century Ottoman army, wrote in his memoires: 'The Turkish emperor holds securely all the fortress in all his lands, having garrisoned them with his Janissaries or protégés, not giving a single fortress to any lord: and moreover the emperor holds any fortified city and the fortress within it, having garrisoned it with his own men.'

These fortified places guarded the frontier and main routes while also serving as administrative centres. Between the larger fortresses were numerous forts, usually earth and timber *palankas* which housed smaller military units. In regions where Ottoman rule was most direct, garrisons were normally organized in a uniform manner. An *Ağa* senior commander would be appointed by central government but these men often appointed their own *Kethüda yeri* 'local lieutenants', selecting them from men with local experience. Konstantin Mihailovic's memoires were based on his experiences in the mid-fifteenth-century Balkans, and reflected this state of affairs; 'The organization in the fortress is as follows: there is one who commands all the others who is called the dyzdar [*dizdar*], like our burgrave [in the Hapsburg Empire]; the second official after him is called the kethaya [*kethüda*] like our steward here; after him are the bulukbasse [*bölük bası*] like decurions amongst us...'

Ottoman records also show that the *timar* fiefs of garrison commanders could consist of entire villages or merely part of a village. The smallest *timars* were those held by a *serbölük*, the commander of a *bölük* unit. The biggest were, of course, allocated to a *dizdar* fortress commander, while that of his *kethüda* deputy was significantly smaller. Many aspects of the organization of fortresses and their garrisons stemmed from Ottoman methods of conquest back in the fourteenth century. It had then been normal for small garrisons to be installed in those fortifications which were not demolished, enabling the main army of conquest to advance further or return to its barracks. Much of the conquered territory was then allocated as *timars* to those of the *sipahi* cavalry who did not already have a suitable fief. Some settled in the conquered villages while others, the *hisar-eri* or *kale-eri*, were stationed in fortresses where they formed the bulk of garrisons during the fifteenth century. It is interesting to note that the majority of *hisar-eri* in the Ottoman Balkans came from Anatolia while most *hisar-eri* in Anatolia came from the Balkans, presumably a security measure to inhibit the development of local power groups.

However, a shortage of Muslim military manpower meant that the Ottomans had to recruit local troops from defeated Christian military elites, especially as the Sultan had no wish to see his army tied down in garrison duties. The faithfulness of these local auxiliaries to the new regime astonished outside observers and was a testament to Ottoman tolerance, justice and indeed effectiveness. While such 'native troops' received privileges, usually in the form of tax exemptions, they were always accompanied by Ottoman regulars. Tax privileges could also be given to entire fortified towns, Muslim and Christian inhabitants included, in return for military and political faithfulness. For example the population of Croïa in Albania was offered tax exemption in return for guardianship of the fortress shortly before the area was attacked by Skanderbeg, the famous Albanian resistance leader.

The backbone of the most important garrisons were, of course, *Janissaries*, but another increasingly element were the *gönüllü* 'volunteers'. They ranged from elite cavalry to servants, 'attendants of castle guards', and *ma'zul* 'dismissed' members of garrisons. Officers' servants who took up arms were listed as *gönüllü*, many in an effort to be accepted into a registered military unit with its increased pay and status. Occasionally men who had been demoted wanted to redeem their reputations and became *gönüllü*.

During the fifteenth and early-sixteenth centuries Vidin, overlooking the Danube in north-western Bulgaria, formed an important part of the *serhad* 'frontier zone' facing autonomous but not necessarily reliable Wallachia and the still powerful Kingdom of Hungary. As a result the fortified town and the forts of its *sancak* province were strongly garrisoned. Most of the local Muslim men belonged to one of its corps, either *timarlı sipahi* cavalry, *mustahfizan* fortress guards or *akinci* raiders. Many local Christians were meanwhile enlisted in paramilitary corps such as the *filurciyan* and the *voynuğan*.

The frontier zones which separated the Ottoman Empire from its European neighbours, and where most of its fortifications were located, had much in common with the frontier zones which had earlier separated the Byzantine Empire from its Islamic neighbours. As a result Ottoman garrisons, especially those of smaller fortified outposts, continued many of the traditions of their medieval predecessors – the Muslim *gazis* and the Christian *akritoi* of Anatolia. In fact during the early centuries many were recent converts to Islam and under these circumstances their code of frontier behaviour remained similar to the military attitudes of the medieval period. They took part in major military campaigns but otherwise tended to ignore official periods of peace by continuing to raid and be raided. Correspondence between governments, complaining about this state of affairs, tended to be couched in general terms whereas correspondence between the commanders of fortified outposts dealt in much more detail. Indeed it soon became clear that garrison troops, especially volunteers, were less interested in destroying the enemy than in capturing booty or prisoners. Casualties also tended to be surprisingly few because, as a recent historian of south-east Europe under Ottoman rule pointed out, a dead peasant could not produce, a dead soldier could not be ransomed, so life, paradoxically, often seems to have been more valuable on the precarious frontier than it was when large armies met in battle.[1] It was a way of life which would characterise the Balkan provinces of the Ottoman Empire for almost four centuries.

---

1 Sugar, P.F., *South-Eastern Europe under Ottoman Rule 1354-1804* (Seattle 1977) 105-107.

Glossary

Adnoumia – Byzantine muster or review.

Akinci – Ottoman light cavalry 'raiders'.

Akoluthos – Commander of the late-Byzantine Varangian Guard.

Akrites – Byzantine frontier warriors.

Alay – Regiment of Ottoman provincial cavalry commanded by an *Alay Bey*.

Allagion – Late Byzantine regiment, commanded by an *allagator*.

Almogaver – Lightly-equipped Spanish Aragonese or Provençal troops, including those operating in the Aegean region.

Archontes – Late Byzantine provincial elite.

Archontopouloi – 'Sons of archontes', Byzantine regiment.

Armamenton – Byzantine imperial arms factory.

Azap – Ottoman naval soldier, marine.

Bailli – Governor or representative sent to a Crusader State by an outside ruler, including the military governor of Crusader Greece under Angevin rule; or the commander of a castle or garrison

Bandon – Byzantine military unit, usually of cavalry.

Bektaşi – Member of a mystical *Sufi* Muslim brotherhood inspired by Haci Baktaş.

Beredarioi – Byzantine government messenger system.

Bey (or *beg*) – Turco-Mongol local and military leader.

Beylerbeyi – Governor of an Ottoman *eyalet* large military province.

Beylik – Small independent or autonomous Turkish state.

Bogomils – Followers of a dualist faith or heresy in the medieval Balkans, believing that the universal powers of Good & Evil were roughly equal in power.

Boyar – Member of the aristocratic elite in some Balkan Slav countries (also in Russia).

Brodniki – Military communities living along southern Russian rivers.

Caliph – Spiritual and originally also the temporal ruler of the *Sunni* Muslim world.

Çauş – Low-ranking Ottoman officer.

Chevauchée – Medieval French term for a raid, usually by a wholly mounted force.

Chosarion – Byzantine term for light cavalry (*hussar*).

Commanderie – Administrative province of a Military Order.

Composite bow – Bow usually made of glued strips of wood, sinew and sometimes horn.

Condottieri – Commander of Italian mercenary troops.

Connétable (*Constable*) – Military commander of a western European or Crusader army.

Çorbaci Başi – Commander of a Janissary company.

Count of the Walls – Byzantine officer responsible for the defence of Constantinople.

Deli – Ottoman frontier cavalry.

Demarchos – Late Byzantine governor of an urban quarter and probably its militia.

Derbendci – Ottoman military families responsible for defence of key communications routes.

Dervish – General term for a member of a mystical *Sufi* Muslim brotherhood.

Despotate – Fragmented Byzantine independent state or autonomous province.

Devşirme – Enforced recruitment of youngsters for Ottoman *Kapi Kulu* corps, including Janissaries.

Divan – Advisory council in the Ottoman and other Islamic states.

Doğanci – Balkan Christian auxiliary cavalry in Ottoman service.

Domestic – Senior Byzantine military commander.

Droungos – Byzantine mobile field reserve or battalion.

Druzhina – Armed retinue of Russian and some other Slav princes.

Dux – Commander of a Byzantine frontier province or Duchy.

Emir (*amir*) – Muslim secular ruler acknowledging the superior authority of another secular ruler such as a *Sultan*.

Eparch – Governor of a Byzantine city.

Eyalet – Largest Ottoman military province.

Fakih – Muslim legal export.

Fatwa (Turkish *fetva*) – Judgement based on Islamic Sharia law.

Fief – Portion of land allocated to an individual (usually a knight) to maintain himself and his family.

Foederati – Byzantine frontier allies or auxiliaries.

Friar – Member of a Catholic Christian preaching rather than monastic order.

Gasmouli – Soldiers and sailors of mixed 'Latin' (western European) and Greek parentage (see also *vasmuli*).

Gonikeia – Form of Byzantine peasant farm.

Goulabion – Byzantine retainers or military followers (from Arabic *ghulam*, soldier of unfree origin).

Grand Domestic – Most senior Byzantine official beneath the Emperor.

Greek Fire – Petroleum-based incendiary weapon.

Gureba – Elite Ottoman cavalry regiments based in the Sultan's palace.

Hamam – Public baths in Islamic towns and cities.

Han (Khan) – Hostel of merchants or travellers in Muslim lands.

Harim – Private section of a house reserved for women and their immediate family.

Icon – Religious painting in the Orthodox Christian church.

Iconoclasm – Fundamental disapproval of pictorial religious illustration.

Imam – Muslim spiritual leader or guide.

Indulgence – Remission of sins offered by the Catholic Church to Crusaders and others.

Janissary (Yeni Çeri) – Elite infantry soldier in the Ottoman army.

Jihad – Individual struggle against evil in Muslim society, or war in defence of Islam.

Jupan (zupan) – Balkan Slav nobleman or local governor.

Kadi (Qadi) – Judge in Islamic society.

Kanun – Secular law in the Ottoman state.

Kastron – Small Byzantine fortified outpost or fortified town.

Kastrophylax – Commander of a late Byzantine fortified place.

Kavallarioi – Fief or pronoia-holding Byzantine cavalry.

Kephale – Late Byzantine commander of local forces or provincial governor.

Khan – Turkish or Mongol ruler.

Kizil Elma – 'Red Apple', a Turkish military goal which always remained out of reach.

Kleisourai – Byzantine commander of mountain passes.

Knezat – Balkan or other Slav governorate.

Koursa – Naval raid, Byzantine.

Kul – Slave or servant of the Ottoman Turkish Sultan.

Lavra – Byzantine monastic retreat, often fortified.

Logothete – Official in charge of Byzantine law courts.

Madrasah (Turkish *medrese*) – Teaching mosque or school.

Mamluk – Elite Muslim soldier of unfree origin.

Magnus archonte – Byzantine senior archon or regional authority.

Megalloallagitai – Late Byzantine 'large regiment', usually based in a city.

Megas konostoulos – Late Byzantine 'Grand Constable' in command of western mercenaries.

Mehter – Military band in the Ottoman army.

Mesoi – Late Byzantine urban middle class and probably its associated militia.

Military Order – Monastic order dedicated to fighting for the Christian faith.

Millet – Faith community within the Ottoman state.

Money fief – Source of revenue allocated to a knight instead of a territorial fief.

Monokaballoi – Late Byzantine locally-recruited regiment, usually cavalry.

Mourtatoi – Byzantine troops recruited from Turkish prisoners converted to Christianity.

Mufti – Islamic legal expert.

Müsellem – Early Ottoman professional cavalry.

Paidopoula – Byzantine page or personal servant, sometimes military (see also *payadeh*).

Patriarch – Senior member of a church hierarchy, one grade beneath a Pope.

Payadeh – Early Ottoman infantry.

Pezoi – Late Byzantine infantry.

Primmikerios – Commander of late Byzantine Vardariot elite guard unit.

Pronoia – Byzantine fief or money-raising estate.

Protostrator – Deputy commander of late Byzantine army.

Qaraçi – Turco-Mongol frontier division, commanded by a *Qaraçi bey*.

Sancak (Sanjaq) – Ottoman military province under a *Sancak Bey*.

Sebastokrator – Byzantine senior commander.

Sekban – 'Dog handlers', Ottoman infantry regiment.

Seneschal – Senior officer in command of castles in a Crusader state.

Sergeant – European professional soldier of non-knightly status.

Sharecropping – Form of land tenure in which farmers gave an agreed proportion of crops to the landowner.

Sharia (Turkish *Şeriat*) – Islamic religiously based law.

Shi'a – One of the two main religious divisions in Islam.

Şihna – Seljuk Turkish military governor.

Silahdar – 'Guardians of the ruler's weapons', Ottoman cavalry regiment.

Sipahi – Ottoman cavalry maintained by *timar* fiefs.

Solak – Ottoman infantry guard unit.

Sous maréchal – Senior officer in the Military Orders.

Stradioti – Byzantine local garrison or frontier troops.

Stratopedarch – Officer of late Byzantine locally-recruited *monokaballoi* cavalry.

Subaşi – Ottoman military rank and also local police chief.

Sufi – Muslim mystic.

Sultan – Muslim secular ruler acknowledging the superior authority of the Caliph.

Sunni – One of the two main religious divisions in Islam.

Symponos – Official responsible for law and order in a Byzantine city.

Theme – Byzantine provincial army and the military province itself.

Timar – Ottoman fief or estate for *sipahi* cavalry.

Tourkapouloi – Byzantine troops of Turkish origin.

Trapezitai – Byzantine light cavalry.

Tsar – Slav term for supreme ruler (from *caesar*, etc).

Turcopole – Light cavalry fighting in Middle Eastern style, usually in a Crusader or Military Orders army, originally of captured Muslim origin.

Tzaggratores – Byzantine crossbowmen.

Tzakones – Late Byzantine infantry from southern Greece.

Tzaousios – Officer in command of a late Byzantine garrison (from Turkish *çauş*).

Tzouloukonai – Late Byzantine military servants.

Uc – Frontier province or march of the Ottoman state.

Varangian Guard – Elite Byzantine military originally formed from Scandinavian, Anglo-Saxon (pre-1066) and English (post-1066) recruits.

Vardariot – Late Byzantine guard unit.

Vasmuli – Soldiers & sailors of mixed 'Latin' (western European) and Greek parentage (see also *gasmouli*).

Vicar – Civilian governor of Crusader Greece under Angevin rule.

Vicar general – Civilian governor of Crusader Greece under Catalan and Aragonese rule.

Voivod (*vojvod*) – Slav, military governor or local ruler.

Voynuq (*voynuk*, *wojnuq*) – Balkan Christian auxiliary cavalry in Ottoman service.

Waggenburg – Temporary field fortification made of wagons.

Waqf (Turkish *vakif*) – Islamic charitable organization and its property.

Yasa – Mongol and Turkish customary law.

Yaya – Early Ottoman infantry.

Yeni Çeri (*Janissary*) – Elite infantry corps of the Ottoman army, commander by the *Yeni Çeri Ağasi*.

Yürük – Turkish Muslim nomad of the southern Balkans.

Zabareion – Byzantine arms factory.

Zanggra (see also *tzaggra*) – Byzantine crossbow.

Zeugelateion – *Pronoia* fief granted in perpetuity.

Zupan (*jupan*) – Balkan Slav nobleman or local governor.

Further Reading

Atiya, A S, *The Crusade in the Later Middle Ages* (London 1938).

Atiya, A S, *The Crusade of Nicopolis* (London 1934).

Babingen, F, *Mehmet the Conqueror and his Time* (Princeton 1978).

Bakapoulos, A, 'Les Limites de l'Empire Byzantin depuis la fin du XIVe siècles jusqu'à sa chute (1453)', *Byzantinische Zeitschrift*, 55 (1962), 56-65.

Barbaro, Nicolo (trans Melville Jones, J R), *Diary of the Siege of Constantinople* (New York 1969).

Barker, J W, *Manuel II Palaeologus (1391-1425): A Study in Late Byzantine Statesmanship* (New Brunswick 1969).

Browning, R, 'A Note on the Capture of Constantinople in 1453', *Byzantion*, 22 (1952), 379-387.

Concasty, M-L, 'Les Informations de Jacques Tedaldi sur le siège et la prise de Constantinople', *Byzantion*, 24 (1954), 95-110.

Curcic, S, & Hadjitryphonos, E (eds), *Secular Medieval Architecture in the Balkans 1300-1500, and its preservation* (Thessaloniki 1997).

De Vries, K, 'Gunpowder Weapons at the Siege of Constantinople, 1453', in Lev, Y, (ed), *War and Society in the Eastern Mediterranean, 7th-15th Centuries* (Leiden 1996), 343-362.

Delaville le Roulx, J, *La France en Orient au XIVe siècle: Expeditions du Maréchal Boucicaut* (Paris 1886).

Doukas (trans Magoulias, H J), *Decline and Fall of Byzantium to the Ottoman Turks* (Detroit 1975).

Dujcev, I, 'La conquête turque et la prise de Constantinople dans la literature slave contemporaine', *Byzantinoslavica*, 17 (1956), 278-340.

Farmer, H G, 'Turkish Artillery at the Fall of Constantinople', *Transactions of the Glasgow University Oriental Society*, 6 (1929-33), 9-14.

Foss, C, & Winfield, D, *Byzantine Fortifications; an Introduction* (Pretoria 1986).

Gabriel, A, *Châteaux turcs du Bosphore* (Paris 1943).

Gibbons, H A, *The Foundation of the Ottoman Empire* (Oxford 1916).

Goodwin, G, *The Janissaries* (London 1994).

Gross, M L, *The origins and role of the Janissaries in early Ottoman history* (Amsterdam 1969-70).

Hess, A C, 'The Evolution of the Ottoman Seaborne Empire in the Age of Oceanic Discoveries, 1453-1525', *American Historical Review*, 75 (1969-70), 1892-1919.

Högg, H, *Türkenburgen an Bosporus und Hellespont* (Dresden 1932).

Housley, N, *The Later Crusades, 1274-1580: From Lyons to Alcazar* (Oxford 1992).

Inalcik, H, 'Mehmed the Conqueror (1432-1481) and his Time', *Speculum*, 35 (1960), 408-427.

Inalcik, H, *An Economic and Social History of the Ottoman Empire 1300-1914, vol. 1, 1300-1600* (London 1996).

Inalcik, H, *The Ottoman Empire: The Classical Age 1300-1600* (London 1973).

Iorga, N, 'Une source negligée de la prise Constantinople', *Bulletin de la Section Historique (Acad. Roumaine)*, 13 (1927), 59-68.

Káldy-Nagy, G, 'The First Centuries of the Ottoman Military Organization', *Acta Orientalia Academiae Scientiarum Hungaricae*, 30 (1977), 147-183.

Kiel, M, 'A Note on the History of the Frontiers of the Byzantine Empire in the 15th century', *Byzantinische Zeitschrift*, 66 (1973), 351-353.

Luttrell, A, 'The Crusade in the Fourteenth Century', in Hale, J R (et al. eds), *Europe in the Late Middle Ages*, (London 1965), 122-154.

Melville Jones, J R, (trans), *The Siege of Constantinople 1453: Seven Contemporary Accounts* (Amsterdam 1972).

Mihailovic, K, (edit & trans Stolz, B), *Memoires of a Janissary* (Ann Arbor 1975).

Mijatovich, C, *Constantine Palaeologus, The Last Emperor of the Greeks: 1448-1453: The Conquest of Constantinople by the Turks* (London 1892).

Miller, B, *The Palace School of Mohammed the Conqueror* (Cambridge Mass. 1941).

Nicol, D M, *The End of the Byzantine Empire* (London 1979).

Nicol, D M, *The Immortal Emperor* (London 1992).

Nicol, D M, *The Last Centuries of Byzantium, 1261-1453* (London 1972).

Nöldeke, T, 'Auszüge aus Neṣrî's Geschichte des osmànischen Hauses', *Zeitschrift für Deutschen Morgenlandischen Gesellschaft*, 15 (1861), 333-380.

Papacostea, S, 'Byzance et la Croisade au Bas-Danube à la Fin du XIVe siècle', *Revue Roumaine d'Histoire*, 30 (1991), 3-21.

Paviot, J & Chauney-Bouillot, M, (edits), *'Nicopolis, 1396-1996': Actes du Colloque Internationale (Dijon 18 Octobre 1996) Annales de Bourgogne*, 68/3 (1996).

Paviot, J, *Genoa and the Turks: 1444 and 1453* (Genoa 1988).

Pertusi, A, 'Le notizie sulla organizazione administrativa e militare dei Turchi nello 'strategicon adversum Turcos' di Lampo Birago (c.1453-1455)', in *Studi sul medioevo cristiano offerti a R. Morghen* Vol. II, (Rome 1974), 669-700.

Philippides, M, (trans), *Byzantium, Europe and the Early Ottoman Sultans, 1373-1513: An Anonymous Greek Chronicle of the Seventeenth Century (Codex Barberinus Graecus 111)* (New York 1990).

Philippides, M, (trans), *The Fall of the Byzantine Empire: A Chronicle by George Sphrantzes 1401-1477* (Amherst 1980).

Pitcher, D E, *An Historical Geography of the Ottoman Empire* (Leiden 1972).

Rolland, M, *Le Siège de Constantinople 1453* (1989).

Rosetti, R, 'Notes on the Battle of Nicopolis', *Slavonic Review*, 15 (1936-37), 629-638.

Runciman, S, *The Fall of Constantinople* (Cambridge 1965).

Savu, A G, (edit), *Pages sur l'histoire de l'armée Roumaine* (Bucharest 1976).

Savvides, A G C, 'Constantinople in a vice: Some notes on Anadolu Hisar (1395/1396) and Rumeli Hisar (1452)', *Acta Patristica et Byzantina*, 8 (1997), 144-149.

Schiltberger, J, (trans Buchan Telfer, J), *The Bondage and Travels of Johann Schiltberger* (London 1879).

Shaw, S, *History of the Ottoman Empire and Modern Turkey, Vol. 1, 1280-1808* (Cambridge 1976).

Soulis, G C, *The Serbs and Byzantium during the reign of Tsar Stephan Dusan* (Washington 1984).

Spinei, V, *Moldavia in the 11th-14th centuries* (Bucharest 1986).

Stacton, D, *The World on the Last Day* (London 1965).

Stoicescu, N, 'Organizational Structure of the Armies of the Romanian Principalities in the 14th-18th centuries', in Savu, A G (edit), *The Army and the Romanian Society* (Bucharest 1980), 165-191.

Sugar, P F, (edit), *A History of Hungary* (London 1990).

Sugar, P F, *South-Eastern Europe under Ottoman Rule 1354-1804* (London 1977).

Tafrali, O, 'La siège de Constantinople dans les fresques des églises de Bucovine', in *Melanges offerts a M. Gustave Schlumberger a l'occasion du quatre-vingtième anniversaire de sa naissance* (Paris 1924), 456-461.

Tsangadas, B C P, *The Fortifications and Defence of Constantinople* (New York 1980).

Turkova, H, 'Le Siège de Constantinople d'après le Seyahatname d'Evliya Celebi', *Byzantinoslavica*, 14 (1953), 1-13.

Vacapoulos, A E, *The Origins of the Greek Nations, 1204-1461* (New Brunswick 1970).

Villain-Gandossi, C, 'Les Éléments Balkaniques dans la garnison de Trébizonde à la Fin du XVe siècle', in Bacqué-Grammont, J-L & Dumont, P (eds), *Contributions à l'histoire économique et sociale de l'Empire ottoman* (Leuven 1983), 127-147.

Weissmann, N, *Les Janissaires: Etude de l'Organisation Militaire des Ottomans* (Paris 1964).

Zachariadou, E, (edit), *The Ottoman Emirate (1300-1389)* (Rethymnon 1993).

Index